M

vitae humanae defensoribus humanitatisque

Moral Theory

A Non-Consequentialist Approach

David S. Oderberg

BLACKWELL PUBLISHING
350 Main Street, Malden, MA 02148-5020, USA
9600 Garsington Road, Oxford OX4 2DQ, UK
550 Swanston Street, Carlton, Victoria 3053, Australia

First published 2000

2   2005

Library of Congress Cataloging-in-Publication Data

Oderberg, David S.
    Moral theory : a non-consequentialist approach / David S. Oderberg.
        p.   cm.
    Companion to: Applied ethics.
    Includes bibliographical references and index.
    ISBN 0-631-21902-1 (hb : alk. paper) — ISBN 0-631-21903-X (pbk. : alk. paper)
    1. Ethics. I. Title.
BJ1012.O34 2000
171'.2 21—dc21   99-045661
                                                                         CIP

ISBN-13: 978-0-631-21902-6 (hb : alk. paper) — ISBN-13: 978-0-631-21903-3 (pbk. : alk. paper)

A catalogue record for this title is available from the British Library.

Set in 10 on 13 Sabon
by Ace Filmsetting Ltd, Frome, Somerset
Printed and bound in the United Kingdom
by Marston Book Services

The publisher's policy is to use permanent paper from mills that operate a sustainable forestry policy, and which has been manufactured from pulp processed using acid-free and elementary chlorine-free practices. Furthermore, the publisher ensures that the text paper and cover board used have met acceptable environmental accreditation standards.

For further information on
Blackwell Publishing, visit our website:
www.blackwellpublishing.com

Contents

Preface and Acknowledgements

In 1995, the philosopher Professor Peter Singer published a book entitled *Rethinking Life and Death*. The subtitle is *The Collapse of our Traditional Ethics*. Professor Singer announced the conquest of the view of morality coming down to us through the centuries, and rooted in what he calls the 'Judeo-Christian' ethical tradition. The 'old ethic', he says with undisguised relief, is dead; a 'new ethical approach' is on its way, though its 'shape' is still to be determined.

The purpose of this book, and of its companion *Applied Ethics*, is to show that traditional morality is not dead. It may not be the official outlook of most moral philosophers, and one might even question how many people in Western societies believe it any more. I suspect, however, that the number is larger than the intelligentsia would have us believe.

In seeking to show that traditional morality is not dead, I do not want to pretend that there has not been something of a revolution in moral philosophy, which has filtered down to the population at large. Indeed, Professor Singer is one of the thinkers most responsible for this startling change in our attitudes to a wide range of topics. Since his seminal work in the 1970s, he has been followed by hundreds of writers in the field he almost single-handedly invented, called 'practical' or 'applied' ethics, all of them in one way or another assisting in the overthrow of traditional morality. Professor Singer's moral theory, known as consequentialism, owes its modern form to the nineteenth-century British ethicists James Mill, Jeremy Bentham and John Stuart Mill (among others), and became the dominant ethical outlook in British moral philosophy in the twentieth century. Whatever the differences among its adherents, and whatever the challenges it now faces in the higher levels of moral theory (for example, from Kantianism), it is still the overwhelmingly pre-eminent theory used in applied ethics in Britain, the USA, Australia, and elsewhere in the West.

Traditional ethics has had its defenders, to be sure, but they are small in number and influence. This book and its companion, it is hoped, will help to redress the imbalance in the kind of material available to students. If I do not succeed in convincing the reader of the truth of the positions I defend, at the very least I hope to show that traditional ethics is a coherent system of thought, that it can be done in the modern age, and that it provides a method for dealing with even the most difficult problems in practical ethics. In other words, the pronouncement of its demise is, I believe, premature.

I will not describe here what the traditional ethic amounts to: that is the work of the following chapters. What I will say, however, is that even if the bulk of moral philosophers find the conclusions I reach unpalatable, disagreeable, ridiculous, absurd, anachronistic, barbaric, bizarre, or just plain wrong, I console myself with the following thought: that every single one of the major positions I defend was believed by the *vast majority* of human beings in Western society for thousands of years, right up until some time in the 1960s, when the Western Cultural Revolution took place. (I do not speak of the non-Western societies, which even today subscribe to most or all of the views defended here.) Naturally, this does not make the views for which I argue right; but it is a fact that offers some solace in an age in which traditional ethics is held up to such ridicule. Furthermore, I also believe that there is such a thing as the common sense of humanity, which extends to morals as well as to everything else. In this I follow Aristotle, for whom the investigation of morality began with common sense and was in large part its systematisation. Hence the much-derided Principle of Double Effect, which is central to traditional moral theory (and which I defend in chapter 3), is nothing but the codification and elaboration of what we all know intuitively to be correct, however much the principle is considered by some to be obscure and repugnant to rationality. Indeed, it has its difficulties, like many other philosophical principles, traditional or not, but it begins with common sense on its side, and therefore starts at an advantage.

Moral Theory and *Applied Ethics* are companion volumes, designed to be read in sequence. Either book makes sense on its own and could be read without the other, but there is a dependence between them that makes this undesirable. *Moral Theory* presents ethical ideas and principles in the abstract, and looks to their application to concrete cases; *Applied Ethics* discusses concrete cases, and presupposes to a large extent the prior defence of the ideas and principles applied to them (although the main lines of defence are recapitulated). They were written together, and are best read together.

The structure of the two books is simple. In *Moral Theory* I set out in elementary fashion the system of traditional morality as I understand it. I start with a critique of moral scepticism, not because I have anything especially new to say or because it has not already been refuted by others. The reason is that scepticism about the very possibility of arriving at moral truth pervades universities throughout the Western world. It has seeped into culture at all levels, in fact, so that students come to university sceptical about moral objectivity and leave with their scepticism intact and even reinforced by their teachers. This is one topic on which traditional moralists, and consequentialists such as Peter Singer, are in substantial agreement. (Although not even consequentialism, on analysis, escapes from ethical relativism born of pluralism about values, resort to subjective preferences, and a lack of belief in human nature. See further Janet E. Smith, 'The Pre-eminence of Autonomy in Bioethics', in D. S. Oderberg and J. A. Laing (eds), *Human Lives: Critical Essays on Consequentialist Bioethics* (London/New York: Macmillan/St Martin's Press, 1997), pp. 182–95.) No student can be receptive to what traditional morality has to say without first shaking off his sceptical prejudices, and this is what chapter 1 is designed to help him to do.

Chapters 2 and 3 of *Moral Theory* set out the basic concepts and principles of traditional morality. The exposition is on the whole elementary and non-technical. It is not designed as a comprehensive or definitive statement of the traditional ethic. I do not engage with all the alternative ideas explored in recent literature on virtue theory, or Kantianism, or natural law ethics. I am concerned only to present the leading ideas of traditional morality in a straightforward way, showing their main interconnections, in order to prepare the ground for a discussion of specific problems in the second volume. The vast majority of applied ethics books share the vice of not giving sufficient space to the theoretical justification of the positions adopted on particular issues. Far too often, an author gives a twenty-page exposition of his ethical viewpoint and then launches into discussion of difficult concrete cases. I believe this is wholly inadequate, hence my desire, at the risk of 'over-egging the pudding', to state and defend at length the traditional ethicist's theoretical presuppositions and general approach and to explain the concepts used in later discussion. Applied ethics is not like riding a bicycle: you don't just 'do it', as some applied ethicists seem to think, and convince your reader by doing it well rather than badly. You start with a theory, explicit or implicit, and you *apply* it. I have, then, stated the theory of traditional morality as explicitly as possible for my purpose of applying it to concrete cases. There is also some discussion that has no direct bearing on later applications, but seemed to me worthwhile for the purpose of elaborating and defending traditional moral theory for its own sake. These passages, some of which are abstruse and somewhat technical, can safely be skipped by the reader who wants to focus on the main points, in particular on the application of the theory to specific problems.

Chapter 4 is the link between the two books, setting out the fundamental moral principle of the sanctity of human life. Here I draw the reader away from general theory and towards my main focus, which is issues of life and death. The doctrine of the sanctity of human life has come under merciless attack in recent years, and is the first principle that most applied ethicists seek to undermine. Without it, there is no traditional morality. With it, much of what passes for contemporary ethical opinion can be shown to be false, even morally repugnant and dangerous to society.

The main negative focus of *Moral Theory* is the critique of consequentialism, which by far dominates current thinking and writing in applied ethics. (For those who doubt that this is the case, a typical example to look at is A. Dyson and J. Harris (eds), *Ethics and Biotechnology* (London: Routledge, 1994), in addition, of course, to the well-known texts by Singer, Glover, Rachels, Harris, Beauchamp and Childress, among many others.) Hence the subtitle of both books: its aim is to make clear that they constitute an alternative to the staple fare of applied ethics books, in which the approach to theory and practice is overwhelmingly consequentialist. I do not set out every flaw in consequentialism, however, omitting even some major ones. Rather, I concentrate on its incompatibility with the basic demands of rights and of justice (due primarily to its 'maximising' and calculative nature), and hence its fundamentally inhuman character, and I explore some other of its more bizarre and morally objectionable features. Of course, consequentialism comes in various forms, and I have not explored the species and sub-species that have been formulated in the attempt to get around certain objections. Instead, I focus on the leading ideas central to any form of consequentialism worthy of the name. The trend in current ethical writing seems to be for consequentialists of a more enlightened outlook to alter their theories to such an extent – in order to make them conform to common sense and basic morality – that they are barely recognisable as consequentialist. This is a research programme with an uncertain future, one to which I am happy to leave its exponents.

In *Applied Ethics* I discuss particular controversies, all of them revolving around issues of life and death. In chapters 1 and 2 I argue for specific prohibitions on the taking of human life. In chapter 3 I draw the boundary separating those beings which possess the right to life from those which do not. Here, although the chapter is entitled 'Animals', the reader will soon see that I focus almost exclusively on the issue of whether animals have rights. There are all sorts of facets to the 'animals issue' which I do not explore. The main reason for this is that by concentrating on the question of rights, and drawing a logico-moral boundary between human and animal life, I aim to highlight, or to place in relief, what I say about rights for human beings. In this sense the question of animal rights is an integral conceptual part of the overall project of expounding traditional morality. Second, however, it seems that the animal rights movement is growing strongly and distorting the common-sense approach that most people still have towards the animal kingdom. Only by seeing the flaws in the idea that animals have rights will society recover a sane attitude both to them and to itself.

It might be thought that my position on the animals issue places me close to Peter Singer's, since he too does not believe in animal rights. Whilst Professor Singer is to be commended for much of what he has written and done about the suffering of animals, it remains the case that his attitude is fundamentally unsound, since it stems from his consequentialist belief that *no* being has rights – 'I am not convinced that the notion of a moral right is a helpful or meaningful one' – and that '[t]he language of rights is a convenient political shorthand. It is even more valuable in the era of thirty-second TV news clips.' (See *Practical Ethics*, Cambridge: Cambridge University Press, 1993; 2nd edn, p. 96; *Animal Liberation*, London: Jonathan Cape, 1990; 2nd edn, p. 8.) Whereas, then, Professor Singer seeks to demote human beings to the same level as animals inasmuch as *none* of them have rights, traditional morality maintains a fundamental conceptual and moral distinction between human beings and every other living creature. Professor Singer's viewpoint may have meant an improvement in the lot of many animals, which is praiseworthy; but it also means, for the traditional ethicist, a change for the worse in the fate of mankind.

In chapters 4 and 5 I argue for cases where it is permissible to take human life. It is at this point that some people who see themselves as partisans of traditional morality will part company with me. They have, according to my diagnosis, overreacted to the contemporary attack on the sanctity of life by falling into the opposite error of regarding all killing as wrong simply by virtue of the victim's being human. Like all overreactions, this one may be understandable in the present death-oriented climate but, like all overreactions, it too is mistaken. It simply is not in conformity with traditional morality to oppose, *on principle*, war or capital punishment. Nor, when the issues are thought through, is it in accord with traditional moral thinking to oppose either activity in certain very real cases that have obtained in our recent history or that obtain today. In other words, it is untraditional to say *either* 'War/capital punishment is wrong' or 'War/capital punishment is permissible in principle, but the circumstances in which it is legitimate today are so rare that it is, for all practical purposes, always wrong.' Chapters 4 and 5 are designed to show why this is so.

The choice of topics for the second volume has given the book a certain natural structure, though it was in the first instance motivated more by personal interest and a concern to present the traditional view of certain hotly debated issues. In each case, I pursue the topic in as much depth as space allows, because it seemed to me early on that an in-depth examination of a limited number of topics would ultimately be more useful to students than a more superficial overview of a wider range of issues. My objective is to show how traditional moral philosophy works, how its fundamental concepts and categories apply to an issue. Also, I have been concerned to tackle at length many of the most common objections to traditional positions, objections that recur time and again in the literature and in popular discussion, and also most significantly in the way students talk about the traditional viewpoint. Hence I have, at the risk of obsessiveness on my part and potential annoyance on the reader's, discussed some apparently minor issues at substantial length. Moreover, it seems to me that the right approach to many disputed topics not covered in the second volume – such as genetic engineering, embryo experimentation, and cloning – depends in a straightforwardly logical way upon the position to be taken on what should be called the *fundamental* issues, such as abortion and euthanasia. I hope this approach will be excused because of its ultimate usefulness, not least for other traditional ethicists. Once it is seen how to tackle a small number of foundational issues in detail in the traditional way, the student may then be in a better position to apply the same method to topics I have not covered. Perhaps, if the opportunity becomes available, I will expand the list myself.

In writing this book and its companion I have benefited greatly from discussions with a number of people, some of whom have also commented on portions of them. In particular I would like to thank (in no special order) John Andrews, Elaine Beadle, Tim Chappell, John Cottingham, Brad Hooker, Andrew Mason and Dale Miller. I am especially indebted to Helen Watt, with whom I have discussed at length the contents of both volumes; and to Jacqueline Laing, for many stimulating and profitable discussions not just on ethics, but on all aspects of philosophy, as well as for her encouragement in the preparation of both books. Finally, I would like to express my immense debt of gratitude to Steve Smith of Blackwell Publishers for his unfailing support and encouragement, even at times that would have taxed an editor with the patience of Job.

Needless to say, the fact that someone has assisted me with these books does not imply that they hold any or all of the views I defend. Some will disagree with almost everything I say. I hope that they find the project encapsulated in *Moral Theory* and *Applied Ethics* of some worth, nevertheless.

David S. Oderberg
Reading, May 1999

Note: References throughout the book to the male 'he' and its cognates are used in the generic sense unless the context suggests otherwise, and are in no way intended to cause offence.

1

Ethics, Knowledge and Action

1.1 Introduction

Ethics, as Aristotle taught, is an applied science. It is a science (from the Latin *scientia*) because it yields knowledge (though it is not an empirical science, like chemistry); and it is applied because it is concerned with the application of abstract principles to concrete problems of human action. So knowledge and action are the two essential objects of ethics, what the person who wants to 'be moral' or 'act morally' has to aim at. But the same goes for, say, building a house. If you want to do it you have to have a certain amount of knowledge, and you have to be capable of translating that knowledge into action. So what is special about morality? The best way of making the distinction between morals and other areas of human knowledge and action is in terms of goodness and badness, and related notions such as right and wrong, praise and blame, approval and con- demnation – not as applied to this or that capacity in which people act, but as applied to people acting *as people*. For instance, a house-builder's essential objective *as a house-builder* is to build a house well, to be a good builder. The same goes for a musician, or a journalist, or athlete – their aim, *as* musician, journalist or athlete, is to be good *at what they do*. But when it comes to morality, our aim is not to be good at a particular trade, or occupation, or pastime – but to be a good *person*, to act in the right way *as a human being*.

In chapter 2 we will explore in some detail just what goodness and badness in morality amount to and how right and wrong, and other ethi- cal notions, relate to them. For the moment, though, we need to look at a more abstract set of questions. I have spoken so far as though the basic concepts of morality correspond to objective reality. Many people would immediately take issue with this way of talking, or at least qualify it in important respects. They would say: 'It's all very well for you to say ethics is about good and bad, right and wrong, but it must be understood that these are not objective concepts like tall and short, black and white – and what other kind of objectivity is there?'; or 'I do not object to you talking about good and bad or right and wrong, as long as you accept that what is good and bad is a matter of opinion, or personal preference, and is not a matter of objective, discoverable truth.' Still others will say: 'If you agree that morality is a cultural phenomenon, with no standard lying outside the beliefs of different societies, then I'm with you; otherwise you're beginning your investigation on the wrong foot'; or 'I don't like the idea of associating ethics with concepts such as praise and blame, approval and condemnation, because our actions are not really free and so we are not really responsible for what we do'; and again, 'You can say ethics is about action, but don't assume that it's free action – we are total products of our genes and our environment.'

These sorts of response mean that before I can set out the moral theory I wish to defend – one that has notions of objective good and bad, right and wrong at its core – I must address the sort of *scepticism* about morality that lies behind the kinds of remark I have just noted. For many decades now philosophy has been generally more concerned about what goes on inside people's heads than what goes on in the world as a whole. This is reflected in philosophy's overriding concerns throughout the twentieth century with the nature of language, knowledge and the mind. These concerns themselves reflect the 'inward turn' philosophy has taken in the last few hundred years, especially since René Descartes and, later, Immanuel Kant. What beliefs about the world are we rationally entitled to have? Can we be *certain* in those beliefs? What, after all, is certainty? Do we have any genuine *knowledge* of reality? Such questions have been the mainstay of philosophical thinking since the Enlightenment and moral philosophy has been equally transformed by them. You may wonder: *Can we have genuine knowledge of right and wrong, good and bad? How does moral knowledge, if it exists, differ from other kinds of knowledge, say in natural science or history? If moral concepts like good and bad are supposed to correspond to reality, what sort of reality could that be? Isn't morality all relative anyway? How can we argue rationally about what is ultimately just a matter of opinion? How can there be any fixed moral truth in such a vague and ever-changing world as ours, which confronts us with radically new problems every day?

For all its superficial appeal, scepticism about morality is unwarranted. The defence of this claim requires a book in itself, but all I propose to do here is consider some of the main issues related to this topic, since my primary concern is to set out and defend the theory of traditional morality, with a view to applying it to concrete problems in the companion volume, *Applied Ethics*. What I hope to do in the present chapter, then, is at least to convince you that the case against moral scepticism, and for moral objectivity and moral reality, is a strong one – and, at best, that moral scepticism is baseless.[1]

1.2   Ethics and Knowledge

I have said that ethics, being a science, yields knowledge. Many people, philosophers and non-philosophers alike, would dispute this claim. Surely ethics is nothing like the other subjects we legitimately call sciences, such as physics, mathematics, chemistry, or even social sciences like history, anthropology or economics (the latter also known as 'the dismal science', for obvious reasons). A field of enquiry, if it is to be a science, must yield genuine knowledge, if not certainty; there must be recognised methods of investigation capable of being used by any enquirer; the results must be *repeatable* – in the same circumstances, using the same methods, any enquirer would get the same result; there is generally *progress* or *convergence* upon the truth, from a previous state of ignorance; and there must be a good deal of (if not unanimous) *agreement* among enquirers as to just what the truth is.

These requirements are correct, as long as they are properly understood. Part of the moral theorist's task is to show how they are satisfied by doing ethics in a rigorous and systematic way, just as any investigator who claims his work is scientific will seek to demonstrate this by his methodology. In this sense, at least, any field of enquiry is known by its fruits – not just its results, but the way those results are arrived at – and ethics is no exception. It is necessary, though, to address these requirements directly, since doubts that they are satisfied in ethics are all too common.

Some of the concern, however, can be allayed by emphasising a crucial point, one made by Aristotle: ethics might be an applied (or practical) science, but every science is only as precise as its subject matter allows. We should not expect mathematical certainty in morality any more than in, say, history, psychology, or any other field of enquiry that deals with human beings and their actions. Nor should we expect the precision we find in chemistry, or in geology. Humans are unpredictable in a way equations are not; their beliefs, habits, tendencies and the like are unquantifiable and unmeasurable in a way molecular structure is not; they form plans and goals in a way that mountains and rivers do not. There is, then, an essential element of *inexactitude* in moral theory, corresponding to the elusiveness and unfathomability of many of the predicaments people find themselves in. It stems also from the mysterious depths of the human soul, with its often dimly understood thicket of motivations, desires, beliefs and emotions. Perhaps in the end every moral question has an answer (I shall not pursue this difficult issue); but even in cases where we are on surer ground, we will find that we sometimes have to deal in approximations and probabilities. The moral theorist should minimise these where possible, but they cannot be eliminated and should indeed be welcomed as indicators that morality is about people, not machines; and we shall see in the course of the discussion that some moral theories go too far in their attempt to find exactness where it is not to be had. All of the above, however, is a far cry from the unwarranted assumption that ethics cannot be a science because it is not as exact as some other sciences.

To take first the least troublesome requirement mentioned above, the repeatability of results was said to mean that in the same circumstances, using the same methods, any investigator will get the same result. Since ethics is not an experimental science, there is no question of empirical conditions being the same. Note that we are not talking here about a different matter: that if it is right or wrong for a person to perform an action in certain circumstances, then it is also right or wrong (respectively) for any other person to perform the same action in the same or relevantly similar circumstances – this is what has been called the *universalisable* character of ethics, and was emphasised by Kant. The point being made here is not about what is right and wrong, but about how we *reason* about what is right or wrong, which may be done by any person about any other person's situation. At this second level of moral theory, all that repeatability means is that any moral theorist starting from the same principles as another and reasoning in the same way (which includes applying the principles in the same way) will reach the same result. Now it might be thought that this is far too strong a claim and so cannot be true. Perhaps as a claim about what moral philosophers actually do this is so – but the same goes for repeatability in the natural sciences. Hardly any experiment ever performed in the history of natural science would pass the repeatability test if this required that all scientists who performed the experiment always got the same result. Mistakes are made; data are misinterpreted; conditions thought to be the same (or relevantly similar) are sometimes subtly not; and so on. It is equally true in ethics that principles are sometimes misinterpreted, relevant facts are not appreciated, logical fallacies are committed, and so on. A more modest claim, however, and one that is more plausible, is that where results diverge even when the same principles and reasoning are ostensibly employed, it is possible in principle to show what went wrong – for instance, where the reasoning was faulty. Similarly, it is a mark of natural science that divergent experimental results can, at least in principle, be explained.

The situation in natural science is of course far more complicated, and I do not claim more in the way of analogy between it and ethics than is necessary for present purposes. What is being claimed is simply that you should not regard ethics as unscientific on the specious ground that there is no constancy in moral theorists' conclusions based on similar reasoning. Ethics is a rational and intelligible discipline; it can be taught; its principles and the conclusions derived from them can be communicated, even between moral philosophers who do not share the same principles – they can nevertheless understand each other's reasoning and see how to get to a certain conclusion given certain assumptions. In this way as in many others ethics, while about people, is far from personal or subjective.

A similar point can be made about the existence of recognised methods of investigation, which is another mark of a science, and here ethics is again at no disadvantage. If by 'recognised', however, we mean that all investigators agree about all the methods to be used, we make too strong a claim. But it is clear that just as there is general agreement about how to carry out research in natural science, so there is in ethics. This can be seen in the possibility of *communication* and *understanding* between theorists in both areas. Two molecular biologists, for example, might have distinct views about the role of induction in genetics (for instance, the forming of conclusions about whole populations from limited samples), or even about what induction *is* (a subject that has exercised philosophers for centuries). But this does not prevent them communicating their results to each other and comprehending the methods each has used to achieve them. Similarly, two moral theorists might disagree about whether ethics involves the calculation of good and bad effects (as the consequentialist believes, about which more later) and they might arrive at radically different conclusions as a result; but they can understand each other's method and argue about which is correct. This is because, at a more general level, they agree about how to go about doing ethics, which is the way all philosophy is done: through reason, logic, the development of general principles, the derivation of secondary principles (and so on) and the application of those principles to particular situations. The more specific the methods in question, the more philosophers will disagree; all one can do in the face of such disagreement is to insist that there are *correct* methods and, if one believes one knows them, to try to convince others. Similarly for natural science, though it must be admitted that agreement between natural scientists holds more firm – as methods are described more specifically – than it does in philosophy in general and ethics in particular. More will be said about the phenomenon of disagreement in a minute; but again the general point is clear and hence disagreement should not prevent you from taking seriously the idea of ethics as a science.

Is there progress in moral philosophy? It seems that in natural science there is the steady accumulation of knowledge: as long as we take suitably long periods of time, it appears that in each period there is ignorance about certain questions that is removed in a subsequent period. In fact this is a simplistic conception of scientific progress and one open to debate; but let us assume that some such picture is correct. Can something similar be said about ethics? First, we must be careful not to confuse two questions, namely whether there is progress in moral philosophy and whether there is progress in how people *behave*. It is quite conceivable that moral theorists should have steadily accumulated a body of ethical truths even though hardly anyone respected them! It is the first question that is our concern, however. Either there is progress in ethics or there is not. If there is, we have no problem. And many people would argue that there *is* indeed progress in ethics. They would say, for instance, that philosophers have been the ideological driving force behind the development of the liberal democratic society, which is an improvement on earlier models of social organisation. They might cite, for instance, the influence of John Stuart Mill on the achievement of equal rights for women or the abolition of slavery. They might appeal to the writings of Jeremy Bentham, which they say greatly influenced prison reform and the improvement of our treatment of animals. Or they may cite the philosophy of Jean-Jacques Rousseau and its contribution to the ideals of democracy as based on the sovereignty of the people. Or perhaps Jean-Paul Sartre's important critique of anti-Semitism. The list that might be appealed to is a long one, which, it will be said, builds an impressive picture of the progress philosophers have made in moral theory.

If the above view is correct, there is no further question about whether there is progress in ethics. On the other hand, suppose there is no progress – that the history of ethics does not demonstrate the neat model of steady accumulation of knowledge said to be evident in the history of natural science. Does this count against the pretensions of ethics to scientific status? Only if there is no *explanation* of the lack of progress. It is perfectly possible to maintain that ethics done properly involves (among other things) the building up of a body of truths and yet that moral philosophers have for one reason or another on the whole not managed to do this, at least in recent history. One reason might be that natural science has an impersonal character that ethics does not. The former is about the cold, hard facts of the operation of nature. True, as recent philosophers such as Thomas Kuhn and Paul Feyerabend have shown, there are far more political and social influences on the way natural science develops than was once thought: like more politically sensitive areas of enquiry, it too is buffeted by the winds of favour and disfavour, by prevailing ideology (witness natural science as it was practised in the Soviet Union and Nazi Germany), by the urgent need to preserve academic reputation, or to fall in with the Establishment.

On the whole, however, natural science, concerned as it is with the impersonal workings of the universe, is able to proceed in a disinterested fashion. And yet if it too is subject to the sorts of forces mentioned above, how much more so is ethics, concerned as it is with matters of human action and character, often of the most intimate kind? Questions of right and wrong are, among other things, questions about whether and in what circumstances human action is *restricted*, whether human behaviour conforms to certain standards, with the inevitable conclusion that it should *change* in the areas where it fails so to conform. What morality *requires* of the individual (or of society) is all too often what the individual (or society) does not want to do. Given that moral theory enters deeply into the life of the individual and the society in which he lives, it is wholly unsurprising that what people want or do is often not what morality tells them they should want or do. Nor is it surprising that moral theorists themselves – who, after all, must see themselves as bound by the conclusions they arrive at, and who are not isolated from society but equally subject to the swings of popular approval and disapproval – might not allow themselves to be led in the direction in which reason leads them.

Further, the factors mentioned above, such as fashion, reputation, ideology and the like, influence philosophy just as much as they influence natural science, and so compound the tendency of ethicists not to be seen to be converging upon the truth. To take but one example, it is clear that the current dominant view of moral theorists in favour of euthanasia, where once it was approved of by no one, happens to coincide with the oft-repeated line of most governments, echoed unceasingly by the media, that there is a growing scarcity of hospital resources and that long-term care of the terminally ill, the elderly, and the severely incapacitated is a growing economic burden on the state. The 'obvious' conclusion does not need to be drawn explicitly – though it sometimes is. Nor is it necessary (or even possible) to try to show that moral theorists have somehow tailored their views on euthanasia to suit Establishment opinion on the economic burden to the state of certain classes of people. All that is being suggested is that it would be simplistic to think that the prevailing winds of social policy do not at least subtly influence the way ethicists think. All of this is enough to explain why, if there is no convergence in ethics even though it is a science, this should be so.

The above considerations apply equally to the phenomenon of *disagreement* among ethicists. Again, there is plenty of disagreement among natural scientists, often on fundamental questions. (Consider some of the great debates of the past, such as whether light is made of waves or particles, or whether the continents move, and debates of the present, such as whether mankind can be traced back to one geographical region.) On the whole, however, more of them seem to agree on more things than do moral philosophers, but as long as there is an *explanation* of the commonness of disagreement, there is no reason for thinking ethics is inherently unscientific. To the above remarks, however, we can add some further ones. First, widespread agreement should not be taken as a sufficient condition of the knowledge-yielding status of a discipline. For instance, there is much agreement as to how to go about astrology: not the generally spurious material found in tabloid newspapers, where there is plenty of divergence, but astrology as practised at a higher level by the aid of immensely detailed star charts, planet guides, and so on. But we would need much further convincing that astrology was a science: mere professional agreement is not enough. The same goes for quasi-medical disciplines such as iridology or reflexology, where practitioners agree impressively about which parts of the body are connected to which sorts of illness, how to diagnose illnesses, and so on. But why, then, should widespread agreement be taken as *necessary* for scientific status any more than it should be taken as *sufficient?*

Second, there is a question of the onus of proof. Methodologically, there is much sense in assuming that where people disagree over a certain question, there is a truth of the matter to be had unless there are good reasons for thinking otherwise. If people express their disagreements in terms of differing opinions, we should assume their opinions are *about* something and can be *justified* – that one opinion might be closer to the truth than another. Would not any other approach involve a certain lack of commitment, a willingness to give up on rational debate where, with perhaps a little hard work, further progress could be made? The appeal to disagreement, then, even if such disagreement be widespread, seems to induce a sort of torpor in the face of rational enquiry. As truth-seeking individuals we should look hard for truth, and assume it is there until convinced it is not.

1.2.1   The fact–value distinction

The widespread scepticism about ethics today – the idea that there is no knowledge to be had about right and wrong (any more than about art – 'there is no disputing matters of taste', it is often said) – owes much to the empiricist tradition in philosophy. Empiricism places the foundations of knowledge wholly in experience, observation, feeling and sensation. If a discipline cannot be understood – at least ultimately – in those terms, it does not have a claim to objectivity. It is arguable whether, understood correctly, an empiricist philosophy should rule out ethics on this count, but it would take us too far afield to discuss empiricism in general. What I want to focus on is the so-called *fact–value* distinction which arises out of it and which is responsible for much modern scepticism.

The distinction finds its classic statement in the philosophy of David Hume. He famously remarked: 'In every system of morality, which I have hitherto met with, I have always remarked, that the author ... makes observations concerning human affairs; when of a sudden I am surprised to find, that instead of the usual ... propositions, *is*, and *is not*, I meet with no proposition that is not connected with an *ought*, or an *ought not.*' And he considered it 'altogether inconceivable, how this new relation can be a deduction from others, which are entirely different from it'.[2] In other words, how is it possible to get from statements of fact – statements about what *is* – to statements about what one *ought* to do, or what *ought* to be? Is there not an unbridgeable logical gap here? If so, then it seems morality is really detached from fact and must be about something else: feeling, taste, emotion, or whatever.

The so-called fact–value distinction embodies various confusions, but only the most important will be mentioned here.[3] The first concerns facts. Proponents of the distinction argue as follows. Facts are the elements of reality that make declarative sentences true. To take a simple example, the sentence 'Charles ate a sandwich for lunch', if it is true, is made true by the fact that a certain individual, Charles, ate a particular thing, namely a sandwich, for his lunch. If reality did not contain this fact (say, because Charles did not exist, or ate ham and eggs for lunch, or ate a sandwich, but for dinner rather than lunch), the sentence would not be true. A similar analysis can be made of any fact, they say. But what about moral facts? What possible elements of reality would make true the sentence 'Breaking a promise is wrong'? Ethical sentences – about what is right or wrong, good or bad – are in a different class from statements of fact, since there is no realm of reality in virtue of which they are true or false. Where is this 'ethical realm'? How do we know about it? How can we check the truth of ethical statements against it? Are we to say that just as the predicate ' . . . is green' refers to a property of the real world, namely the colour green, so there is a property of the real world, namely wrongness, to which the ethical predicate ' . . . is wrong' refers?

The above line of argument is a familiar one. Although it has been refined and complicated in various ways, and more subtle versions have been developed, the basic idea is always the same. It is also easily countered in several ways, but only one need be proposed here. The proponent of the fact–value distinction is in the dilemma of having to provide an account of 'fact' that neither begs the question against the believer in ethical facts nor allows such facts to be philosophically respectable after all.

Suppose the Humean (which I shall call the believer in the fact–value distinction) understands facts to be elements of concrete, observable reality that can be used to verify (or falsify) propositions. On such an understanding, it seems ethical facts do not get to first base. One would be hard pressed to say that we could check the statement 'Breaking a promise is wrong' against the fact that breaking a promise is wrong in anything like the way we could check the statement 'Charles ate a sandwich for lunch' against the fact that Charles ate a sandwich for lunch. The Humean is right: Where do we check? How? What do we look for?

The problem for the Humean, though, is that this account of facts simply begs the question against the ethical realist (as I shall call the believer in moral facts). All it amounts to is the insistence that if there were moral reality it would have to be just another part of empirical reality, which is supposed to close the debate. But the ethical realist does not share this insistence. If the only philosophically respectable facts are observable elements of concrete reality, then moral facts seem to be ruled out from the very beginning and nothing else the realist can adduce in favour of moral facts will count. But by claiming that there are moral facts, the realist is not thereby *assuming* that the empiricist view of facts is correct. If the sceptic about moral facts wants to use the notion of a fact to cast doubt on realism, then, he must not rely on a conception that the moral realist does not share in the first place.

Of course, the Humean is bound to justify his belief that the only genuine facts are observable elements of concrete reality, and he may well try to do so. This would involve a full-blown justification of a view of empiricism that supports such a belief, a view which there is no space to canvass here. The point is simply that, short of doing this, he will need to rely on a less controversial conception of facts, one which does not foreclose the debate against the realist. Again, without going into detail, it should be noted that the more deeply we look for a substantial view of facts as elements of reality, the more we realise how complicated our conception must be and the less probable becomes the claim that there is no space for moral facts. Where in reality would we look for facts to make true or false statements such as: 'If Alan had bet on horse number five, he would have won'; 'One day the universe will come to an end'; 'Mountain climbing is a dangerous sport'; 'Brian is a peculiar sort of chap'; 'The joke Alan told me is very funny'; and so on? The more one thinks about such statements, the harder it is to point to an element of concrete observable reality that verifies or falsifies them. Let us leave it to the Humean to try to perform the impossible task of accounting for such cases while retaining a conception of facts that straightforwardly rules out the ethical.

A different way of understanding facts is possible, however. Instead of thinking of them as elements of concrete reality, we might plausibly think of them as *true propositions*. Part of the motivation for this approach is the notorious difficulty of *individuating* facts. One theory is as follows: sentences express propositions (for instance, a proposition is what is expressed by two sentences, in different languages, that say the same thing); it is propositions that are the primary entities that are true or false, with sentences deriving their truth or falsity from them; and a fact is whatever it is to which a true proposition corresponds. We can individuate facts, then, by means of the true propositions that correspond to them. For instance, the fact that snow is white is distinct from the fact that snow is cold because the propositions that snow is white and that snow is cold are themselves distinct. But the problem then is that in order to know whether a proposition is true, you need to know if it corresponds to a fact; but in order to know whether there is a fact to which it corresponds, you need to know whether the proposition is true in the first place! So, in order to know whether the proposition *that snow is white* is true, you need to know if there is a *fact* that snow is white. But to know the latter, it seems you need first to know the former. It appears, then, that one cannot really separate facts from propositions.

This might make one move to a view of facts that does not take them to be anything over and above true propositions. (Let us leave aside false propositions, since the point can be made without considering this complication.) The fact that Charles ate a sandwich for lunch, then, just *is* the true proposition that he did so. If we take this less metaphysically robust notion of facts to be correct, however, moral facts begin to look philosophically respectable. For the fact that breaking a promise is wrong just is the proposition that breaking a promise is wrong, which is true. Moral facts, on this account, suffer from no special metaphysical problems. Just as the proposition about Charles can be asserted, denied, believed, entertained, and argued over, and conclusions can be drawn from it, the same goes for the proposition about promise-breaking. These are *intrinsic features* of all propositions.

The second point concerning the fact–value distinction can be dealt with more briefly. Proponents of the distinction often argue that morality is about *reasons for action*. For instance, the truth of 'Pornography is morally objectionable' is a reason not to promote it in any way, say by selling it or financing it. We can look further at the facts on which this reason is based, such as that pornography is a cause of sexual crime; but what about the reason itself: isn't it over and above the facts that give rise to it? When talking about reasons, are we not also talking about *norms* or *rules* of behaviour, and not facts?

To the extent that this objection is merely a repetition in a different guise of the first one, namely the supposed strangeness of moral facts, we need not go over the same ground. What should be added, however, is that there is nothing peculiar in something's being both a fact *and* a reason. Reasons are about *explanation* and *justification*. The reason why Charles got food poisoning, for instance, is that he ate contaminated meat. The fact that he ate contaminated meat is also an explanation of his becoming ill. The fact that the meat was contaminated and the fact that he ate it give a justification for claiming that there is a causal connection between them and his becoming ill. The fact that the meat was contaminated can be used as a premise in an argument to the effect that he became ill because of what he ate. These are all familiar characteristics of the enterprise of giving reasons, but they are no less important for being familiar. Facts can be reasons for saying certain things, for putting forward certain arguments, for drawing certain conclusions, for holding certain beliefs, and so on. A fact is no less a fact, as it were, for being able to do duty in these different ways. On the contrary, something would not be a fact if it did *not* have such features. Why, then, are moral facts to be discounted because they have precisely the same features? To say that morality is about reasons for *action* as opposed to thought, belief, assertion, and so on, is spurious; for these are all kinds of action as well. In short, the so-called duality of facts and reasons is an illusion.

This brings us to the central problem with the fact–value distinction, of which the above points are really just aspects. Taken one way, the distinction does imply an unbridgeable conceptual gap between facts and values – but the cost of forging it, for the Humean, is that he loses his grip on reality. Taken another way, however, there is still a distinction that can be made – this time one we are bound to accept, but not one the Humean can make any use of in supporting his sceptical position.

Consider the following description. Charles picks up a shiny metal object. The object contains several movable parts, one of which can be rotated. Charles rotates it. He then places his finger on another, curved movable part, holds up the object in front of him, and points at another object further away. He then moves his finger towards him while keeping it in contact with the curved movable part. This is a perfectly coherent factual description. Does it enable us to know what Charles is *doing*? Not completely; but then no description of any situation can be complete. So why should we ask for any more information? Well, Charles might be doing a number of things – for example, he might be playing Russian roulette with a friend. To say that this is not important extra information is absurd: it is information of the highest importance, which allows us to realise that Charles is doing something dangerous.

Consider another description. Alan digs a hole in a meadow. Is there anything else of any importance that we need to know? It might be wondered – what else *is* there to know? But suppose I tell you that the meadow in which Alan is digging a hole is an ancient religious burial site considered sacred by the local inhabitants, and that digging a hole in it is a gross profanation. Does that extra information not enable us to realise that Alan has offended the local inhabitants?

The point that such examples make clear is that there are various ways of describing a situation, ways which are more or less precise and more or less inclusive of important information – important because it may enable us to know what is *really* going on. It might be thought that no philosopher has cast in doubt such an obvious and vital point, but it is precisely this that was famously denied by Hume in his discussion of whether morality is something which can be *recognised* by the intellect in factual situations. He supposes:

> Let us choose any inanimate object, such as an oak or elm [by 'inanimate' he means 'not an animal' as opposed to 'not alive']; and let us suppose, that by the dropping of its seed, it produces a sapling below it, which springing up by degrees, at last overtops and destroys the parent tree: I ask, if in this instance there be wanting any relation, which is discoverable in parricide [the murder of a parent] or ingratitude? Is not the one tree the cause of the other's existence; and the latter the cause of the destruction of the former, in the same manner as when a child murders his parent?

And he concludes that as the 'relations are the same' in both cases, and 'as their discovery is not in both cases attended with a notion of immorality, it follows, that that notion does not arise from such a discovery'.[4]

At one level of description, Hume's analogy between a sapling killing its parent tree and a child murdering his parent is correct. Indeed, Hume himself does not describe the case at the right level since he uses the word 'murder', which itself connotes wrongdoing. But if we think of them simply as cases of one living thing killing another, it is hard to see where morality can be 'discovered', to use Hume's word. The problem is that the only levels of description at which Hume's point has any force are those that involve a radically impoverished apprehension of reality: not an impoverished conception of *morality*, but of *what exactly is going on*. Only if we ignore crucial facts, properties and features of Hume's analogy, or of the examples I gave above, can we hope to divorce fact from value. Of course there is nothing unusual about such examples – they can be multiplied indefinitely. *Any* situation can be redescribed, or described at such a level of incompleteness, that it leaves out precisely those aspects that enable one to 'discover' its moral characteristics. We need not speak of *murder* – we can instead talk about killing, or perhaps termination. We need not talk about *cowardice* – we can instead talk about the conscious avoidance of situations involving minimal risk to life and limb. We need not speak of *lying* – instead we can speak of being 'economical with the truth', as a high-ranking British civil servant told the court in a famous legal case in the 1980s. Indeed, it is bureaucrats who are specially trained to describe situations at such a level of abstraction and incompleteness that they do not actually say anything *false* – but neither do they tell the whole truth, how things *really* are.

The proponent of the fact–value distinction, then, can purchase his distinction, but at the high cost of having only a partial grasp of reality. A more complete grasp is called for, but it is not one according to which the distinction is remotely plausible in the sense that the Humean requires it to be to support scepticism. With a more complete appreciation of reality, there will still be a distinction between facts and values; there will still be a way of describing the world that only pays attention, say, to microphysics, to chemistry, to the movements of particles, to the interaction of objects, to pure cause and effect, and so on. But these descriptions will only capture a *segment* of reality, one which has a definite but limited place in ethical theory.

More generally, ethics is about good and bad. (I will be more precise about this in chapter 2.) But goodness and badness are fundamental features of reality as much as any other. Why is it good to look both ways before crossing the road? After all, how can there be any objective goodness in the mere turning of the head while crossing a piece of bitumen? And why is it good to eat green vegetables? Where is the objective goodness in the mere ingestion of organic matter containing chlorophyll which contributes to cell repair and regeneration? The questions need only be posed for their answers to be self-evident. Both actions are *good* for human beings, because they prevent bodily harm and promote health. And the prevention of bodily harm and promotion of health are themselves *good* for human beings, which is where the actions which realise them derive their goodness. In this sense, then, the Humean can forge no relevant distinction between fact and value. Indeed, it is value 'all the way down'.

1.2.2   Relativism

Scepticism about ethics is widespread. There is a pervasive belief that there is simply no objective good and bad, or right and wrong. By 'objective' I mean the feature a statement has when it is true (or false) independently of whether anyone believes it to be true (or false). By far the most common form that moral scepticism takes is the espousal of one or another version of *relativism*. There are numerous varieties of relativism, but what they all share is the central dogma that moral propositions, instead of having objective truth – truth for all people in all places at all times – are true relative to one standard but not another. While it is impossible to examine all the species of relativism, the doctrine is so common that some of its general features and problems should briefly be stated, problems that affect every specific version.

Perhaps the most widespread form of relativism, again deriving from the philosophy of David Hume, is what I shall call *personal* relativism, more usually called subjectivism. The central claim of personal relativism is that the truth or falsity (truth value) of moral statements varies from person to person, since morality is merely a matter of *opinion*. Now there are various ways in which subjectivists have elaborated this basic thought, developing more or less sophisticated semantic theories linking moral judgements with statements of opinion. It is impossible to look at them all, but since the sorts of objection I will raise can be applied in modified form to different versions, let us take just one kind of subjectivist theory. It is one of the more simple varieties, and while many philosophers would say it was too simple, it also happens to be the sort of subjectivism that the vast majority of students of moral philosophy believe; and it is an approach that many will continue to believe even after they have finished studying philosophy!

According to this version of subjectivism, there is no objective truth to the statement, for instance, 'Child abuse is wrong': all that a person is entitled to claim is something equivalent to 'I disapprove of child abuse.' Instead of saying 'I disapprove of child abuse', Alan may say 'Child abuse is wrong for me', or 'Child abuse is wrong from my subjective viewpoint', but he is not then allowed to say 'Child abuse is wrong, pure and simple', since it might be right from Brian's subjective viewpoint – he will say 'Child abuse is right for me, though it is wrong for Alan, who personally disapproves of it.' Generally speaking, moral judgements can never be considered apart from the question of who makes them. A moral judgement, 'X is wrong', made by a person P, can only be assessed for truth or falsity by relativising it to P: the subjectivist says that 'X is wrong', uttered by P, is equivalent in meaning to 'I disapprove of X' uttered by P. If an observer were to report on P's opinion, he would say, 'X is wrong for P, or as far as P is concerned; in other words, P disapproves of it.' But the observer can still say, 'However, I personally approve of it, so "X is wrong" is not true for me.'

For the subjectivist, to claim that there is a fact about the morality of child abuse, which transcends mere personal opinion, is a philosophical mistake. Certainly, there are facts about what is wrong for Alan, right for Brian, and so on. These facts are genuine – they are reports of the opinions (or 'sentiments', to use Hume's term) of individual moral judges – but since each judge makes law only for himself, he cannot impose his view of things on others. For the subjectivist, once the facts are in concerning the moral opinions of those engaged in a disagreement, there is no room for further argument. More accurately, there might be room for argument over *other* facts: Alan might claim 'I approve of child abuse' because he does not know the psychological damage it does to children. Had he known, he would have claimed 'I disapprove of child abuse'; and another person might change Alan's mind by pointing out the relevant facts. But what the personal relativist holds is that as long as there is no dispute over the facts, two people can make opposing claims about the morality of a certain action or type of behaviour with no room left for rational dispute. They have, as it were, reached bedrock.

As was said, the version of subjectivism just outlined is a simple one and all sorts of refinements can be added. Still, it is the view held by very many philosophy students, not to say quite a few philosophers (and certainly vast numbers of the general population), and should be assessed in that light. Further, as was also noted, the general kinds of objection that can be raised against it apply to the more sophisticated versions. We can only consider a few devastating objections here, but it should be noted that the validity of any one on its own is enough to refute subjectivism, whatever the strength of the others. Given the weight of all the objections, however, it is surprising that personal relativism should be so widely held.

First, there is a semantic problem. A proposition of the form 'Doing X is wrong' uttered by P (for some action or type of behaviour X and some person P) is, according to the personal relativist, supposed to *mean* no more nor less than 'P disapproves of doing X': the latter statement is claimed to give the *meaning* or *analysis* of the former. But 'P disapproves of doing X' cannot, on this analysis, be equivalent to 'P believes that doing X is wrong', since 'Doing X is wrong' is precisely what the relativist seeks to give the meaning *of*; in which case the analysis would be circular. On the other hand, the relativist might again analyse the embedded sentence 'Doing X is wrong' in 'P believes that doing X is wrong' as 'P believes that doing X is wrong', and so on, for every embedded occurrence of 'Doing X is wrong', thus ending up with an infinite regress: 'P believes that P believes that P believes . . . that doing X is wrong.' This, of course, would be no analysis at all, being both infinite and leaving a proposition of the form 'Doing X is wrong' unanalysed at every stage.

Such an obvious difficulty might make one wonder that any relativist should support such a way of trying to analyse 'Doing X is wrong'; but if he is committed to the idea that morality is a matter of *opinion* or *personal belief*, it seems that he tacitly invokes just such a pseudo-analysis. The only other route the relativist can take is to assert that 'P disapproves of doing X' needs no further gloss: it is a brute statement of disapproval that does not itself invoke the concept of wrongness (or rightness, goodness and the like). But then personal relativism collapses into *emotivism*, the theory that moral statements are just expressions of feeling or emotion and only *appear* to have the form of judgements that can be true or false. Emotivism is a different theory from relativism, however, and more will be said about it in the next section. Unless the personal relativist can give an analysis of disapproval that is neither circular, nor infinitely regressive, nor collapses his theory into emotivism, he is in severe difficulty; and it is hard to see just what such an analysis would look like.

Second, the concept of disapproval is inherently incapable of capturing the various kinds of moral statement that one can make. In particular, there are three broad types of proposition concerning moral obligation: one of the form 'Doing X is wrong' (or bad, impermissible, and the like); another of the form 'Doing X is right' (or good, obligatory, and so on); and another of the form 'Doing X is permissible' (neither obligatory nor forbidden, and perhaps neither good nor bad). (Note that this is highly simplified for the purpose of the argument. I will paint a fuller picture in later chapters.)

The personal relativist might analyse 'Doing X is right' uttered by P as 'P approves of doing X.' He might also analyse P's utterance of 'Doing X is wrong' as 'P disapproves of doing X.' But what about P's utterance of 'Doing X is permissible'? One obvious possibility is 'P neither approves nor disapproves of doing X.' But this is also compatible with P's *not know-ing whether* doing X is right, wrong, or permissible, which is different from the settled opinion that it *is* permissible. P might neither approve nor disapprove because he is confused about the issue, or feels he has not gone into it far enough, or simply does not *have* an opinion. The relativist might reply that we can indeed analyse 'Doing X is permissible' uttered by P as 'P neither approves nor disapproves of doing X', but also analyse P's state of uncertainty, confusion or lack of opinion as 'P both approves *and* disapproves of doing X.' But this will not do, since one cannot both approve *and* disapprove of something at the same time: it is logically im-possible. What about the possibility of mixed feelings? But mixed feelings do not involve simultaneous approval and disapproval; rather, they in-volve first approving, later (perhaps almost immediately after) disapprov-ing, then perhaps approving again, and so on. But a series of statements of approval followed by disapproval will not do as an analysis of P's lack of certainty, lack of an opinion, or whatever: for on the relativist view each statement corresponds to a *distinct* and *unequivocal* opinion by P: first P disapproves of doing X, then he approves, then he disapproves, and so on. These are not states of uncertainty, nor do they collectively *add* up to a state of uncertainty, any more than variations of opinion *between people*. For the relativist, the varying states of approval and dis-approval, both between people and within one person's mind, correspond to distinct facts about the wrongness of doing X: it is wrong for Alan, but right for Brian, but wrong for Charles; and it is wrong for Alan on Tues-day, but right for Alan on Wednesday, and so on. In short, then, the personal relativist cannot distinguish between an opinion that something is definitely permissible and a lack of opinion or state of uncertainty as to whether it is permissible.

Third, the personal relativist wants to give a *complete* analysis of all moral statements into statements of approval and disapproval; and he must, or else he will not have given an analysis at all. What, then, does the relativist say about the principle of *tolerance*, or the freedom of each per-son to express whatever moral opinion he likes? Relativism is tradition-ally motivated by this very idea: if morality is simply a matter of personal opinion, then no one can be allowed to impose his sincerely held belief on someone who believes differently. But is the principle of tolerance *itself* simply a matter of opinion? Alan might *disapprove* of tolerance: is he then allowed to impose his moral beliefs on others, even by physical coer-cion? Either the relativist says that he can, or that he cannot: but it is hard to see which view the relativist is logically bound to take, in which case relativism is compatible both with tolerance and with oppression, which is not a conclusion the vast majority of relativists would countenance. Suppose, however, that the relativist bites the logical bullet and says that, *logically* speaking, tolerance or oppression is open to each individual in respect of others. Then relativism collapses into moral *nihilism*, the view that there are no objectively valid moral rules whatsoever governing interpersonal behaviour. I do not propose to give a critical analysis of nihilism here, merely to note that relativism could not then be seen to be a stable alternative to the view that 'anything goes' in morality, which, again, is not how relativists see their theory. Further, the view that anything goes is quite simply morally repugnant, which should be sufficient to deter rational people from giving it, or any form or relativism that leads to it, further consideration.

Suppose, on the other hand, that the relativist is able logically to resolve the problem of tolerance versus oppression, and opts – one would hope – in favour of the view that you may not coerce others to believe what you believe; and that this is an *objective moral truth*. Then the relativist will have countenanced at least one objective moral truth, contrary to his own theory that all morality is a matter of opinion. Now he might say, 'But tolerance is the *only* objective moral truth I recognise.' Why, however, should we believe him? If tolerance is objectively right, this is a big principle to concede – why are there no others? Why should there be only one moral truth? To reply, 'But that's what my theory implies' is no answer. Rather, it is the theory itself which then comes into doubt. One would need a convincing explanation indeed as to why there is only one moral truth, as much as if a physicist were to say there is only one truth of physics (which would *not* be the same as saying there is only one 'supertruth', say a grand equation, from which all the other *distinct* truths can be derived); or the historian that there is only one historical fact. In the words of the philosopher W. V. Quine (himself a relativist of sorts both in ethics and in other areas of philosophy, and here speaking about cultural relativism, though his remark applies to all forms of relativism): 'He [the cultural relativist] cannot proclaim cultural relativism without rising above it, and he cannot rise above it without giving it up.'[5]

The other primary form of relativism is not personal but *social* (usually called cultural relativism). The social relativist holds that morality is not a matter of personal opinion, but of the opinion of society. More precisely, 'Child abuse is wrong', for example, uttered by person P in society S, means 'S disapproves of child abuse.' Often the social relativist will say, 'Child abuse is disapproved of in such-and-such a *culture*', or such-and-such a group, or such-and-such a country, and so on. This gives rise to a problem that will be mentioned shortly, but what must be noted at once is that whatever the social relativist's favourite word, the theories are all variations of one another and of the general theory that morality is relative to a social standard.

Fortunately, we can be brief in our discussion of social relativism, because all the above problems – each one on its own being fatal to personal relativism – apply equally to social relativism. Some further remarks, however, are in order. First, there is a purely factual point worth making because of its historical and continuing importance. The rise of social relativism to its prominent place today was motivated in large part by the huge influx of information this century concerning the behaviour, customs and habits of cultures around the world. A prime example of this is the work of the famous anthropologist Margaret Mead, whose book *Coming of Age in Samoa* had a remarkable influence both on social science and on philosophical thinking. It was (and still is) widely thought that she had proven that there was nothing sacrosanct about Western moral standards by adducing evidence of wide divergence from them in the case of the Samoans. She concentrated, among other things, on sexual behaviour, family arrangements, warfare and rituals, and she seemed to show that the Samoans were an example for the West of an almost idyllic form of social arrangement – peaceful, trouble-free and unrepressed, lacking the taboos and strict moral code that hindered the personal development of Western man.

Influential though her work was, it has now been effectively demolished. Most notably, the anthropologist Derek Freeman has demonstrated that Mead's research was shoddy, ill-informed and painted a far from accurate picture of Samoan life, one that was almost patronising in its depiction of the Samoan as a 'noble savage' (to use Rousseau's expression). Contrary to Mead's alleged findings, for instance, the Samoans condemned adultery and premarital promiscuity, and practised warfare on a far wider scale than she claimed. Freeman concludes, 'We are thus confronted in the case of Margaret Mead's Samoan researches with an instructive example of how, as evidence is sought to substantiate a cherished doctrine, the deeply held beliefs of those involved may lead them unwittingly into error.' Indeed, Freeman even goes so far as to claim that Mead was *hoaxed* by the Samoans, having been fed spurious tales of their sexual and other behaviour![6]

A grave conceptual problem for the social relativist is the determination of the standard he is using. Is morality relative to the beliefs of a culture, a society, a nation, a country, an ethnic group, a religious group, a tribe? None of these necessarily coincide, though sometimes they do. Certainly, in the world as it is today, with greatly increased migration and multiculturalism, it is even harder to find a well-defined 'unit of measurement' that the social relativist should use. Is the morality of adultery, for instance, to be identified by reference to the common opinion of each member of the UN? Does 'the West' count as a standard, and if so, which countries are included? If Alan is in the United States, does he speak truly or falsely when he says 'Abortion is wrong where there is no threat to the mother's life or health'? This statement might be denied by the majority of US citizens, but it is also affirmed by significant and well-defined subgroups, both religious (for example, Christians of various denominations, Moslems, orthodox Jews) and geographical (large parts of the Southern states). Does Alan speak falsely when he is in California, but truly in Georgia? Or is his standard the group *he* belongs to? In which case, if he is an orthodox Jew, does he speak truly even in California because he has the common opinion of the majority of orthodox Jews around the world on his side? What if he is in Africa, where the multiplicity of tribes and systems of belief makes it almost impossible to speak of a single moral standard? Make the relevant unit of measurement small and one result is obtained; larger, and another is obtained. The social relativist cannot dismiss this problem by saying that it shows how moral standards vary greatly: the problem is of *identifying* a moral standard in the first place, especially in an age of enormous diversity of opinion; and also of avoiding contradiction or hopeless vagueness when someone utters a moral statement. The identification of standards seems, then, to be an arbitrary matter that can yield whatever result the relativist wants. And this is a good reason why the personal relativist insists that all measurement should come down to the beliefs of the individual.

Further, even if a particular standard is identified, what is the quantum of measurement to be? Is abortion wrong in society S if 51 per cent of the population has that opinion? Or 50.1 per cent? Perhaps in grave moral matters a larger threshold is required – say 75 per cent? Do we look at the *laws* of that society and say that abortion is wrong if it is illegal, because legality best reflects S's belief system? But it is a common fact that what the law says and what a society thinks often diverge. Do we look at S's *practices* as well as stated beliefs (perhaps as expressed in opinion polls)?

There is no sociological reason why practice as opposed to stated beliefs should be excluded – but again, what the members of a society *do* is often different from what they say they believe (obvious cases being adultery or promise-keeping). Social relativism, then, is arbitrary both with respect to the determination of a standard and the degree of measurement within that standard.

1.2.3   Prescriptivism and expressivism

Before ending our discussion of ethics as a knowledge-yielding discipline, two other theories should be mentioned. Both deny that ethical statements are in any way *reports* of facts, whether about an objective moral realm, about a person's state of mind, or about the beliefs of a society. Expressivism, like most other sceptical theories about morality, derives its motivation from Hume, who remarked, 'Morality, therefore, is more properly felt than judged of.'[7] It was developed in the 1920s and 1930s under the name 'emotivism' or 'the emotive theory of ethics' by Ogden and Richards (writing in 1923), A. J. Ayer (writing in 1936) and C. L. Stevenson (writing in the late 1930s and early 1940s). The idea behind all versions is that when, for instance, Alan says 'Child abuse is wrong', all he is *really* doing is *expressing* his emotional repulsion: what he is saying is, to put it somewhat crudely, 'Down with child abuse!' And when he says, for example, 'Promise-keeping is good', he is expressing his emotional attraction and so saying, in effect, 'Up with promise-keeping!' Thus moral utterances are not statements of fact at all: they are more similar to grunts and groans than to propositions, despite their outward appearance.

Prescriptivism is associated with the influential philosophy of R. M. Hare (writing first in 1952) and it too denies the fact-stating character of moral utterances. Rather than being like grunts and groans, however, for Hare they are really *imperatives* or commands. So when Alan says 'Surrogate motherhood is wrong', he is saying 'Do not be a surrogate mother' (and perhaps also, 'Do not support surrogate motherhood in any way'); and when he says 'Paying taxes is right', he is saying simply, 'Pay your taxes.'

Both theories have beguiled more philosophers than they have non-philosophers, and various reasons could be given as to why the beguilement is unjustified. I shall, however, state only one objection that is fatal to both. It is a well-known one and was put forward in its original form by Peter Geach, deriving his idea from the German philosopher Gottlob Frege.[8] Both expressivism and prescriptivism equate the assertion of a moral proposition with something other than the statement of a fact: in one case an expression of emotion, in the other a command. However, one can do more with moral propositions than assert them: one can use them in the context of other more complex propositions, so that the moral proposition that is a component of the more complex one is not asserted at all. For example, not only can Alan say, 'Prostitution is wrong'; he can also say, 'If prostitution is wrong, then so is living off the earnings of prostitution.' Suppose he says both things. From them he can conclude, by *modus ponens* ('If A then B; A; therefore, B'), 'Living off the earnings of prostitution is wrong.' The conclusion follows with absolute certainty, assuming the first two propositions are true. But it could not follow if the proposition 'Prostitution is wrong' had a different *meaning* in the first premise of the argument (where it is stated on its own) from its meaning in the second premise (where it is preceded by 'If . . . ' and followed by 'then living off the earnings of prostitution is wrong'). If the meanings were different, the argument would suffer from the fallacy of equivocation and so be invalid.

The expressivist analyses 'Prostitution is wrong' as 'Down with prostitution!'; and the prescriptivist, as 'Do not be a prostitute.' (Problem: what if Alan, who says 'Prostitution is wrong', is referring only to female prostitution, but is talking to a man? How should the prescriptivist analyse his remark?) Suppose we replace the first premise with either of the alleged equivalents. Since the meaning of the original proposition must be the same in the second premise for the whole argument to be valid, we must make the same substitutions respectively. In the expressivist case, the argument will then run: 'Down with prostitution!; if down with prostitution, then down with living off the earnings of prostitution!; therefore, down with living off the earnings of prostitution!' For the prescriptivist, the argument runs: 'Do not be a prostitute; if do not be a prostitute, then do not live off the earnings of prostitution; therefore, do not live off the earnings of prostitution.' We can immediately see that the second premise of both arguments is meaningless: what is the meaning of 'If down with prostitution, then . . . ', or of 'If do not be a prostitute, then . . . '? One simply cannot place commands or expressions of emotion in such a context. But then the original proposition, 'Prostitution is wrong', *cannot* be equivalent in meaning either to a command or to an expression of emotion. In a word, the emotivist and prescriptivist propose analyses of moral statements which, if used consistently, turn into nonsense obviously meaningful premises in obviously meaningful arguments. If not used consistently, the analyses fail for incompleteness. If, on the other hand, they are supplemented by the use of a different analysis for the same moral statement in different contexts (asserted in the first premise of the above argument, and unasserted in the second), they render obviously valid arguments invalid because of equivocation. In any case, expressivism and prescriptivism are false.

One response which is sometimes made to the Frege/Geach point is to assume, as does Jonathan Bennett,[9] that it denies the existence of entailments between commands or expressions of attitude. Bennett argues that it is wrong for the anti-expressivist (anti-prescriptivist) to try to gain mileage from the idea that compound ethical propositions (such as 'If prostitution is wrong, then living off the earnings of prostitution is wrong') are turned into nonsense when their component propositions are replaced with expressions of attitude or with prescriptions. Of course there are entailments between commands or attitude expressions, he retorts: 'The command "Bring peace to all people" entails "Bring peace to all poor people" for exactly the same reason that the statement "You will bring peace to all people" entails "You will bring peace to all poor people".' R. M. Hare recognised and explained this matter ages ago. So what is Geach getting all excited about?

The problem with Bennett's response, however, should be clear: it changes the subject. Let us suppose – plausibly, though there is room for argument – that there are indeed entailments between commands or attitude expressions. They are *not* the entailments between ethical propositions such as those found in the above 'if . . . then . . . ' argument (sometimes called moral *modus ponens*). It is *one* thing to say that 'Don't be cruel' entails 'Don't be cruel to animals', and *another* to say that 'Cruelty is wrong' entails 'Cruelty to animals is wrong.' The underlying logico-linguistic reasons for each entailment might be the same (although notoriously difficult to spell out), but it simply does not follow that 'Cruelty is wrong' *means* 'Don't be cruel.' The Frege/Geach point is not about the logical relations between prescriptions or attitudes, but about argument forms such as moral *modus ponens*, whose premises contain indicative component propositions such as 'Prostitution is wrong' which have a semantic form, unlike prescriptions and attitudes, that does not prevent them from being assessed as true or false, agreed or disagreed with, and themselves used as premises in arguments. ('Prostitution is wrong' looks like the sort of proposition that can be assessed as true or false, agreed with or disagreed with – it has the same indicative or fact-stating form as 'Grass is green.' As such, it can serve as a free-standing premise in an argument, such as the first premise of the example we are using, as well as being embedded within a compound proposition, such as the 'if . . . then . . .' proposition which is the second premise of the sample argument.) It is *these* arguments that we perfectly well understand, and which we assess for validity (we *know* that the prostitution argument above is valid), but which, if prescriptivism or expressivism were true, would turn out to be incomprehensible at worst, or implausibly have to be deemed invalid at best.

The prescriptivist or expressivist might therefore rejoinder:

> So, ditch moral *modus ponens* and all argument forms that mimic arguments involving fact-stating propositions, and replace them with their parallels using expressions of attitude or commands. What you should be arguing is (something like): 'Don't be a prostitute; "Don't be a prostitute" entails "Don't live off the earnings of prostitution"; so don't live off the earnings of prostitution.' If you insist on calling *this* argument form "moral *modus ponens*" go ahead, but forget about what *you* were calling moral *modus ponens*, or at least think of your version as *really* being, on analysis, my version.

This sort of reaction, however, won't do. To 'ditch' moral *modus ponens* and similar argument forms in favour of others is simply to 'ditch' reality, that is, real arguments with perfectly good meanings, in favour of *other* arguments with *other* meanings. Further, to *think* of moral *modus ponens* as 'really' being an expressivist or prescriptivist argument form is no easier to do than to think of an orange as *really* being an apple (even if they are, at a more basic level, both fruit!). That is not a healthy way of doing philosophy.

The message of the Frege/Geach point, then, is not that we necessarily have to rule out logical relations between commands or expressions of attitude, but that there are *other*, arguably more basic, argument forms which *cannot* be accounted for, in terms of meaning or validity, by an expressivist or prescriptivist reduction. Arguments such as the one above concerning prostitution abound in ethics as in other areas of discourse. Moral propositions are not always asserted: they are embedded in unasserted contexts like 'if . . . then . . .' statements, but they are also assumed, wondered about, entertained, and the like. In *all* such contexts, treating them as commands or expressions of emotion produces nonsense. (I leave it to the reader to think of argument forms other than moral *modus ponens* that also show the absurdity of the analytical reductions proposed by the expressivist and the prescriptivist.) This is not to say, of course, that commands and expressions of emotion have no part in ethics: on the contrary, they are a central feature of ethical discourse and practice. Moral propositions allow certain commands to be made: for instance, the Ten Commandments, stated as they are in the imperative form, are meaningful and can be obeyed or disobeyed. They are, though, not *equivalent* to the propositions (such as 'It is wrong to bear false witness') that license them. Similarly, moral statements are often, if not usually, accompanied by emotional responses: disgust, attraction, delight, horror, and so on. Expressivism and prescriptivism err by reversing the true order of explanation: it is the truth and falsehood of moral statements that *justify* the having of certain emotional responses and the issuing of commands. Any moral theory (such as Kant's) that ignored the role of emotion would be severely deficient. It is a far cry from the acceptance of these truisms, however, to try to dissolve moral truth and moral falsehood, and so the possibility of rational debate, into the cauldron of emotional reactions that accompany them and are justified by them.

1.3   Ethics and Action

As well as being a discipline that yields knowledge, ethics is concerned with the application of that knowledge to human conduct, which is why it is an applied (or practical) science.

Not every type of human conduct is the proper object of morality, however; for morality is concerned only with *free* conduct, or *action*. We can speak of actions that are not free, such as the action of the circulatory system, or the act of digesting food; but in ethics 'action' has a technical sense that excludes those bodily happenings that are not under the control of the will.

One of the presuppositions of the present work is that human beings have free will. I do not propose to defend this claim, or to refute determinism. Instead, it will be taken for granted that human beings are capable of acting freely, of making *choices* about what they do. In particular, they are capable of choosing between right and wrong, good and evil. Is this fact itself a good thing? This is a complex question, but in at least one sense the answer is, perhaps surprisingly, that the existence of human freedom is neither a good nor a bad thing. It just is. On this view, it is a tautology to say that choosing evil is bad and a contradiction to say that choosing evil is good. More particularly, since the choice of evil can never be good, the fact that people choose it is not to be admired as proof of human freedom; perhaps such a power is a *sign* of freedom, but only in the sense in which disease is a sign of life. One can imagine a world in which people chose only good and yet were still free, just as one might imagine a world in which mathematicians never made mistakes though they were free to do so: it would be the high level of development of their reasoning that kept them from error. In any case, one cannot say that a world of free people who chose only the good would by that very fact be worse than our own world.

Two types of freedom must not be confused: physical and psychological freedom on the one hand, and moral freedom on the other. A mathematician is psychologically free to deny Pythagoras' Theorem; but he is not *mathematically* free to do so. A soldier is physically free to go on what he knows will be a disastrous mission that serves no military purpose and will lead to his certain death; but he is not free, from the point of view of *military tactics*, to do so. Similarly, a person is psychologically free to decide to walk into his neighbour's house and insult him gratuitously, and he is physically free do so; but he is not *morally* free to do it. Moral freedom, then, is a species of *rational* freedom, as is mathematical freedom or tactical freedom. In that sense, one is only ever morally free to do the right thing, just as one is only mathematically free to believe what is mathematically true. The freedom of the will, then, is a type of physical and psychological freedom: the freedom to choose right or wrong.

There are, nevertheless, influences on the freedom of the will that should be mentioned as they are relevant to all moral questions, including those we will be looking at. First, there are what might be called *individual* influences on free will, the main ones being age, temperament and natural talent. For instance, the younger person is typically prone to impulsive behaviour: a child tends to grasp at whatever is in front of him, or to cry the minute he does not get his own way. Similarly, an adolescent tends to act wilfully and stubbornly in the face of parental authority, choosing what is forbidden precisely because it *is* forbidden. In the case of temperament, some people are, for instance, more prone than others to anger, or to depression, or to light-heartedness, which affects the choices they make.

So, too, natural talent is an influence. Some people have greater aptitudes for certain things than others, be they intellectual, artistic, physical, and the like. The presence or absence of such talents obviously influences a person's moral development: for instance, a person's choice of profession is largely conditioned by his talents, which thereby present him with certain types of moral choice he might not otherwise have to make.

All of these tendencies, inclinations and circumstances influence the choices we make, but they do not destroy our freedom. We are bound to try to know ourselves as best we can, including facts about our individual situation, and to develop our characters in ways that compensate for them where they are likely to interfere with the making of good choices about how we live. A person remains master of his choices despite the various influences talent, age, temperament and other characteristics have upon him.

As well as individual influences on free will there are *social* influences, the main ones being upbringing and society. No one has the same upbringing as anyone else, not even identical twins brought up by the same parents, let alone someone born into a life of poverty and hardship and another born into a life of privilege. In particular, individuals are subject to different examples and role models. A child might throughout his childhood be faced with one bad example after another set by his parents. Upbringing is the single most important influence in a person's moral development, and yet the will is still free despite this influence. Even a child of reprehensible parents can develop into a right-thinking and right-acting adult; and with the best role models in the world, a child can still make many wrong choices and end up living a reprehensible life. These are facts almost too obvious to mention, but they are also too often ignored by those who claim that a person's will is thoroughly constrained by his upbringing.

Almost as important as family upbringing is society in affecting the choices a person makes. Fashions, trends, public opinion, prevailing ideology – all are powerful influences on a person's actions. And yet no person is simply a product of society – he remains a free agent, responsible for his actions, in spite of it. People can, and regularly do, rise above societal influences. Further, the sociological fact that so many people are 'slaves' of fashion, public opinion, and so on, does not prove they have no liberty of choice in the matter. Statistical analyses of mass behaviour under similar conditions are limited to external acts, whereas the wellsprings of human action, namely the inner inclinations, intentions and motives of the individual, continue to elude empirical enquiry of the most sophisticated kind. All that sociology and allied disciplines can ultimately show is to what extent people agree or disagree in certain practices; this is not the same as proving them to be unfree.

That a person is essentially a *free agent* means that he is *responsible* for his actions; he *answers* (responds) for them. Being responsible means that a person's actions are *imputable* to him: in other words, the person is properly blamed or praised for how he acts, and liable to reward or punishment as a result. The freedom that entails responsibility, however, contains two essential components: *knowledge* and *voluntariness*. A person is responsible for his action if and only if it is done knowingly and voluntarily; the complete absence of either or both of these elements destroys freedom and hence responsibility. A partial lack of either or both *lessens* or *diminishes* responsibility, but does not destroy it.

A couple of simple examples illustrate the above principles, though the matter is in fact far more complex than space will allow for discussion. Alan is visiting Brian and takes home the wallet he saw lying on the table. Alan thought it was his, but in fact it was Brian's. Alan is not guilty of theft, because he did not know the wallet was not his: here the requisite knowledge is lacking and Alan is not responsible. As Aristotle pointed out, one does not will what one does not know. Suppose Brian's wallet had been lying on the floor and Alan, walking along, accidentally kicked it into the open fire. Here, while Alan might have known what was happening – he may have watched in dismay as his foot pushed the wallet into the fire – what he did was an *accident* and so not voluntary. Although freedom, as was said, incorporates knowledge and voluntariness, we can speak more loosely of a voluntary act's being a free act, in the sense that the agent has *control* over what he is doing – he can choose to act or to refrain from acting.

Not every external action requires a presently occurring choice or act of will (or intention, as it can be called) for it to be voluntary. If Alan does not know what to have for breakfast, and then decides upon muesli, he eats the muesli because of an actual choice to do so. Brian, who has been rude to his work colleagues often in the past, resolves one morning to be as pleasant as possible at work that day. But he is so absorbed at work that he forgets his morning resolution. Nevertheless, he might still be polite all day, in virtue of the decision made earlier, without having an actual intention on each occasion specifically to be polite. In such a case we might call the intention or choice *virtual*, since the power (or virtue) of the early-morning resolution persists throughout the day; Brian is still responsible, and to be praised, for those acts of politeness.

Suppose Celia, having been well taught as a child, forms the intention to look both ways before crossing the street, but it is not something she thinks about at all once she has been taught. Years later she still looks both ways without a moment's reflection. Clearly the intention formed years ago is not directly efficacious, but Celia acts in accordance with it because she has acquired a habit of looking both ways: hence she acts with what we can call an *habitual* intention, and every act of looking both ways is voluntary and to be praised as a prudent thing to do. The habitual intention is, as it were, worn like a forgotten piece of jewellery, and is a sign of a certain attitude of mind.

While the total absence of relevant knowledge, or voluntariness, destroys freedom and hence responsibility for one's actions, there are also factors that *limit* responsibility for actions and hence lessen blameworthiness or praiseworthiness. Thus moral praise and blame are not all-or-nothing matters – they are matters of degree. Ignorance in particular is a case in point. Alan's lack of knowledge that it was Brian's wallet he took absolves him from blame for theft: he has not freely (that is, voluntarily *and* with advertence to what he is doing) stolen Brian's wallet. But he might be guilty of something else (in the moral sense – it is not *legal* guilt we are concerned with). If he realised that the wallet was probably Brian's and not his, but still took it, he is guilty not of theft but of something less, perhaps a *careless* or *reckless* taking of the wallet. Although he was actually ignorant that the wallet was Brian's, his ignorance is *culpable*, since he realised it was probably Brian's. If he did not realise it, but *ought* to have – suppose Alan did not even bring his own wallet with him, and knew perfectly well what Brian's wallet looked like, and so on – then he is guilty of a *negligent* taking of the wallet. His ignorance is culpable, since due and reasonable enquiry could have remedied it. Both reckless and negligent behaviour are blameworthy actions, but the lack of actual knowledge prevents the careless or the negligent person from being fully responsible for an intentional or deliberate action, which is more serious.

Similar observations can be made of other factors that might lessen responsibility for actions, though they cannot all be considered here. A good example is acting from fear. Suppose Donald threatens to shoot Fred if he does not rape Celia, and that Fred, acting purely from fear for his own life, does so. Fred still acts freely – he *could* have refused, though it would have meant his own death. Thus he is responsible for the rape;

but there is a sense in which his act is what might be called *conditionally* involuntary, since he *would* have refused point-blank were it not for his fear. This does lessen his blameworthiness to *some* extent: we would blame him less than if he had simply decided to rape Celia because he hated her. Fear, however, does not excuse an evil act that results from it. It does make choices more difficult, but then human acts are not necessarily easy acts: sometimes you have to refuse to do something no matter how scared you are of the consequences. Further, as Aristotle again pointed out, people are more than ready to take the credit for their good actions when done from emotions such as love or joy; so why should they not take the blame for bad acts done from fear, anger or despair? Of course, if a person under the influence of an emotion literally takes leave of his senses and simply does not know what he is doing, or acts almost like an automaton, directed wholly by whatever passion or emotion is controlling him, then he is not to be blamed at all for acts done under that influence. Nevertheless, he might be blamed for *allowing* himself to get into a certain state (say, by brooding over some past humiliation). And if he is not wholly consumed by emotion, he might still be responsible for something less than deliberate action (manslaughter rather than murder, for instance). We can contrast acting from fear with acting from violence, where responsibility is usually destroyed. If Alan pushes Brian into Celia, knocking her over, Brian has not acted voluntarily and so is not to blame; similarly if Alan forces Brian to shoot her by wrapping the latter's finger around the trigger and squeezing it. Nevertheless, if Brian were not at least to *resist* the violence internally (and externally if he had the chance) or to *regret* what happened after the event, he would be blameworthy, if not for the act itself, then for concurring in it.

Many of our acts, perhaps *most* of them, are done from habit; but again, habit does not destroy freedom and responsibility as long as the habit is *allowed* to endure. If Alan has a habit of using offensive language in front of other people and makes no effort whatsoever to disown the habit, then he is acting freely: he knows what he is doing, and is acting under an habitual intention (as explained above). If, however, Alan decides to overcome the habit, then he disowns it. But, as the saying goes, he who wills the end wills the means to that end, so for Alan to be sincere he has to be watchful of what he is saying, to monitor his remarks in public. If he is, then any offensive words that slip out are *not* ones for which he is to be blamed, since he is not responsible for them – in any than a merely bodily or behavioural sense. More will be said about habit in the following chapter, since it is central to ethics: morality is not just about individual actions, but about the *character* of the person who acts.

It was said that there are degrees of blameworthiness and praiseworthiness. This does not mean, however, that the boundaries of right and wrong are somehow blurred or confused. It does not mean there are no clear limits that, if crossed, make the agent guilty of a wrong act pure and simple. For instance, although Alan's killing of Brian might be something less than murder if done, say, out of extreme provocation, it will still be a wrongful killing. And if he *had* murdered Brian it would have been an evil act, perhaps the most evil a person can perform, and so warranting the fullest blame. In morality, then, there are certain *base levels* of conduct that make certain actions right or wrong whatever the circumstances. Murder, manslaughter, rape, child abuse, fraud: these are examples of acts that are wrong and to be condemned without qualification, and although factors such as those mentioned above might affect how we *classify* an act (say, as manslaughter rather than murder) or how severely we condemn it (condemning acts done from fear less than those that are coolly calculated), it remains that there are base levels of moral conduct that humans must observe. To take an analogy: suppose an engineer wants to build a bridge. In order to do so, the engineer will have degrees of freedom as to how he goes about building it. If the blueprint does not specify what material to use, he has a choice. If it does, he has no choice in that respect, but he may have a choice as to the width of the bridge, or its height. No blueprint will specify *everything* he has to do. Nevertheless, there are certain limits he cannot cross if he wants the bridge to do its job properly, and indeed if it is not to collapse altogether. There are certain rules of engineering he simply must obey – they are essential to successful bridge-building and so are, as it were, in the nature of things.

Similarly, both morality and circumstance give a person degrees of latitude in what he does – for instance, what means to use to achieve a desired end. But if morality, and so human relations, are not to break down altogether into an incoherent morass of meaningless behaviour, there must be rules that cannot be crossed; and moral theory itself supplies those rules. Perhaps the vast majority of people agree with general observations such as these. Where they are more likely to disagree is over precisely *what* those rules are. In the following three chapters, the fundamental concepts of morality will be set out from which rules can be derived and applied to the concrete (and controversial) cases that will occupy the companion volume, *Applied Ethics*.

2

Basic Concepts In Moral Theory I

2.1   Introduction

Before we can go on to consider the concrete problems that will be discussed in *Applied Ethics*, it is necessary to provide an overview of the fundamental concepts and principles that govern the reasoning to be employed in solving those problems. It is impossible in the limited space available to provide a comprehensive defence of the principles to be enunciated, or of the plausibility and centrality of the basic concepts. Also, I will at this stage omit some important ideas and principles, but they are more in the nature of secondary notions, to be stated and briefly defended in later discussion when they are put to use in particular situations. The primary task, then, is threefold: first, to state, explain and briefly defend the basic concepts of moral theory; second, to show how they form a *network* – how they interconnect to constitute a *system* that is coherent, reasonable and usable; and third, to give a more detailed but indirect justification of this system by showing how it can actually be employed in our concrete ethical decision-making.

2.2   The Good

Aristotle famously began his *Nicomachean Ethics* with the claim that 'every art and every inquiry, and similarly every action and pursuit, is thought to aim at some good; and for this reason the good has rightly been declared to be that at which all things aim'.[1] We can do no better in understanding this most basic ethical concept – the good – than by unpacking Aristotle's axiom. But first let us begin *outside* the axiom, as it were, and work our way into it, as this will clarify its metaphysical context. We will then be able to see that the *fundamental principle of morality* is: Do good and avoid evil.

There are some things in the universe of which it makes sense to say that things go *well* or *badly* for them. At the level of inanimate objects, the concepts of going well and going badly make little sense. What would it mean to say that things went well or badly for a rock, or for a pool of water? Inanimate objects cannot suffer a *lack* of anything, nor do they have a natural *appetite* for anything, since there is no lack to be filled by the satisfaction of the appetite.

When we move to the level of *living* things, however, matters become more complex, since they can want for certain things necessary for their proper functioning. Bacteria, for instance, are governed by laws concerning their reproduction, nutrition, and other operations – they tend to multiply in appropriate media, to die in inappropriate media, to feed on certain compounds, to infect other organisms in certain conditions, and so on. Without the appropriate nutrition, they starve; when placed in the wrong medium, they can be poisoned, or they can stop reproducing and so die off. Plants, too, are governed by biological laws of growth, decay and reproduction. When conditions are right, and they want for nothing, they flourish; when conditions are in some way deficient, they become diseased, or stunted, or die. Indeed, at the biological level the concepts of *disease* and *health* have general application, so that the proper functioning of an organism fundamentally involves its health in appropriate conditions and its disease in others; and all of its various types of behaviour, including its reproduction and the propagation of its species, are subordinated to its ability to remain healthy, to have its natural appetites satisfied, to be free of abnormal functioning.

At the level of *animals* the laws governing behaviour are even more complex: animals can feel pain and pleasure, acquire certain kinds of knowledge, learn skills, form elaborate social groupings, and so on. The laws are still biological, but take in sensory and cognitive capacities that have no parallel in the plant kingdom. The more complex a creature, then – the more the kinds of things needed for it to operate well in its environment – the more complex the ways in which its operation can go wrong, or break down: the more complex the ways in which things can go *badly* for it, rather than *well*.

Matters are at their most complex, however, when we consider one type of living thing – human beings. Human beings are complex in just the same way all living things are complex, inasmuch as they are subject to physical, chemical and biological laws governing growth, nutrition, reproduction and related processes. A person's digestion is good if it works as it should, processing food and supplying its health-giving ingredients to the body in an efficient way. It is bad if this process is impeded or damaged, thereby preventing an adequate supply of nutrition – this could be due to anything from a relatively minor problem such as gastric reflux to a life-threatening complaint such as stomach cancer. But bodily processes such as digestion are not under our control: they simply *happen*, because the body has inbuilt systems whose purpose is to sustain life and health.

Man, however, is far more than the subject of automatic natural processes: he has a *rational nature* (hence the truth of the Aristotelian definition, 'Man is a rational animal'). Now, I will consider in chapter 3 of *Applied Ethics* to what extent it is proper to speak of reason in the case of non-human animals; but the point here is that man has an *intellect* unlike any other kind of creature on earth. He is capable of *reasoning about how he should live his life*. He spends much of his time *ordering* things so that he lives a certain kind of life. He *reflects* on how he wants to live and *proposes* certain things to himself as worthy or as not worthy. Whether it be in the area of work, social life, family, health, or mental or physical pursuits, from the moment he is capable of thinking *about* his life he *does* so think, and therefore thinks about how he should arrange those ingredients that go to make up what he believes will be a *good life* for him.

Man does not, however, simply use his intellect to propose certain things to himself as necessary to a good life – for the living of a good life is not a matter of mere intellectual curiosity. He also makes *decisions about living* in accordance with what his reason tells him is a good way to live. And he usually *acts* on those decisions, or at least *tries* to. Why? Precisely because he believes that living in the way his reason tells him to live will satisfy all his appetites, so that he lacks for nothing – in other words, he believes that he will be *fulfilled* by living in a certain way. Just as he uses his reason to learn how the world works (even if only that limited part of the world that is his immediate environment), and acts on its deliverances, so he uses his reason to work out what will fulfil him, and acts accordingly. Human beings, then, as well as having intellect, possess *will*: they are free to *choose* how to order their lives – not just what objectives to pursue, but how best to achieve them. In other words, we deliberate about *ends* and *means*, and try to do so in a rational way, in accordance with the deliverances of our intellect.

We can now return to Aristotle's axiom which began this section. It should be noted first that he has often been accused of committing a simple logical fallacy – of concluding that there is some one thing, the good, at which everything aims, from the fact that everything aims at some good (called in logic books a 'quantifier shift' fallacy). But would this not be as fallacious as arguing from 'Every material object has some colour' to 'There is some colour that every material object has'? This is precisely what Aristotle is *not* arguing, however. His argument, rather, parallels the following valid inference: 'Every material object has some colour; therefore, there is some property, namely *being coloured*, that every material object has.' He is saying that since every activity aims at some good, there is some property, namely goodness (or the good), at which all things aim. Now what the precise form of goodness is for every activity may vary (and often does) just as much as the particular colour of each material object. Nevertheless, just as being coloured is itself a single property capable of definition (in terms of light absorption and reflectance, and also in terms of hue, saturation and luminance), so too the good is a single property capable of definition as *that which satisfies a thing's natural appetites*, or *that which fulfils a thing's nature*.[2]

Notice that Aristotle does not speak about the idea of *living well*, that is, about *life's* aiming at the good. He only talks of arts, inquiries, actions and pursuits, in other words, of human activities. For instance, when a person plays the piano he aims at playing it *well*. Of course in a given case a person might fool around on the piano and not try to play well, or might simply play in order to annoy the neighbours – but in such cases he is either not seriously practising the art of piano-playing, or is doing so for an extrinsic objective having nothing to do with the art itself, but which he deems worthwhile or desirable in the circumstances. The point is that the art itself, and every serious attempt to practise it, has good execution as its intrinsic objective. Similarly, when a person takes a job, he aims to do it *well* considered in itself. Again, if he aims to do it badly, it can only be for some other objective he deems worthwhile at the time, such as frustrating his disliked employer's own desires. We need not multiply examples, since the general principle is clear: everything that a person does, *everything*, aims at something deemed good or worthwhile, whether that good be intrinsic to the activity itself (performing it well) or extrinsic (for some other objective deemed good); and in nearly all cases, the good aimed at is a combination of both the intrinsic and the extrinsic (I want to play the piano well, but I also want to please my audience). More precisely, it is *free human acts* that aim at some good. You might drum your fingers on the table, or whistle a tune, or sneeze, without aiming at some good – but all such acts are either spontaneous, involuntary, subconscious, or in some other way less than fully intentional, meaning done with knowledge and advertence, and without physical compulsion.

Although not all people play the piano, or study philosophy, and so on, there is one thing we all do, and that is *live*. And just as philosophy can be studied well or badly, and the piano played well or badly, so one can live well or badly. Why should living be an exception? Why should it be the one activity not capable of being done well or badly? Aristotle, of course, though he does not mention living in his axiom, spends the rest of his *Nicomachean Ethics* elaborating precisely this point, namely that living itself is an activity that aims at the good just like every other, and so can be done well or badly. And by living he does not mean the unreflective continuance of our existence by means of automatic bodily processes, but the full, conscious, reasoned living of our lives that every normal person either undertakes or is capable of undertaking, in no matter how incomplete a fashion.

The same point can be made from the perspective of the individual. Everything a person does is for some objective proposed as worthwhile: Alan takes a job so he can earn money; he earns money so he can pay his bills; he pays his bills so he can support his family. Why does he support his family? Here all that he can rationally say is that it is *good* to support one's family – irrespective of any pleasure, or gratitude, or other desirable results it may bring. If you pick any other example, you will see the same phenomenon: every act terminates in something done simply because it is *good* and for no further end. But this ultimate good, as we can call it, is simply the good that corresponds to the ultimate human activity of which every other activity is but an ingredient: the living of the human life in all its fullness, that is, taking into account all the tendencies, capabilities and characteristics (such as rationality and freedom) of the human being.

Since the intellect always proposes an objective that it deems worthwhile or desirable for every activity, and the intellect is not infallible, it can make mistakes about what is a good objective and about whether an activity is done well if done in a certain way. I might think that playing Schubert well on the piano consists in thumping the keyboard with my elbow – but I would be wrong. I might think that I will do my job well if I turn up five hours late every day – but I would be wrong. But I might also think that the objective of eating is simply to swallow as much food as possible, or that the end of study is simply to know enough to be able to make a lot of money. In both cases I would be wrong. I might *have* these objectives, but I would be mistaken about whether they were *good* ones, whether they contributed to my living well, *all things considered.* This last phrase is crucial, because when we reason about living well we must take in the *whole* of what a person is and does, not simply this or that aspect. Making a lot of money might be a worthwhile objective of study if all that we think about are the material comforts we desire, or the power and prestige that go with wealth. But when we attend to some of our other appetites rather than the appetite for material comfort – the desire for knowledge, for understanding of the world around us, for example – we see that study (conceived broadly to include more than just reading books and attending lectures, and even types of learning that do not involve such activities at all!) is uniquely able to satisfy those appetites. Material comfort might be a reasonable further end of study, but it cannot be the only end, nor can it be study's intrinsic end.

People are not simply capable of *misrepresenting* to themselves what is good for them, though they do it often and moral education consists in learning what is and is not good. Being free, they can *choose* not to do good and so be *responsible* for acts that are not good. Not every choice not to do good is evil, however: food is good, but I can choose at a given time to read a book instead of eat. The choice to do evil, rather, is the choice against a good *as such*: the choice not to eat well or not to take any exercise, for instance. It is important not to think of evil in the narrow, sensationalised sense of popular thought. Whatever evil's association with the idea of dark forces, pure malice, and so on, evil correctly considered is any lack of something that is necessary for a thing's fulfilment.

While it is possible – and common – for people to choose evil over good, and to do so knowingly, it is not possible for them to choose evil *because* it is evil. Whether this necessity is metaphysical or merely psychological is not something we can explore here: it is simply a truth that whenever a person knowingly chooses evil, it is not for the *reason* that it is evil, but either because the thing chosen brings with it some good, real or apparent, that the person decides to trade off against the evil itself, or because the thing chosen itself is seen to have a good aspect, real or apparent, as well as an evil one. If I choose not to eat well, for instance, I act against a good as such to the extent that I am aware of the contribution of diet to health and of the damage I do to my own health by not having a healthy diet. But although I may be attacking the good of health as such, I do not choose to damage my health *because* it is evil. Rather, I will have some other motive, which I think *good*, for acting the way I do: for example, I prefer to work long hours and so give less importance to sensible eating. Alan might say hurtful things to Celia, knowing it is bad to do so, because he is acting out of spite and delights in the short-term satisfaction or pleasure of being hurtful. Brian may disobey his employer, say, by lying about a colleague's activities, knowing it is bad to do so, but because he sees the act of disobedience also as an act of kindness in the protection of his colleague. Again, if you think of other cases, you will soon see that all knowingly bad acts are chosen because of some good, genuine or phoney, that the agent tries to obtain. The ubiquitous and complex problem of weakness of will, a distinctively human phenomenon, exemplifies the activity of doing something bad for the sake of usually short-term and transient satisfaction.

Morality, then, is concerned primarily with the study and elucidation of what is good and bad for human beings, and hence with what are good and bad actions, choices and motives. But is the good something monolithic? And if so, is it not inadequate to account for the immense diversity of human endeavours, pursuits, choices, and so on? Thomas Nagel, for one, thinks he sees a problem here: some objects are multifunctional, such as a combined corkscrew and bottle-opener – so how can everything operate well in only one way?[3] There is, however, no problem. The good is monolithic, both for all things to which goodness can be attributable at all, and for humans in particular, but only in the sense that there is a single property, namely operating well or in accordance with a thing's nature. For human beings, this is simply living well *as* human beings. The property, however, consists in a complex of other properties that together mark out the distinctively human life. More precisely, it is *happiness* that is the good of man. ('Flourishing' is also an appropriate word.) There is no new concept being introduced by the term 'happiness', just a specification or clarification of what the good for man *is*. It is happiness for which we all strive, which we all want from life (at least on rational reflection), and which consists in the well-lived life in which our appetites, capacities and potentialities as human beings are satisfied in an harmonious, well-ordered way. Perhaps no more truistic thesis can be found in moral theory.

Since human life is multifaceted, and human appetites diverse, so too the good for man, or happiness, has many aspects. (Note, as should be apparent by now, that by 'appetite' is *not* meant simply 'bodily or sensory desire', as the term is commonly used today, but 'tendency of a thing towards some action or operation for the securing of some good', which of course subsumes bodily or sensory desires and tendencies.) Every general, distinguishable aspect of human happiness, or human flourishing, is one of the goods that go to make up the good for man as a whole.

Is the list of human goods infinite? If goods are thought of as including every sub-operation of every operation, and if we assume an infinite number of these, then there will be an infinity of goods: good health, for example, includes good digestion, which includes good intestinal operation, which includes the good operation of each part of the intestine, and their parts, and so on indefinitely. But the primary concern of moral theory is the most general distinguishable features of human activity that make up human flourishing (which are themselves still recognisably complex), and there is no reason to think *this* list should be infinite. We need not delay ourselves with this question, however, as mention of some of the most important and obvious will suffice for the purpose of considering the sorts of problems in applied ethics to be discussed in the companion volume.

Life (in the narrow biological and physiological sense) is one of the fundamental human goods; and in a sense to be explained in chapter 4, it can be considered the most important. I shall postpone detailed discussion of life until then, noting here simply that, being complex like all goods, life encompasses more than just biological *existence*. For it is not simply existence that we tend towards, but *healthy* and *integrated* existence, and numerous physiological processes and operations are continually taking place, or capable of taking place, to maintain or restore the body to optimal functioning. Hence the good of life encompasses such sub-goods as proper diet, exercise, fresh air and rest. Loss of bodily parts is bad for the individual, as is disease, too much stress, overwork, loss of energy, and so on. It is therefore good for a person to attend to all of these and the other factors necessary for optimal existence.

Being rational creatures, having an intellect, we naturally have a tendency to *use* it. More exactly, from the moment we *can* use our intellect we *do* use it in the pursuit of one thing – truth. Human beings are enquiring creatures, naturally curious, always looking for new and better ways to solve problems, to understand themselves and the world around them. None of us can know everything, just as none of us can attain perfect health (as any doctor will confirm, there is always *something* we can do to make ourselves more healthy!). But we want to know as much as we can, *within the limits imposed on us* by ability and environment, including all the other matters that require our daily attention. The pursuit of truth, then, or the acquisition of *knowledge*, is one of the goods that contribute to our happiness. It must be emphasised that there is nothing necessarily academic, pretentious or high-flown in the concept of this good. Even a person whose occupation, surroundings, interests, and the like require very little knowledge of the world around him, and little in the way of lofty intellectual pursuits, still has to know *very much*, both in quantity and quality, in order to be able to get on even minimally. Nevertheless, while many people's pursuit of knowledge does not extend into loftier zones, many others' does, and one need hardly remark on the ability of individuals, and of humanity as such, to reach sublime heights of intellectual endeavour. Again, it is not knowledge merely in the sense of acquired information, but *understanding* which the pursuit of truth encompasses: we want to know *how* and *why* things are as they are, not merely whether, what, when or where (though understanding can accompany the answers to such questions too). Further, among the objects of knowledge is *knowledge of the good itself*. Without knowledge of the good, the good life as a whole could not even begin to be lived. But there is no reflexive paradox here: just as the mind can reflect upon itself and try to understand itself (one of the marks of self-consciousness), so too the mind, in knowing the good, can know that this act of knowing is itself good. In short, just as life and health are what perfect our bodies (and fulfil us thereby), so knowledge and understanding perfect our minds.

As man is a rational animal, so he is also a *social* animal (though the latter is a mark, rather than a definition of being human). Everywhere and at all times people have come together and stayed together in groups, united by one or more features: mutual protection, assistance or prosperity; commonness of background or origin, be it ethnic, national or cultural; similarity of outlook or belief, be it religious or political; similarity of interests, occupation, socio-economic status; the list is perhaps endless. People are not naturally loners, in the sense of eschewing all attention from and interest in others: to be sure, there are degrees of self-imposed aloneness and history is replete with individuals who largely withdraw from social life, usually in pursuit of some nobler aim such as spiritual fulfilment. But even the most reclusive of hermits needs others, and human flourishing requires at least some level of wanted interaction with others. More generally, we can identify a good sometimes called the good of *friendship*, since it focuses primarily on those wanted interactions that involve fellow-feeling, sympathy, kindness, love and care. But it subsumes also friendship in the broader sense of social living, in particular living in a self-governing community, or perhaps state, whose sole purpose is to promote the peaceful and harmonious coexistence of its members. Hegel was therefore wrong to say, 'Man owes his entire existence to the state, and has his being within it alone. Whatever worth and spiritual reality he possesses are his solely by virtue of the state.'[4] On the contrary, man does not exist for the state – the state is not his extrinsic ultimate end. Rather, the state exists *for* man, in order to enable him to flourish, and so is good *for* man. On the smaller scale, the distinctive social grouping that contributes to flourishing is the *family*, which provides a natural locus for the promotion of other goods, such as life (via procreation and physical and economic sustenance) and knowledge (via education of children). Much contemporary social-scientific research has belatedly rediscovered the benefits of the *extended* (as opposed to nuclear) family, which has of course been the traditional small-scale social unit in all cultures and at all times. There is no space here to recount those benefits and so to demonstrate the extended family's unique capacity to promote social life at the micro-level; the reader is encouraged to seek out this research for herself.

Many people think that the only reason they work is to obtain enough money to support themselves and their families. These people tend also to think that the only reason they relax is to forget about work. There is reason to think that, at least in the West, the stresses and strains of work, with its drudgery for so many people and the ever-present insecurity of employment, encourage such feelings. But on both counts people who think this way are wrong, because *work* and what we might term *play* (in the broad sense encompassing leisure and relaxation) have their own intrinsic value. They occupy and exercise our minds and bodies, engage us in enjoyable endeavours, and bring their own special satisfactions. In this sense work and play are but two aspects of a single component of the happy life and are plausibly distinguished from other goods, with work at its best a form of play and vice versa, although they both serve, of course, in the promotion of other goods such as life, knowledge and friendship.

Mankind has at all times and places appreciated beauty, both in nature and in the products of human activity. The appreciation of beauty also brings its own special pleasures and satisfactions and satisfies the highest appetites of the mind. It does not appear reducible to any other good, though again it contributes to their promotion and often overlaps them –

for the professional artist, to take an obvious case, work and aesthetic experience go hand in hand. We can then identify *the appreciation of beauty* as another in the list of goods that satisfy man's nature.

Similarly, *religious belief and practice* are an integral part of the happy life. Religion is as old as humanity itself and has been practised by the overwhelming number of people in all places and at all times. Even now, despite the virtual collapse of religion in the West, the vast majority of people alive are religious believers and practitioners. Moreover, many who would call themselves atheists nevertheless readily testify to an appreciation of some sublime principle of the cosmos that surpasses understanding, but is real, and dwells behind everything that happens. Much of modern popular science, for example, though written by self-professed non-believers, testifies to a mysterious and irreducibly transcendent aspect of reality to which even the most hardened materialist is drawn, the more he appreciates the awe-inspiring complexity of the universe. It would be wrong simply to class this sort of apprehension as aesthetic, though an appreciation of the beauty of nature overlaps it. It is, then, reasonable to regard such an experience as truly *spiritual or religious*, and the practice that follows from it as distinctive, as rooted in all cultures at all times, and as thereby reflecting an innate and special tendency of the human being. And when this religious tendency is taken together with man's quest for truth mentioned earlier, we can see that what perfects human nature is not mere religious belief and practice of one sort or another, but only *true* belief and the practice which best expresses it.

Much, much more could be said about the good, but it is enough for present purposes if the reader has an outline understanding of how it forms the basis of ethical decision-making. Further elaboration, where necessary for the argument, will occur at the appropriate places; in particular, the good of life will be explored in depth in chapter 4. Before we move on, however, it is necessary to make explicit what was implicit in the above discussion. Every human good *can be*, and often *is*, used as an instrument for the pursuit of some other good (Alan stays healthy so he can work; Brian plays chess so he can make friends; and so on). Some goods – the possession of money, for instance – are purely instrumental. But no *basic* good is solely instrumental in character; each good mentioned above is basic precisely because it itself is a component of the happy life. If any one of them is turned away from, rejected, or compromised *in general*, life goes badly for the person who does so. And often, though not always, if a good is turned away from, rejected, or compromised *in a given instance or circumstance*, life again is not lived well. More will be said about this later.

2.3   Virtue

It is a truth of human nature that a person does more easily what he does more often: frequent repetition makes performance easy. This is well known in the sphere of physical activity, especially where much skill is involved: an athlete must train in order to perform well; if you want to ride a bicycle well, you must ride it often; you can never hope to be a good skier without skiing frequently. Where mental skill alone is required, the same is true: how could someone be good at solving crossword puzzles without doing many of them, or at writing term papers without writing them often? How could you learn a language without practising it as much as you can? And when mental and physical skill are both required, of course, mind and body have to be trained to respond competently and easily to the demands of performance – you need only think of playing a musical instrument, or building a model, or drawing a picture. The simple fact is that frequent repetition of an act, in *any* sphere of human activity, is a prerequisite for good performance, since the agent learns how to do the thing required, learns how to avoid mistakes, works out ways of doing the same thing more quickly, more efficiently or with less stress. Further, repetition *inclines* the agent towards the act concerned, since easy and efficient performance is intrinsically satisfying, reinforcing among other things the agent's confidence in his own skill and ability.

Why, in the sphere of the good life as such, should things be any different? It is here that the idea of *virtue* comes into play: those deep-seated (and hence difficult to change) habits of behaviour that govern every aspect of life, mental, physical or moral. Again it is to Aristotle that we owe the first (and in many ways unsurpassed) detailed definition and exposition of the virtues and how they contribute to the life of happiness. Only a very brief account of the most general principles can be given here, sufficient to pave the way for their application in later discussion of specific problems.

Although the examples just mentioned suggest that all ingrained inclinations to good performance of an act are *acquired* through instruction and practice, this is not the case. At its most general, a virtue is simply a deep-seated inclination *as such* towards performance, and so it might be *innate*. Some people are born with a quick mind – this is an innate intellectual virtue. Others are born strong – an innate physical virtue. Being born quick-witted or strong will not necessarily make you *good* at, say, study or weightlifting, to take but two of many possible applications of those virtues, not least because many other factors are involved in such activities. But the inborn inclination to use the skills nature provides certainly makes success in application more *likely*, as long as the skills are fostered and improved, and not neglected or damaged.

Some virtues (perhaps most of them), however, are *acquired*. A person of normal strength can become stronger through physical training, and someone not especially quick with his mind can become better through practice at problem-solving. There are far more good pianists than there are people born with a gift for piano-playing, and no one was ever born a good electrician – any skills the latter has are wholly learned. All virtues are kinds of *habit*, where a habit is defined as an ingrained behavioural trait, difficult to change, and inclining a person to a certain sort of activity. A habit can be quite narrowly focused, as when we speak, for instance, of a person's habit of brushing his teeth at six o'clock every evening. The habits that we call *virtues*, however, are ingrained behavioural traits that reflect a certain broad aspect of *character*. In this sense, brushing one's teeth at six o'clock each evening could be a virtue if it reflected a character trait of, say, careful regard for health, or attention to routine. But there is no possibility of virtue without the possibility of *vice*: the same person's tooth-brushing behaviour might, rather, reflect an unnecessary obsessiveness about routine, so that even a small or urgently necessary deviation was something he found hard to accept. Only knowledge of other facts about the person could help one decide which interpretation was more accurate.

In ethics we are primarily concerned with acquired habits. (Perhaps there is something odd about the term 'innate habit'. It is true that we tend to reserve the term 'habit' for traits that are learned, but it is not hard to think of ingrained behavioural traits with which people are simply born – it is just that such traits are inevitably influenced, modified and shaped by subsequent learning in the broad sense, such as reinforcement by example.) In particular, we are concerned with acquired *moral* habits, in other words those that are necessary for the good life. Thus neither strength nor quickness of mind are necessary for living well, even though they can be an *aid* to living well, insofar as they facilitate the achievement of the basic goods of life.

But if some innate virtues can be aids to the good life, does this not mean that some people are born *luckier* than others in terms of whether they possess those aids? Is there not, then, what has been called 'moral luck'? And are all *moral* habits acquired, or are some of these innate as well, and if the latter, does this not also confirm the existence of moral luck? Is not moral luck paradoxical, or just plain objectionable, especially if the good is supposed to be within the reach of everyone who uses reason?

A brief response to these questions should sufficiently dispel worry about moral luck. First, aids such as those mentioned above are of limited usefulness. They must be harnessed and employed precisely for living well before they can be of assistance in the moral sphere. For every person who can so harness them, there is another who does not. Some let such abilities shrivel through neglect to the point of their uselessness. Others use them only for frivolous activities, bringing no more then short-term satisfaction. Even worse, some positively employ them in the service of *evil*. (Consider the quick-witted person who devotes himself to finding ever better ways of defrauding his employer.)

Second, it is highly doubtful whether any moral habits are innate. Are people really born lazy? Or selfish? Or generous? A person might have an innately short concentration span, and this can be a *factor* in laziness; a person might be born with good looks, which can be an *inducement* to selfish behaviour; a person might be born with an innate disposition to share what he has with others, and this can lead to generous behaviour in later life. But none of these innate characteristics are virtues or vices *in themselves*. Some, such as the disposition to share, can lead equally to virtue or vice – one might end up being loose and improvident with money, for instance. More importantly, though, even if no moral habits are innate, or 'in the genes', as it were, there will still be a certain amount of luck in whether one's environment shapes non-moral traits for good or bad. In particular, the acquisition of virtue depends in large part on whether you have parents who set a good example, and teachers who give correct instruction, and whether you have other role models. So no matter how environmental the development of good moral habits is, luck will be an ineradicable feature of the development of one's character. In this sense, there is and must be 'moral luck'. But as long as we remember that human beings are free, this should not strike us as paradoxical. For every person exposed to the most dangerous of moral environments, and who consequently leads a bad life, there is another, equally unfortunate, who goes on to live a life of virtue. Thus the 'consequently' is never one of *causa-*

tion. Just as no one is born good or bad, so no one is *made* good or bad. Everyone is born with the desire to know the truth and the desire to live well. Even if their surroundings work against them, they can employ their native reason to rise above those surroundings (as so many do) and to live well and do what is good.

It is, then, the moral habits or moral virtues and vices (which I will now call simply virtues and vices) with which ethical theory is concerned. What distinguishes them from all the other traits of character and behaviour? The quick answer is that they essentially involve our dealings with other people, since ethics is precisely about our dealings with others. The answer is indeed quick – it is only roughly correct. Strictly, the moral habits are distinguished by the fact that in displaying them we can act against our reason. We cannot use our intellect to make a judgement against what our intellect tells us – we cannot believe to be false what we *know* to be true. We can, however, use our *will* against what we know to be true. Hence the phenomenon of weakness of will, mentioned earlier. Intellectual mistakes result from lack of knowledge, either of general truths or their particular applications, or perhaps from carelessness. But the will *can* act against what the intellect proposes. In a world without temptation, without distraction from pursuit of the good, mere knowledge of the good would suffice for the virtuous life. But that is not our world, and so good moral habits are required to keep our emotions, our sensations, our bodily desires, and the like, harnessed to the pursuit of human happiness. Even Robinson Crusoe (without Friday) could develop bad moral habits though he had no one to deal with – he might, for instance, suffer from despair and begin neglecting his health. (I leave it to you as an exercise to think of how else he may not live a good life.)

Virtues are not mere dispositions: a person who has just had some good news might be disposed to be kind for a while, but this does not make him virtuous. (It is only correct to speak of his actions as virtuous in the sense that the individual acts of kindness, say, are *good*, and would be a natural concomitant of the truly developed virtuous character.) Nor is virtue simply a mood, or passing whim. Such things are transient and easily changed. Habits, being ingrained, are difficult to change and so it is best to acquire good ones as early as possible, no matter how adverse the circumstances. Nor is virtue the same as *instinct*. While there is no freedom in purely instinctive behaviour, virtuous behaviour is free, no matter how deep-seated it is. You are free to change your habits, acquire new ones, modify old ones. Nor is virtue the same as *routine*: there is little or no skill in routine, but virtue requires sound judgement and the skilful application of principles to particular moral problems. The American philosopher and psychologist William James sums up the notion of habit as well as anyone (and its application to virtue is evident):

> The great thing is to make our nervous system our ally instead of our enemy. For this we must make automatic and habitual, as early as possible, as many useful actions as we can and guard against growing into ways that are disadvantageous to us. The more of the details of our daily life we can hand over to the effortless custody of automatism, the more our higher powers of mind will be set free for their proper work. There is no more miserable human being than one in whom nothing is more habitual than indecision and for whom the lighting of every cigar, the drinking of every cup, the time of rising and going to bed and the beginning of every bit of work, are subjects of express volitional deliberation.[5]

But automatism in this context does not mean that habitual actions are mere *reflex* actions not intentionally brought about. As mentioned in chapter 1, *habitual intention* is a kind of intention and habitual acts are thus in a deep sense performable *at will*. Habits *feed on* acts: the more often you act, the more ingrained becomes the habit. Similarly, habits languish or even fade away with non-use, or more effectively, with acts *contrary* to habit. This is, of course, immensely useful if you want to give up a bad habit, otherwise you would be stuck with it for life; but in the moral sphere, where we want to develop good moral habits, neglect or frustration of habit can be destructive of happiness.

How does the idea of virtue square with our sense that morality often involves the overcoming of difficulty? This is a common charge laid against the idea of virtue, one going back at least to Kant. Are we to say, to take a familiar example, that if Alan visits his sick uncle in hospital because he has the virtue of kindness he is more praiseworthy than Brian, who does the same even though he dislikes his uncle and hence the thought of visiting him, and so finds the act hard but knows that it is right to visit the sick? The answer is that, in a narrow sense, Brian's act might be worthy of admiration, but in a broader sense, Alan's is more praiseworthy. Brian has indeed performed an act of kindness (diminished if he lets his dislike affect his manner during the visit) and has demonstrated, for a time, self-mastery. However, his feeling of difficulty would indicate a more general problem of having to overcome contrary inclinations in order to do good (something we have to deal with often). This would at least make more probable his following his inclinations and turning *away* from good, than would Alan's more integrated personality. Of course, when a person is on the way to acquiring a virtue he almost always has to overcome contrary inclinations and desires, and to turn difficult actions into easy ones; and if that were Brian's position he should be even more praised as walking the path of virtue. But a life of *continuous* attempts at self-mastery, where good behaviour rarely comes easily, is not a good life to that extent: it involves much inner conflict and turmoil, making a person uneasy with himself and almost certainly with others. Further, it is wrong to think, as do some objectors to the idea of virtue, that all virtuous actions are completely easy and effortless. To take our familiar example, even the most skilled and well-trained pianist will find it difficult to play certain pieces, will feel nervous in front of an audience even if he has played in public hundreds of times (many artists say that without *some* level of nervousness one cannot play well!) and will experience creative tension. The same goes for virtue, where temptation to act against habit, in the pursuit of short-term or transient pleasure, is an ever-present obstacle. The virtuous person can rely on his habits to serve him well, so that he acts predictably, effectively and smoothly in the face of obstacles which the non-virtuous can never hope to cross. This does not mean, though, that he will not experience difficulty in some cases, that in others he might not fall away altogether, or that in all cases he will not be aware of the need for some effort at the slightest hint of rebellion by his emotions and inclinations.

Two other questions must briefly be answered before mentioning some principal virtues. The first is whether one can be virtuous in the pursuit of evil. The usual example is of the bank robber who displays the virtue of courage as he commits his evil deed. What, then, has virtue to do with morality? The answer is that a bank robber *cannot* display courage *qua bank robber*. Virtue is not a mere feeling of bravado, nor the mere taking of risk with complete self-assurance. Being a *good* moral habit, virtue is displayed *only in the pursuit of noble and worthwhile ends*, namely the ends of the good life. If the objective is evil, then although many of the elements of a virtue such as courage may be present in its pursuit, the virtue itself will not be present. This can also be seen in the fact that *mere* daring, *mere* confidence in the face of risk to life and limb, unregulated by the goodness of the objective sought, can shade over into behaviour that looks less and less like courage and more like rashness, for instance, in which a person exposes himself to unnecessary danger. Or one can end up recklessly exposing *other people* to danger – hardly virtuous behaviour. We have an answer, now, to the second question – are virtuous acts good because they are virtuous, or virtuous because they are good? They are virtuous because they are good, but not just because of this: they are good, they are repeated, they become habitual, but they are never beyond the control of the will.

There are many virtues, corresponding to the multifacetedness of human life itself, and almost every moral act displays more than one of them. They cannot all be discussed here and many are not directly relevant to the problems we will be looking at in *Applied Ethics*. Where necessary they will be mentioned in subsequent discussion, but for the moment I want to note three of them that have a fundamental explanatory role in applied ethics: the latter two, especially, will be the subject of greater discussion and application.[6]

Since knowledge and understanding of the good is itself a good, as explained earlier, its habitual pursuit is a virtue, usually called 'practical wisdom' or 'prudence'. The latter term, as used today, tends to signify only the ability to be careful and skilful in the choice of *means* to an arbitrary end, whether that end be good or bad, important or trivial. This is not what the true good of prudence consists in, however. Rather, prudence or practical wisdom involves primarily the ability to use one's intellect to appreciate that the human goods *are indeed goods* and hence to be pursued. Only secondarily does it involve the ability to work out the best *means* to achieve those goods. If practical wisdom were not itself a virtue, this would handicap one's ability rationally and reliably to pursue the good, and so the whole of the good life would be unachievable except by accident at worst, or by singular and isolated efforts at best. Hence there is a necessity and benefit in being able to use one's reason to come to know just what the good life consists in and how to choose the best means to achieve it.

The second virtue is *justice*, which is the virtue that inclines a person always to respect the rights of others. Since I have not yet explained rights, not much more should be said at this stage save that justice is essentially a *relational* virtue, concerning one's dealings with other people, singly or in groups. It also concerns one's dealings with the state as a whole and the state's dealings with the individual. Hence one cannot be unjust to *one-self*. One can love oneself, or feel sorry for oneself, but one cannot be unjust to oneself. What would it mean to say that a person respected his own rights? Where justice is concerned, a person considers other people *as others*, with lives of their own and goods to pursue, and one respects and is sensitive to those facts *irrespective of how one feels about those other people*. One may dislike another person intensely, or wish him nothing but ill (not that this would be virtuous!), but one must respect his 'moral space', as it were, in spite of that, and one must do so as a matter of course.

The third virtue is *charity* or *love* (they mean the same, one deriving from Latin and the other from Anglo-Saxon). The eviscerated vocabulary of modern moral discourse has narrowed the term 'charity' (as it has narrowed 'prudence') to cover certain special acts of kindness to those less fortunate than ourselves, and we speak of 'giving to charity', or of an organisation's being a charity even if it has limited moral objectives. None of this usage is incorrect as far as it goes, but it ignores the broader concept from which such narrow applications derive their point. Whereas justice involves treating another person *as another*, charity or love involves treating another person *as at one with oneself* – one loves the other just as one loves oneself. This idea is encapsulated in the biblical formulas that you should 'do unto others as you would have them do unto you' and that you should 'love your neighbour as yourself'. Thus the first act of love is *towards oneself*, since a person would find it all but impossible to love anyone else if he did not first love himself. Self-hate, a common contemporary phenomenon, is usually all-consuming and debilitating, and so undercuts most of a person's efforts to show love toward others. Self-love, on the other hand, is not (contrary to popular misconception) the equally consuming vice of vanity, conceit or inordinate pride. Rather, it is that measured and confident respect for and appreciation of oneself as a human being that breeds peace with oneself as well as an appreciation of the equal dignity of other human beings, leading naturally to a desire to do well by them.

Love is not a mere emotion, contrary to what is virtually the modern definition of the term. Strictly, love is an act of the *will* and may or may not be associated with affection or emotion. Emotions and affections are notoriously fickle and changeable, but love is an enduring thing, a habit – a virtue. It can be and often is demonstrated in quiet, unspectacular behaviour, in which one puts oneself at the service of others. All the expressions of affection in the world cannot replace or surpass the simple acts of kindness a person performs for those around him, whether friends, family, or even enemies. For there is no great difficulty in loving those close to you, to whom you are naturally disposed by affection. The true test of character (which we all fail too often) is to love, not merely strangers, but even those who *are actively set against us*. Morality, of course, allows us to protect ourselves against the threats of others (about which more later), but we must love another even while he attacks us, whether verbally, or physically, or in whatever subtle manner. Human beings belong to a single family, something recognised by great moralists of every stripe throughout history, and we must desire the welfare of every person, just as we desire our own.

2.4   Rights and Duties

So far we have looked primarily at morality as founded on the idea of goodness, where goodness is explicated in terms of what satisfies the nature of an individual human being. Where does the idea of *obligation or duty* come in? How, in the examination of the good for a person, do other people enter the equation? Morality being about our dealings with each other as much as about the way we live as individuals, there must be a connection between the two.

There are a number of ways of drawing out this connection, but the central one involves the concept of a *right*. Rights are perhaps the most misunderstood aspect of moral theory: there are those (mainly consequentialists, of whom more later) who frankly deny their existence while at the same time paying them regular lip service, even appealing to them when their own interests require it; others give them exaggerated prominence in ethics, sometimes basing their entire morality on them; yet others abuse the term 'right', claiming to find rights where really there are none, hurling it at their opponents on this or that issue, or elevating rights to such a status that the mere utterance of the word is supposed to silence all debate.

Perhaps some of the confusion surrounding rights derives from their prominence in most of the written constitutions of the post-Enlightenment era. The French Revolutionaries trumpeted the idea of rights, notably in their Declaration of the Rights of Man. The US Constitution fairly bristles with the term 'right', and its first ten amendments are known as the Bill of Rights. The UN General Assembly, in 1948, passed a Universal Declaration of Human Rights and in 1966 an International Covenant on Civil and Political Rights, as well as another on Economic, Social and

Cultural Rights. The term 'human rights' is now common currency in political and moral debate, and it is rare to find any public discussion of a pressing moral issue in which there is not at least one participant who appeals to 'the right to do X'.

The frequent and often conflicting uses of a philosophical term are a sure sign of misunderstanding, and I will return often to the concept of a right in various contexts, trying to clarify its proper meaning and application. But we must start with an outline of the concept, in order to demonstrate the place of rights in moral theory.

Morality, as I am presuming (and have given reasons to show), is objective and rational: moral truths hold independently of whether anyone knows them; they are not mere constructs of the human imagination or of language; and they can be discerned by the use of reason. I have also presented an outline of the good as the fundamental concept of morality. The question then arises: Why should it not be the case that a person can pursue the good life irrespective of concern for any other person? Why, in other words, should morality – the pursuit of the good – not be a highly individualistic activity?

The assumption that morality is rational means no more nor less than it does in any other field of knowledge. To say that a field of knowledge is rational is, among other things, to say that it provides of its own accord (or on loan from other disciplines) *all* the concepts and principles that unify it, that make it an orderly and workable system amenable to human reason, and (where appropriate) applicable to particular problems or situations. We should expect, then, that morality too, if it is to be an orderly and workable system of knowledge, should not be deficient in any concepts or principles whose absence would render it incoherent or unworkable.

Morality provides us with the concept of the good. Suppose also, however, that its pursuit was something morality *itself* did not guarantee. Suppose that, *as far as morality was concerned*, every person could pursue the good in any way they chose, without regard for others. To use a metaphor suggested earlier, suppose that morality gave no 'space' to an individual to pursue the good – he was constantly under threat of, and regularly suffered, intrusions or interference by *other* individuals in *their* pursuit of the good. Would such a system of morality be incoherent or unworkable? It seems that it would be both. First, it would be unworkable since morality would not provide the individual with *principles for action*. Morality is a guide to action – it is supposed to guide a person in his pursuit of the good, which involves showing him what is and what is not a good to be pursued. Now suppose you lived in this imaginary society, in which morality itself allowed you to interfere with others *at will* in your pursuit of the good. What, then, would the good *mean* to you? You needed to support yourself and your family, say, so you took whatever you could from other people. At what point ought you to stop? On the supposition I have made, there would *be* no point: even if you chose to *kill* another person to get his possessions, morality would be silent. But then how would you know *when* you had successfully pursued the good and when you had done more than was necessary? When you felt satisfied? When you had no more use for the booty you had won? When you no longer felt pleasure at killing others to get what you wanted? None of these could be the proper criterion, for the good is not a matter of simple pleasure, or feelings of satisfaction, or utility. The good, as we have supposed, has inbuilt limitations, demarcating what fulfils you as a human being from what does not – from, among other things, what is *excess*. But if morality did not *decree* any excess, by staying silent on your invasion of the space of others, you would not have any concept of the good, not because *nothing* was good, but because *everything* was good: killing innocent people to feed yourself and your family, theft, fraud, exploitation, and so on.

But, you might reply, why can't morality simply decree that excess is reached when you do not *need* any more than you have, so that you must not kill another to obtain more than your fair share, or more than what is required to support yourself? The reply begs the question, however: What *is* my fair share? What *do* I need and what is surplus to requirements? People differ notoriously over what they think they need, and if morality has nothing to say about when not to interfere with others, you can as rationally regard your proper portion as the lion's share rather than the lamb's. Suppose you kill ten people and take all their possessions – morality does not tell you not to. Are you satisfied? Perhaps – perhaps not. You might *think* you do not need any more, but then you see your neighbour, who is able to kill fifty people and make good use of everything they own. If he can do it, why can't you? Maybe you were *wrong* to stop where you did. Maybe you should kill hundreds of people, maybe you should try to extinguish as many people as you can and make use of everything you can get hold of; human ingenuity certainly does not make this impossible, as history as shown. Of course, we would all rightly regard such behaviour as abhorrent, but that is not the point. What emerges from this small thought experiment is that since *morality* did not provide any limits, how could you come to a workable understanding of what was and was not good for you? Transient feelings of exhaustion or satiety would be no guide, and you would be in a constant state of confusion and anxiety.

Suppose you come under attack from another in *his* pursuit of the good. Morality, on our supposition, is silent on whether you may defend yourself. After all, *the very concept of defending yourself presupposes that you have a moral claim to what it is you may defend* – in other words, a *right*. What would morality say then? Perhaps that you must *yield* to the other person's attack. But then in what sense could what you yield be said to be good? The best morality can proclaim in this imaginary situation is that your food, your possessions, even your loved ones, are, as it were, 'nice to have while you have got them'. This is not the same as saying that they are good, however – that they fulfil human nature unconditionally or absolutely. Such things would merely be transient pleasures, fleeting satisfactions rather than unconditional fulfilments. You might think it was good to have a family. But then your family is killed by another in his pursuit of an apparent good. Since morality was silent, you could legitimately ask: In what sense was it good to have a family? Maybe this was just a fleeting pleasure, since morality (not merely *misfortune*) allowed it to be taken away. Again, you would soon see that you had no concept of the good at all on such a scenario, and hence morality would be unworkable as a guide to action.

Second, morality in our thought experiment would be incoherent, in the sense that it would be self-defeating. The important thing to bear in mind is that the relevant ability of individuals to interfere with each other in their pursuit of the good is not, on the imagined scenario, *physical* ability: some will be strong enough to intrude upon others' lives at will, others will have the physical capacity to do it some of the time, and yet others will be so weak as to be capable of interfering hardly at all. We are imagining that the ability is, rather, conferred by morality itself, in the sense that morality is *silent* on the matter, and just as man-made law permits what it does not forbid, so morality has to be construed as permitting what it is silent upon. But we are not supposing, on our imaginary scenario, that morality gave people the *right* to interfere with each other, since that would *plainly* be self-defeating: Alan, for instance, would have the right to steal Brian's car and Brian would have the right to stop him – morality would be utterly self-contradictory. This is arguably the way Thomas Hobbes saw the state of things before mankind organised itself into a society under government: it is not clear whether he saw morality in this world in which 'might is right' as *logically* contradictory – which it would be – or merely as practically intolerable or physically self-destructive.

Nevertheless, morality would also be inconsistent if its silence were mere *permission to interfere* rather than the conferral of a right to do so, for the following reason. Morality has, on our scenario, provided the concept of the good for man as such and for every person in particular. However, it has not given any person *protection* in his pursuit of the good, or of anything necessary to obtain it. Again, the protection morality will have failed to provide is not *physical* – that is a matter both for nature and for personal ingenuity. It is its *own* special protection that will be lacking, that protection which binds each individual *in conscience* to respect every other person's pursuit of the good. How, then, could morality *itself* say the following: 'Reason decrees that it is worthwhile pursuing that which is good for you, such as life, health, liberty, knowledge – but you have no protection in that pursuit. Others are not bound in conscience to allow you to pursue it, nor are you given the justification to defend yourself and what you have or do in its pursuit.' Clearly, in our thought experiment, morality would be taking away with one hand what it gave with the other – and this would make morality incoherent.

Some people might object that the very theory of the good I am defending is undermined by this problem, since rights would have to be 'pulled out of a hat', as it were, to make the good meaningfully pursuable. These moral theorists see the very notion of a right as mysterious: Where do rights come from? What sort of strange moral thing are they? As with most 'arguments from queerness' (such as that famously used by J. L. Mackie against the very idea of objective morality), there is no real argument, merely a statement of metaphysical prejudice. No more basic and transparent answer to the question of 'where rights come from' can be given than to reply, 'They come from morality itself; they are a conceptually indispensable part of the correct moral system.' What more can be said? Further, the incredulity evidenced by the belief that rights are 'strange moral entities', if it is to be accorded any serious attention, is no more nor less than the demand for a definition.

A right, then (and by right I mean 'moral right' unless otherwise stated), is best defined as a moral power of doing or having something. By 'power' is meant a capacity or potentiality of doing or having something *according to law*. Thus a physical power is the capacity of doing or having something according to physical law, and a legal power is the capacity of doing or having something according to man-made law (sometimes called positive human law, and which I will call simply 'law' unless otherwise stated). A *moral* power, then, is distinct from physical or legal power because possession of neither of the others entails *its* possession, and its possession does not entail possession of either of the others. Nevertheless, it is of course desirable that a moral power be *accompanied* by physical and legal power, in other words that a person be both physically capable and legally empowered (in at least the most important types of situation) to do what he has a moral right to do. But all people are physically incapable of exercising all of their rights all of the time (which is certainly true in a special class of cases to be discussed in *Applied Ethics*), and no legal system in history has ever been so comprehensive (or, more significantly, intrusive) as to protect everyone's rights all of the time, or so well-crafted as never to confer rights that morality itself does not confer (for example, the right to own slaves, or to exploit certain minorities because of their race or origin).

Might does not make right and man-made law does not make right. A moral power, then, is a power to do or to have something according to *moral* law, and which enables one to act licitly before its tribunal, before one's conscience, and before all other people. A right can be thought of as a *claim* or *title* to certain things and actions against other people, namely those things necessary for the achievement of happiness. With this title or claim come certain other rights, which, as it were, cluster around the primary right to a thing or action. The most obvious is the right to *defend* oneself against any intrusion intended to deprive one of the primary right. The idea of defence must be taken broadly. It does not mean simply the right to use physical force. Sometimes you have the right to use force, for instance to protect yourself against physical assault or threat of death. But there are many things you have a right to that you may not protect by force, such as the right to your reputation or good name, or the right not to be treated with undeserved contempt, or the right to have a promise kept that another has made to you. I am speaking here of the personal resort to force, but it might be supposed that if force is understood to include resort to the legal system (that is, the power of the state in its administration of justice), then it is allowed even in these cases. That this is not so is easily shown. As we noted above, the legal system does not protect every moral right: not every promise can be legally enforced, only the special class of promises called *contracts*; not every attack on reputation can be legally redressed, only special kinds such as libel and slander; and the law does not give a remedy for insult or personal offence.

As well as the resort to force, defence includes such actions as the physical, economic or psychological 'ring-fencing' of what one has a right to. Taking the example of property, you have the right physically to secure it against theft, say by concealing it or guarding it. You are morally permitted to demand fair payment for property you sell (this can be seen as a form of defence, since you are protecting the property's *value* to you) and to have your property assessed fairly as to its economic worth (say, if you wish to sell it at a later date to a third party, or to use it as security for a loan). You have the right to warn other people not to take your property, to demand its return if taken, to publicise your ownership to the community at large, and so on.

As well as defence, a person has the right to *reparation* for rights that are violated. If the law provides, you may use it forcibly to demand restitution of a thing taken, or compensation. If it does not, morality sometimes allows you forcibly to secure restitution in person, just as it allows you to use force to defend yourself: for example, it is arguable that a Jew who had had his property stolen by the Nazis but could not have secured restitution from the courts, would have had the right forcibly to take it back, whether or not he was *physically* capable of doing so. (Do you agree?) A person who is insulted without justification has the right to an apology, and if his name is blackened he has the right to demand that the offender clear his name (even though the victim may not use force to secure this, and the offender may have done too much damage to be able to restore the victim's reputation in its entirety). You have the right to compensation for unprovoked physical assault, even if the legal system fails you; and you have the right to an apology, of course. If a person breaks a promise to you, you have the right to demand that he make it up somehow, say by offering to help you with a problem or doing some other favour. And so on.

Another way in which rights are protected is by the general right to *respect* for the primary rights involved in your pursuit of the good. This involves the doing by a person of all those things, no matter how small, that *acknowledge* the existence of the rights of others. It is at least part of what William Blake had in mind when he said, 'He who would do good to another, must do it in Minute Particulars'.[7] Every day we engage in transactions with others that require respect for their rights and their respect for ours. Even if the thing or action is of no great significance materially, financially, psychologically, or to society, if the individual has a moral claim to it then the claim must be respected. An obvious way in which respect is shown is by asking *permission* to interfere with another's right. One must ask permission to use another's property; or to reveal to a third party something told in confidence; or to be relieved of the burden imposed by a promise. *Apology* can be seen as a mark of respect as well as of reparation: by apologising for interfering with another's right (obviously where permission was not sought, or was denied) one thereby acknowledges the existence of the right in the first place. If the matter is serious a *public* apology is sometimes called for, which is also a mark of respect as it involves the difficult task of acknowledging before the (sometimes harsh) tribunal of public opinion that a right existed and was intruded upon. The *admission* of the existence of rights, in our daily conversation and exchanges, is another mark of respect: we condemn acts by others that intrude upon rights, we praise the respect shown by others, we try to persuade people not to intrude upon rights, and so on. No matter how small the matter may seem, respect for the rights of all people should be shown in our words and in our deeds, and it is in this important way that we acknowledge the binding force of morality.[8]

As should be clear from the discussion so far, rights bring with them *duties* or *obligations*. Every right imposes a duty on every other person to respect it. Without duties correlative to rights, morality would again be self-contradictory, for it would permit what it prohibited – interference by others with the legitimate pursuit of the good on the part of an individual. Duties correlative with rights are simply the logical mirror of those rights – they reflect those rights into the eyes of other people. But there is more to duties than rights, contrary to the opinion of some philosophers who have an exaggerated conception of the role of rights in moral theory. And there is more to morality than justice. If you believe that the whole of morality is founded upon rights, you will naturally conclude that there can be no duty that does not correspond to some right. That this is not the case, and that ethics is not just a matter of duty either, can be seen by reflection upon the basic concepts of morality and the way they fit together.

The most basic concept of all, as I have claimed, is the good. But one is not *duty-bound* to perform every act that can be called good – not every kind of good act is obligatory. A person might devote her whole life to the selfless care of deprived people in a remote part of the world; or to some difficult and laborious study that prevents her from enjoying some of the good things in life as much as she would have liked. We properly say that *these* sorts of good acts are in some way *heroic*, or *beyond* the call of duty and, as such, they are admirable, even if not obligatory.

Duty is correlated with all of the virtues that go to make up the good life as such, that is to say the life which fulfils human nature even if it does not display heroism. For instance, the virtue of generosity inclines us to give what we can spare in the assistance of those in need, and imposes a duty on us so to do. We can see that duty is not coextensive with right because it would be wrong to say that in the absence of some specific relationship into which two people have entered (such as an agreement) or in which they find themselves (such as parent and child), one person has a *right* to another's generosity. If you walk past a needy person who asks you for money in the street, when you have plenty to spare, you have not violated that person's *rights*, or done him an injustice – he does not have a *claim* against you for your money. But you will have neglected an important duty springing from the general duty of charity or love of one's neighbour.

The virtue that is exclusively concerned with rights is the virtue of *justice*. It is too often forgotten that justice is a virtue. We often speak of justice as a *state of affairs* or a *condition* of things: we speak of a just society, a just war, a just distribution of goods, or a just wage. Such ways of speaking are not incorrect, any more, to use Aristotle's famous analogy, than it is wrong to speak of a healthy diet: as long as we remember that a diet is only healthy insofar as it promotes the health of the *person* who follows it, and that a wage, for instance, is just only insofar as the action of the person who provides the wage is just. (The case of society is more complex, since it involves the actions of the state as a 'moral person' as well as of individual human beings.) Justice, then, involves a form of moral behaviour, and all moral behaviour contributes to the development of some virtue.

In our examination of concrete moral problems in *Applied Ethics*, it is justice which we will be concentrating upon. Justice, as I suggested earlier, can be defined as that virtue by which a person is inclined to accord another his rights. It divides into three components, traditionally called *commutative* justice, *distributive* justice and, for want of a better term, *civic* justice. It is the first with which we shall mainly be concerned, as it is central to the major problems of applied ethics I will be discussing in the second volume. Commutative justice concerns the relations between individuals, and is the virtue which inclines them to accord one another their rights. Distributive justice concerns the relationship of the state to the individual, in particular its obligations to respect the individual's rights. *Civic* justice is the converse of this, being concerned with the individual's obligations to the state – specifically, to contribute to the common good, about which more later.

It is important at this point to emphasise the proper way of looking at justice and rights, on the one hand, and *law* on the other. In its broadest sense, a law is a binding rational principle governing behaviour, whether it be the behaviour of molecules or of people. The *moral* law is that subset of principles which direct human beings towards their ultimate end of happiness. Rights and duties, then, originate in the moral law and govern human beings in their pursuit of happiness in all its particulars. *Man-made* law, or positive human law, as it was called earlier, is brought into being by the legitimate authority charged with governing a community, for the purpose of securing or promoting the common good of the members of that community (or at least the common good as it appears to the authority). The fundamental principle governing the relationship of human law (or simply 'law') and morality is as follows: it is morality that determines what is and what is not a just law, hence law *always* follows morality. It is the duty of the legislator to frame laws that *reflect* morality and therefore provide the citizen with the state-authorised powers to do what morality *already* allows him to do, the state-authorised duties to do what morality already obliges him to do in conscience, and the state-authorised sanctions against those who would already be morally at fault for interfering with another person's pursuit of the good.

There is much more to law and its relation to morality than these axioms; the point is that they are so often forgotten that they cannot be restated enough. It is assumed by many people, for instance, that the rights proclaimed by the UN's Universal Declaration of Human Rights are rights *precisely* because they have been proclaimed by that body; or that there *must* be rights to life, liberty and the pursuit of happiness because they are in the American Declaration of Independence. This is not the case, for the simple reason that rights are not creations of human legislation or politics, no matter how careful the deliberation that goes into framing them. The most obvious evidence for this is that the laws of different states, such as their constitutions, sometimes contradict each other: for instance, the constitution of a socialist country might prohibit private property, while that of another country proclaims the very same right – clearly they cannot *both* be correct. (Whether or not this is historically the case is irrelevant – the mere *possibility* of contradiction is enough to show the problem.) One could, of course, fall back on a form of relativism about rights, which is itself indefensible (see chapter 1), but the point here is that if rights are features of an objective morality, they cannot at the same time be creations of human legislation.

Similarly, the fact that there is a right to X does not mean that this right will be proclaimed by any constitution or other legislation. There are many rights, for instance, that are not in the Universal Declaration – the right to have promises kept, for example. Indeed, no legislation anywhere recognises such a right, because legislation is rarely enacted where enforcement is known in advance to be virtually impossible. There is a difference between rights as such and rights that the state is competent to protect or, indeed, justified in protecting. Since the state's sole purpose is to protect and promote the common good (that is, the harmonious pursuit by all its citizens of the good), it may be that legal enforcement of certain rights would be dangerous to the common good. In such a case their protection is best left to the individual and to the numerous communal sanctions, such as custom and public opinion, that assist him in the protection of his rights.

It is, then, neither necessary nor sufficient for the existence of a law that it conform to morality generally, or that it respect rights in particular. Sometimes it is said that an unjust law, one that does not respect rights, is not a law *at all*: there is a sense in which this is correct, but we cannot explore this topic here. The important principle to remember for the moment is that although the legislator may, as a matter of fact, enact an unjust law, his *duty*, the requirement of *morality*, is that the laws he enacts conform to it. To the extent that a constitution, or a solemn declaration such as that of the UN, correctly proclaims the rights of the person, it is only because its drafters have used their intellects to *apprehend* the pre-existent rights that morality confers. If reason dictates that this or that clause does *not* proclaim a genuine right, then to that extent the clause is morally deficient. The law must *follow* and *reflect* morality, just as any command given by one person to another must reflect morality.

2.5   Rights and Contracts

As with most philosophical concepts, it helps to understand what rights are by understanding what they are *not*, and what sort of moral theory is incompatible with their existence.

According to contractualism, which has enjoyed a revival in recent years, rights originate in a contract between members of society that is entered into for the benefit of each of them as individuals. There is reason to think that most of the seventeenth- and eighteenth-century contractualists, such as Locke, Hobbes and Rousseau, believed that there was at least *some* historical truth in the existence of the social contract. Kant, on the other hand, and his recent followers such as Rawls, are clear that the contract is not an historical fact, but a theoretical *device* for determining or revealing the most rational moral principles and social structure.

To the extent that morality in general, and rights in particular, are said to *originate* in a social contract, even if it be merely hypothetical, the proponent of such a theory adopts a *conventionalist* attitude to morality. The question the contractualist asks, then, is: 'What sort of arrangement would people enter into if they thought about their needs hard enough?' Various conditions and stipulations are built into this general question, such as that no person knows more about anyone else's situation than he knows about his own (so as to avoid bias). The answer to the question will then contain the panoply of rights and duties that govern human life. Like all forms of conventionalism about morality, such an approach must be rejected, since it renders morality variable according to the contingencies of human imagination and belief about need. For instance, a person might, if he knew he was weak, agree to a society in which he was a slave, since the loss of liberty would be compensated by the gain in physical security of having a master. Or, if the contractualist decision procedure prohibited him from knowing that he was weak, he might agree to a society in which the weakest people, *whoever they were*, were slaves for the same reason.

The contractualist might reply that the decision procedure is governed by certain principles that prevent such arrangements, such as Rawls's famous 'difference principle', according to which every legitimate social arrangement must guarantee the greatest benefit for the least well-off. But apart from begging the question as to what constitutes such a benefit (why wouldn't slavery?), such a reply brings in subsidiary principles of an *ethical* nature for limiting the range of options the hypothetical contractors hypothetically agree to. And this raises the question of whether the decision procedure is supposed to be determinative or revelatory: does it *determine* what rights and duties there are, or does it *reveal* rights and duties that already exist?

Connected with this last question is that concerning the *bindingness* of the contract. How can a merely *hypothetical* contract bind the *actual* members of society? (How can a hypothetical promise to pay bind actual people who have made no such agreement?) If the answer is, 'Because it is rational to do so', the question is then, 'Why is it rational?' The answer given by some recent contractualists is that the theory is not conventionalist: there is an unchanging, prior notion of individual benefit and harm from which follow the foundational and subsidiary principles governing the contractualist decision procedure. But then what part does the contract *itself* play in the ontology of rights and duties? If it is revelatory of a prior notion of what is good for an individual, then it is this prior notion that is doing the theoretical work, not the hypothetical agreement that discovers it. The contractualist, then, faces a dilemma. On the one hand, if a social arrangement is desirable because it is binding, then the theory falls into conventionalism, or else it reverses the true order of explanation by making the goodness of the arrangement depend on the bindingness of the contract – contrary to the reality that the contract can only be binding in the first place *because* it is good. If, on the other hand, the arrangement *is* regarded as binding because it is good, then the notion of a contract itself is theoretically dispensable.

By 'theoretically dispensable' I mean that it does no work in accounting for the *origin* of morality in general and rights in particular. The work is being done by a *prior* notion of the good and of the rights and duties flowing from that notion properly analysed. This does not mean that there is no place for the idea of a social contract in moral theory, however. Any social arrangement, to be just and desirable, *must* be ordered according to the true system of morality. To the extent that many of our actions in society are in the first instance explained by consent (I pay my taxes because I tacitly agree to their use by the state; I vote because I tacitly agree to be governed by whomever wins the election; I allow myself to be conscripted because I tacitly recognise the state's authority to wage war on my behalf and to compel me to fight for others whom I implicitly acknowledge as my compatriots) – that consent depends at a more basic level on our recognition, or at least belief, that what we agree to is good. If it were not, we would rightly protest that the social arrangement under which we lived violated the pre-existent norms of morality.

2.6   Rights and Consequentialism

Rights are not a matter of physical force – might does not make right. Nor are rights whatever custom says they are – there can be rights with no customary recognition, and customs can be immoral. (Nevertheless, some rights are *customary*, in the sense that they arise from a particular way of

doing things – Alan might acquire a right of way over Brian's land because Brian has let him go that way for many years.) Nor are they simply
a matter of contract, as we saw above. (Yet some rights are *contractual*,
since they arise from a particular agreement entered into and would not
have existed otherwise.)

Nor are rights the encapsulation at a given moment in time of the current opinion (if there is one) concerning what is valuable, or of emotional
responses to this or that situation. Opinions shift with intellectual fashion, and emotional responses are transient and inconsistent, but rights are
permanent and inhere in their subjects because of what their subjects *are*.
Hence nothing could be further from the truth than the legal philosopher
Hans Kelsen's statement that judgements concerning rights and justice
'cannot be answered by means of rational cognition. The decision of these
questions is a judgment of value, determined by emotional factors, and is,
therefore, subjective in character, valid only for the judging subject and
therefore relative only.'[9]

Perhaps the starkest case of the incompatibility of rights with a certain
way of moral thinking is shown by consideration of the dominant moral
theory in applied ethics, namely consequentialism. According to
consequentialism, the criterion of the rightness and wrongness of actions
is whether they *maximise* good consequences. What are those good consequences? This is one of the first matters on which consequentialists differ. Some believe that what is to be maximised is pleasure (classical
utilitarianism). Others opt for the satisfaction of desires or preferences
(preference utilitarianism). Others choose the satisfaction of people's interests. Yet others recognise something like a plurality of goods on the
model that has been defended here (though the lists differ significantly
from the present one), which they see as ingredients in the life of 'well-
being'. Because consequentialists are deeply divided on just what it is that
should be maximised, I shall refer henceforth simply to the maximisation
of ingredient X, unless some particular consequence needs to be mentioned for the purposes of argument. (Note also that the terms 'utilitarianism' and 'consequentialism' should be taken as interchangeable
throughout the discussion, unless the context suggests a difference between them. In fact, 'consequentialism' is simply a word that was coined
several decades ago by Elizabeth Anscombe as a term of derision for utilitarians. They have taken to wearing the badge with pride, though they are
far from being an oppressed minority.)

Although many recent forms of consequentialism are so watered-down that it is difficult to say just in what sense they are consequentialist, I shall take it that any consequentialist *must* be committed to a certain set of principles that make the theory distinctive. I shall set out the principles as they apply to one standard kind of consequentialism (the 'act' variety, to be explained shortly) but it will be apparent how, in modified form, the principles apply to other versions (especially the 'rule'-based variety). (The discussion will be abstract and technical at some points; the reader can focus on the main claims if so desired, skimming through the rest.) One principle is that it is possible to *evaluate states of the world* in terms of the goodness of the consequences present in those states as a result of actions. More precisely, the consequentialist believes this can *always* be done, for any state whatsoever, so that there are no gaps in the theory. If there were gaps, the consequentialist decision procedure would not always produce a result prescribing one action or another; but the consequentialist is committed to there always being a correct answer to the question, 'What should I do?', for any situation I find myself in. Even questions concerning relatively minor matters of life, such as whether I should take a walk or read a good book, have a determinate answer based on a theoretically available *calculation* of the consequences of doing one thing rather than another.

Another principle is the one guiding action. Every moral agent's overarching rational duty is to maximise X by selecting the unique action, in a given situation, that produces the best overall state of the world – the state containing the most X-ness, as it were. Combined with this is a subsidiary principle to which we will return, which says that it does not matter for the morality of his action how an agent fails to maximise X in a given situation: he may deliberately choose an act that is sub-optimal (less-than-X-maximising), or he may simply refrain from performing the act that is optimal (X-maximising), with the result that, in one way or another, a sub-optimal state of the world eventuates; either way, he is equally guilty of immorality.

There are various other principles that most consequentialists adhere to, or that go with this or that version of the theory, but the above are its defining characteristics. (I shall mention other principles, where necessary, in the course of later discussion.) Two features implicit in what has been said need to be emphasised for our purposes. One is the distinctively *calculative* aspect of consequentialism. In its cruder forms, adherents claim that it is possible to assign a *numerical value* to states of the world: one can say that action *a* will produce (or can reasonably be expected to produce) a state of affairs with a moral value of *n* units of X, whereas *b* will produce (or can reasonably be expected to produce) a state with only $n -$ $- m$ units of X, making b worse than a because one state of affairs is worse than the other. Some claim that even though not every state can be given a numerical value, states can be *quantitatively compared* for their value: a produces more X-ness than b. In its less crude but correspondingly more vague form, consequentialists appeal to an intuitive apprehension of whether a given act is optimal or not: for instance, though we might not, they argue, be able to say what the numerical value is of hard study for an exam (in a given situation with all things being equal, for example, that the student is not already well prepared), we know that it is better than watching television, and moreover that if the best choice open at the time is study, and the student chooses it, he has maximised X; and if he does *anything* else, he has failed to maximise, and so has acted immorally. Whether a crude numerical approach is used, or an intuitive one, or something in between, the consequentialist is committed to the idea that *everything can be compared with everything else*, in order to arrive at a judgement of what action is X-maximising in the circumstances.

The other feature that must be emphasised is the *impersonality*, or what is often called the *agent-neutrality* of consequentialism. For the consequentialist, every person has exactly the same moral obligation: to procure the best state of affairs in the circumstances – to maximise X. It can never be the case that an agent is placed in a situation in which he has a specific duty that is incompatible with maximisation. For instance, it can never be the case that Alan is placed in a situation in which *his specific duty* is to keep a promise made by him to Brian, even though the result of Alan's keeping the promise will be that bad things happen that far outweigh, in the consequentialist calculus, the goodness of Alan's act. Conversely, there can be no situation in which it is *specifically wrong for Alan* to break a promise made by him to Brian, even though the result of his breaking it would be that good things will happen that far outweigh the badness of that act. Alan's *sole duty* is the same as everyone else's – to maximise X – and all his actions must be subordinated to that master requirement: whatever he does, he must maximise.

Put in a more transparent way, the defining feature of consequentialism, built into the theory by definition, is that there is no such thing as an action that is *wrong whatever the consequences*, and conversely, there is no such thing as an action that is *right irrespective of the consequences*. No actions are *absolutely right* or *absolutely wrong*: they take whatever moral complexion they have from their contribution, *in the circumstances*, to the maximisation of X. Hence the morality of an act will vary from circumstance to circumstance: breaking a promise in one situation will be right because it maximises X and in a different situation will be wrong because it fails to maximise X. Every action, no matter what, is simply one ingredient that goes into the melting pot of consequentialist calculation of the overall state of affairs that will be (or can reasonably be expected to be) produced.

Since consequentialism requires the procurement of the greatest amount of X, it is clearly incompatible with the existence of rights, which prohibit certain kinds of act no matter what the consequences are. It is irrelevant for present purposes whether rights *always* involve such prohibitions, or only *sometimes*: let us postpone the general question of the inviolability of rights to the next section. All that is needed to show the inconsistency of rights and consequentialism is *one* case where there is an absolute prohibition, that is, one that holds whatever the consequences.

First, however, it is worth noting what has been said by some prominent consequentialists about rights and justice. Peter Singer, for instance, says: 'I am not convinced that the notion of a moral right is a helpful or meaningful one.'[10] Elsewhere, he claims: 'The language of rights is a convenient political shorthand. It is even more valuable in the era of thirty-second TV news clips.'[11] J. J. C. Smart, one of the most lucid of contemporary consequentialists, says: 'however unhappy about it he may be, the utilitarian must admit that he draws the consequence that he might find himself in circumstances where he ought to be unjust'.[12] Again, John Harris says: 'I do not accept that there are any "absolute" or "natural" rights ... the use of the word "right" more often serves to obscure the rights and wrongs of an issue than to elucidate them.'[13] For the consequentialist, either rights have no place in morality, or they can be *redefined* in such a way as to be consistent with and embraced by his theory. (The latter is the hallmark of R. M. Hare's approach to rights.)

Consequentialism, as is well known, has two main versions, *act* and *rule*: both are incompatible with rights, for overlapping but partly distinct reasons. For the act consequentialist, the criterion of rightness (or at least permissibility) of an act is that it be X-maximising (right if it is the sole X-maximising option in the circumstances, permissible if it is one of at least two equally X-maximising options); otherwise it is wrong. For the rule consequentialist, the criterion of rightness of an act is that, whether or not it is itself X-maximising, it conforms to a rule that, if followed, is X-maximising; an act is permissible if it conforms to conflicting rules that are equally X-maximising; otherwise it is wrong. Many rule consequentialists now speak not of the evaluation of individual *rules* for their maximising effects, but of *systems* of rules; in which case, an act is right if it conforms to a rule that is part of an optimal system, permissible if it conforms to a rule belonging to equally optimal but conflicting systems, and wrong otherwise. This is a highly simplified outline: there are all sorts of complexities that various theorists have built into their versions of act and rule consequentialism, but these are the basic distinguishing features.

We can see how the act consequentialist cannot recognise rights. His overriding concern is to maximise X with every act, but respect for rights can and does conflict with this requirement. For instance, he would be acting morally if he took part in the enslavement of an ethnic minority where the enslavement produced overwhelming benefits for the majority of which he was a member, even though the minority suffered as a result. He would be obliged to break a promise, or reveal a confidence, if the overall advantages outweighed the harm done to the promisee or confidant. He would be under a duty to kill an innocent person, even his own mother, if the overall benefit required it (suppose a riotous mob were searching for her, and threatened mayhem if she were not killed by him or at least handed over to them to be executed). It is irrelevant that such cases might be rare (though they are all too common, in fact, especially if we take an historical perspective) or that they are extreme: the mere fact that act consequentialism *requires* or at least *permits* such behaviour, even *in theory*, is enough to show its incompatibility with rights. Should we say, on the other hand, that the act consequentialist does recognise rights, only they are not inviolable, merely one factor among others to be considered in the calculus (in other words, rights have only *prima facie* moral force)? Here we can agree with the consequentialist Jonathan Glover when he says:

> a doctrine of *prima facie* rights is of doubtful value . . . in general there is a very strong presumption that killing someone is wrong. A doctrine of absolute rights goes further than this and excludes the possibility of ever justifying killing by its consequences. But the claim that we have only a *prima facie* right to life does not exclude this possibility. It is thus not clear that it significantly differs from the view argued for here [in his book].[14]

Consequentialists are often keen to point out that they recognise one or other of the traditional moral categories, such as rights or justice: but merely saying so does not make it so. It is necessary to be sensitive to the *definition* of the concept as used by the consequentialist. If he redefines a given concept, then although he may use the same expression, such as 'rights', he will not be using the same *concept*. So, if the consequentialist insists on speaking of rights, but defines them as just another thing to be placed into the melting pot of general calculation of whether an act maximises X, then whatever he is talking about, it will not be *rights*.

Rule consequentialism is a little more complicated; nevertheless it, too, cannot recognise rights. A rule consequentialist will propose something like the idea that there are rights on his theory because an agent has a right to do whatever a given rule sanctions. (*Mutatis mutandis* for systems of rules, which will not be discussed here.) Typically, he will work backwards from duties not to interfere with the actions of others: A has the duty not to do F to B if not doing F accords with a rule to which obedience is X-maximising. From this he concludes that B has the *right* not to have F done to him.

Rule consequentialism, like its act-based counterpart, is undermined by numerous criticisms, many of which have been well canvassed by moral philosophers, and I do not propose to go over this ground again except where directly relevant to the discussion. One point does need to be mentioned, however, concerning the rules themselves. Critics sometimes say that rule consequentialism simply proposes the adoption of those rules that are accepted in society, perhaps backed by tradition and custom, or those rules that in practice seem to maximise; and it is said that this is just relativism, making the rules subject to fashion or public opinion. Perhaps some rule consequentialists think this, but they ought not to. The more enlightened version proposes what are sometimes called *ideal* rules, that is, rules that rational reflection would sanction as optimal, and these rules, for all we know, may not have been adopted by any society. Even on the ideal version, however, rights will have no place. First, there might not *be* any such ideal rules, on any consequentialist calculus. (How far into the future the maximising effects of a rule should be calculated, is, of course, itself notoriously unclear.) If not, the rule consequentialist cannot even *begin* to verify the sorts of duties from which rights could be derived. Second, even if there were such rules, their optimality (their X-maximising character) would be merely a *contingent* feature. A rule that sanctioned respect for the liberty of others, for instance, even if it was optimal in one society, might not be optimal in another; and even if it was optimal in all actual societies, it still might not be optimal in some *conceivable* society. It is not difficult to think of a society in which the enslavement of a minority was optimal, or provided overall benefits to that society as a whole. In such a society, there would be no right to liberty as such, at best only a right to liberty for certain of its members. Indeed, it is not hard to think of historical examples, which serves to show that the sorts of right that the rule consequentialist would like his theory to imply, traditional rights to life, liberty, property, privacy, reputation, and so on, are not merely conceivably non-existent but actually non-existent in very real situations. Thus whatever rights end up being recognised by the rule consequentialist, they are certainly not going to be the traditional ones.

To the reply that a rule must be optimal in all actual *and possible* societies, we can point out that this requirement is too strong, because it seeks to make maximisation logically necessary, whereas obedience to a rule can only ever be *contingently* maximising if it maximises at all. Which is where the main problem lies, since a rule that ceases to maximise will no longer be a rule for that society (or world, or universe, or whatever), and so the 'right' sanctioned by it ceases to be a 'right'. Rather, it was never a right in the *first* place, since true rights do not mutate in this way: if you have the right to liberty, you have it no matter whether general respect for liberty maximises X or not.

Another reason why the rule consequentialist cannot recognise rights is that some, indeed most, rights are far too simply stated to count as rights on his theory. For instance, every person has a right to the peaceful use and enjoyment of his personal possessions or chattels (subject to law). This is a right pure and simple, without qualification, but it is hard to see how the rule consequentialist can countenance a corresponding rule that is equally plain and simple. The circumstances in which the loss of a person's (or some people's) peaceful use and enjoyment of his chattels would maximise ingredient X are so vast that any suitable rule would have to allow for numerous exceptions and qualifications. There might, for instance, be a rule consequentialist right-to-the-peaceful-use-and-enjoyment-of-one's-chattels-as-long-as-they-cannot-be-put-to-better-use-by-the-state-or-by-other-people-or-are-not-an-obstacle-to-some-beneficial-action-by-the-state-or-by-other-people, and so on and so forth. But a correct theory of rights *must* countenance the plain and simple right to the peaceful use and enjoyment of one's chattels, not the sort of hedged and conditionalised 'right' that the rule consequentialist is bound to derive from his maximisation calculus. (The well-known charge applies here that the rule consequentialist's rules would all have to be so qualified that they would not be rules in any meaningful sense, whereby his theory simply collapses into act consequentialism.)

The best the consequentialist – of whatever persuasion – can come up with, then, are *prima facie* duties not to interfere with the actions of others, and to these duties correspond *prima facie* claims which he calls 'rights', but they are no more than one ingredient in the melting pot of maximisation, liable to sacrifice whenever the overall, impersonal and agent-neutral good demands it.

Some moral theorists have tried to reconcile respect for rights with an overall consequentialist decision procedure by arguing that it does not prevent the taking into account of actions that are intrinsically good rather than good because of their consequences. Amartya Sen, for instance, has proposed such an account.[15] The problem, though, is that regarding an act as intrinsically good does not prevent its being treated as a *consequence* to be maximised, so that an act that does not maximise respect for rights in general, *even if it is itself an act that respects rights*, will, all things being equal, be morally deficient. So, to take a case mentioned above, if a person refused to kill his own mother, even though a riotous mob threatened to go on the rampage if he failed to do so, his act would, on a theory such as Sen's, still involve moral failure on his part. Conversely, if he sacrificed his mother's right to life, then if it maximised respect for rights in general by quelling the riotous mob, the sacrifice would be morally praiseworthy. A similar criticism can be made of a theorist such as W. D. Ross, for whom an action like promise-keeping is good because of its intrinsic features, not because of its consequences, and yet whose theory implies that you would be permitted, if not obliged, to breach the *prima facie* duty to do what is intrinsically good, namely keep the promise, if the act procured the greatest amount of obedience to *prima facie* duties in general. For instance, if Alan promised $100 to Brian, but then promised the same amount to be divided equally among Charles, Donald, Eric and Fred, he would, on a theory such as Ross's, be permitted, if not *obliged*, to break his promise to Alan and give $25 each to the other four: he would have maximised the number of promise-keeping acts. (Of course Ross could say, as he should, that the subsequent promises were not genuine promises, since there was no money to promise in the first place as Brian already had a title to it. The case could easily be modified, however, by imagining that Gary has made the promises to the other four and told Alan that he will only keep them if Alan breaks his promise to Brian.)

It is worth mentioning another, more subtle, attempt to reconcile rights and consequentialism, in a recent paper by Philip Pettit.[16] He argues that the consequentialist should want to maximise *dignity*, but that dignity is such a fragile and, as he terms it, 'elusive' feature of human relations, that infringement of the rights of another, even on a single occasion, would not maximise dignity. The reason is that it would put people in fear of being similarly treated by the infringer, and place the whole host of intimate human relationships at risk of sacrifice on the altar of the calculation of overall benefit. A person might try to dissemble, to hide his infringement of rights, so as not to jeopardise his other relationships, but 'every hesitation and reservation' by the consequentialist will 'give the game away'; if some people 'see him play games with others then they will expect him to do the same in his behaviour towards them'.

Again, Pettit's proposal, clever as it may be, only serves to demonstrate the sheer impossibility of turning the trick as the consequentialist would wish. First, why should Pettit have alighted on 'dignity' as that which consequentialists should promote? More precisely, what could be meant by 'dignity' in this context? In Pettit's sense, it seems to mean simply the respect for others that does not place stronger claims on the agent than consequentialism itself allows: in other words, the agent must not 'play games' in his relationships with others because of the high likelihood of detection and the subsequent weakening of relationships detection would bring about. This is clearly an attenuated sense of 'dignity', since it is merely the canonisation of the perennial consequentialist idea that human relationships are never good *for their own sake*, but for what overall good they procure. Even if detection is not merely highly likely, but absolutely certain due to some as-yet-undiscovered laws of human behaviour, the fact remains that, *qua* consequentialist, the agent does not see friendship, or love, or loyalty, or justice, as intrinsically good, but as good for what they can produce in the world as a whole. (Hence the attempt to divorce the notion of intrinsic good from consequence-based reasoning, as Sen and arguably Ross try to do, is self-defeating, given their overall consequentialist approach.) The notion of dignity Pettit is employing, then, is consequentialist in its very essence, and so his proposal amounts to no more than bootstrapping: what the consequentialist must maximise, namely 'dignity', is simply that order of human relationships which is consistent with consequentialist thinking in the first place.

On the other hand, Pettit may be tacitly appealing to a stronger notion of dignity, the non-consequentialist one, according to which the moral claims one person has on others are not grounded in what respect for those claims can procure as an overall benefit (which, it must be noted, may or may not involve the benefit of the claim-holder), but in the inherent and unassailable dignity of the claim-holder himself, apart from all other considerations, as a human being in pursuit of the good. Now if *that* is the notion Pettit is relying on – and his brief remarks about dignity as a form of 'dominion' over one's life, and as the ability to 'block' sorts of behaviour that 'invade his personal space', suggest that it might be – then his use of it will not work. The non-consequentialist concept of dignity does not ground the value of human relationships involving love, friendship, loyalty, justice, and the like, in what overall state of the world they can produce. It therefore does not demand condemnation of rights violations because of the fear or instability they will create in others with whom one is (or is not) intimately related, even if that fear or instability are a *certain* consequence; *a fortiori* if they are highly likely, or so difficult to avoid as to make rights violations an 'implausible strategy', or 'hazardous', in Pettit's words. The non-consequentialist sense of 'dignity', then, involves a recognition *in the first place* that rights are not a mere ingredient in a general consequentialist decision procedure, and so appeal to it by Pettit would vitiate his very project of reconciling consequentialism and rights.

Second, Pettit is far too sanguine about the likely disruption to human relationships or social order from a policy of consistent infringements of the rights of some for the benefit of others. It is not hard to imagine a society in which the vast majority were secure in their 'dignity', in Pettit's sense – in which they had no reason at all to expect their dominion of their lives, or the stability of their relationships, to be vulnerable to a state policy of infringing the rights of, say, a well-defined minority of the population. If the majority benefited tangibly from such a policy, they might even approve of it; but even if they did not approve, for all their condemnation they could be convinced that *their* rights were not vulnerable. And neither scenario depends on the policy's being *hidden* from anyone, so the difficulty of dissembling does not arise. Since maximisation is what consequentialism requires, 'dignity' could well be maximised in such a society, contrary to Pettit's supposition that it never could. Again, it is arguably the case that such societies have existed as a matter of historical record; but even if they have not, given the fact that whether a policy maximises ingredient X is always a *contingent* matter, whereas the inviolability of rights is not, it is sufficient that we can *conceive* of a world containing beings who are recognisably human, with human needs and wants, and in which the consequentialist decision procedure no longer underwrites the integrity of a person's rights, for it to be apparent that rights and consequentialism are conceptually irreconcilable.

Finally, Pettit overlooks something to which probably all consequentialists would subscribe, namely that there is more to ingredient X than just 'dignity'. Whatever X is (and, as cannot be emphasised strongly enough, it varies from one consequentialist to another), it will involve more than – and for some not even – one particular aspect of the human character, such as the need for stable relationships or control over one's life. For the consequentialist who wishes to maximise some or other plurality of 'intrinsic goods', 'dignity' will only be one member of the list; so on an overall calculation 'dignity', and the integrity of rights that is supposed to go with it on Pettit's account, may lose out to other things which the consequentialist wishes to maximise.

2.7   Collision of Rights

Rights are not limitless. There are no, so to speak, 'sky-blue' rights: I cannot go beyond what is mine, or my neighbour beyond what it his. Rights are limited because they exist solely as a concomitant to a person's pursuit of the good, which is itself finite, bounded by what fulfils his nature. Living well may be an endless task, in the sense that one is forever trying to order one's life, to overcome temptations, to resist pressures to go against one's nature. Aristotle was correct to remark that one cannot assess whether a person has lived happily until his life is over: it may be that only the very last thing a person does before he dies makes it possible to say that he has indeed achieved happiness. A person might live a reprobate existence full of wrongdoing and yet be so contrite on his deathbed, so desperate to receive the forgiveness of those he has hurt, that his contrition enables him to die at peace with the world and his fellows. Nevertheless, this limit that is so hard to approach is indeed a limit. No person has endless needs, and there does not exist an infinite number of goods that are necessary for a happy life. Hence a person's rights are limited, both by the rights of other people and by the common good, whereby every member of society is enabled to pursue his own finite good life in an orderly and harmonious way.

We must therefore be careful not to place undue emphasis on the rights of individuals or of society as a whole. In particular, two extremes are to be avoided: on the one hand libertarianism, which attributes to the individual exaggerated rights as against the just claims of society to preserve the common good; and on the other totalitarianism, which attributes to the state an unlimited power to intervene in the lives of its members, recognising no prior individual rights that the state is bound to respect.

Even with a proper and necessary understanding of the individual's obligations to society and of society's obligations to the individual, one is still faced with the problem of rights that, as it were, collide. I say 'collide' rather than 'conflict', because there can be no true conflict of rights. Morality cannot be an objective system if it is internally contradictory, which is what it would be if a person both had the right to do X and did not have the right to do X, or if he had the right to do X and someone else (including the state, acting on behalf of its members) had the right to prevent him from doing X. Morality cannot, if it is objective, contain inconsistencies any more than physics, or chemistry, or psychology.

All there can be, then, are *apparent* conflicts of rights, or collisions. There are two situations in which collisions can arise: (a) One person may claim the right to do X and another the right to prevent him; (b) two people may claim the same thing. It is the first that is of most concern in the present context, though the second does raise interesting questions. Suppose Alan promises his spare $10 to Brian and then promises the very same money to Celia. Who has the right to the money? Or suppose Alan promises $10 to Brian, and then $10 to Celia, and he later discovers he only has enough money for one of them. There are various principles for dealing with these and other cases, which we cannot dwell on, but some plausible ones are as follows. (1) If a person undertakes an obligation to do X and then undertakes an obligation to do Y, where Y is logically incompatible with X, then only the temporally prior undertaking imposes a genuine obligation *in justice*; in other words, the later undertaking does not confer a right. (2) Nevertheless, the obligation imposed by the prior undertaking can be *superseded* in certain circumstances. For instance, if the later promisee has an emergency need for the money which the prior promisee does not, then even though the later promise has not conferred a *right* to the money, there may be an obligation *in charity* to provide it which *overrides* the prior obligation, or more properly causes it to be suspended. It is important to recognise that, all things being equal, justice comes first and charity second. By 'all things being equal' is meant, among other things, that the subject matter of the obligations of charity and justice are of equal importance. Brian's strict right to the \$10, which he intends to use, let us suppose, to go to the cinema, may be superseded by the requirement of charity that Alan give the money to Celia, who needs the money to pay a parking fine and will go to jail if she does not. Even in such a case, however, Alan is bound in justice to attempt to seek a release from his obligation to Brian and, if he cannot, to apologise after the fact, and perhaps to make amends where appropriate.

This brings us to the more important case, for our purposes, of collisions of rights where a person claims the right to stop another from doing X and yet the other claims the right to do X. The first thing to note is that rights are conferred by laws: just as positive (civil or man-made) rights (for example, the right to park one's car in a certain place) emanate from the positive laws of a society, so moral rights (which the legal system is, as we have noted, bound to reflect) emanate from the laws of morality. A collision of rights, then, is really a collision of laws, and since rights cannot genuinely conflict, neither can the moral laws that confer them.

Some writers have, in discussing these matters, made a distinction between the *infringement* and the *violation* of a right, which is useful for present purposes (though my employment of it does not necessarily conform to that of the writers themselves).[17] Let us say that a person infringes another's right if he interferes with the pursuit of its object; and he violates the right only if he does so *wrongfully*. Not every infringement, then, is a violation, but every violation is necessarily an infringement.

Examples readily come to mind of the permissibility of infringing the rights of others. Suppose Brian has been in a car accident and his leg is trapped in the wreckage – perhaps the wreckage is even about to explode. Can Alan, a paramedic, amputate Brian's leg if that is the only way he can free him and save his life? Surely he can. But would the amputation not be an *assault* on Brian, a violation of his right to bodily integrity? And must that right not be respected, no matter what the consequences? There is a clear principle that shows that this would be a mistaken and exaggerated understanding of rights: it is always permissible to sacrifice a part to save the whole. (This is sometimes called the Principle of Totality.) Brian's right to life *overrides* his right to his leg. Without such a principle it is hard to see how the defender of rights could handle such a case, but the principle is not ad hoc: it is simply a reflection of the evident metaphysical truth that the parts of a thing are subordinated to the thing itself; in the moral sphere, this is mirrored by the idea that the fundamental unit of concern is the human being, so that the parts of the person are morally important only insofar as they contribute to the person's normal functioning. If the person can only survive without a certain part, then the part must go even if the functioning is thereafter impaired.

Apart from the Principle of Totality, however, there is a broad class of cases in which rights collide and in which infringement is permissible without being wrongful, in other words, without constituting a violation. Suppose Alan has to take his dangerously ill child to hospital in a hurry and the only way he can get there in time is to trespass on Brian's land. May he do so? Brian has the right to exclude people from his property, and certainly Alan should ask permission if he can; but if he cannot? Morality allows that he can trespass (though again, he should apologise later if possible) in order to save his child's life, in defence of his right not to be prevented from doing so. Suppose Charles is starving to death: may he take food from David? The latter has a right to his personal property, but this must yield to Charles's right not to be denied the necessities of life. Eric has the right to protect himself against danger to life and limb; but the state may command him to go to war, in defence of its right (exercised on behalf of the members of that society) to protect the common good.

These are cases that are, I submit, uncontroversial: but it is not to say that this area of moral theory is by any means clear-cut. Nor should we expect absolute precision, as remarked in chapter 1. What if the best enquiries cannot determine which of two rights prevail? Alan may trespass on Brian's land to save his child. But suppose Brian obstructs him: can Alan push him out of the way? Can he assault him? Can he cause him permanent injury? Can he forcibly break into Brian's house, if that is the only way he can escape Brian and find passage to the hospital? Can a starving man *force* another to give over his food? It does not take much imagination to think of all sorts of difficult cases and grey areas. But the moral theorist must *not* start out in his investigation with the attitude of *pessimism*: he must assume a solution can be found until convinced of the contrary; and in the vast majority of cases, a consideration of circumstances, competing rights, motives and so on will enable a resolution. We need not, for present purposes, be persuaded that these sorts of hard case are *in principle* insoluble – it is not clear just *how* imprecise ethics is. All that needs to be said is that *some* cases are such that *diligent* inquiry, motivated by a genuine desire for the truth of the matter, may not resolve a problem. Further, we must note that the requirement of diligence on the part of the *agent* who has to decide what to do, often in a hurry, will not be as great as that on the part of the moral theorist with the leisure of the outside observer. We can say, however, that in general, if a determination of which right prevails is impossible despite diligent investigation, a person does no wrong whatever right he respects, be it his own or another's. Since it is really the collision of *laws* that is at issue, as noted above, the same goes for any collision of obligations: a person does no wrong no matter what obligation he fulfils, if diligent inquiry cannot determine which obligation prevails. (Note that some rights entail obligations on the part of the *right-holder* as well as others. In particular, some rights oblige the right-holder to pursue the good protected by the right, whereas other rights do not impose such an obligation. I will call the former 'duty-rights' and the latter 'option-rights'. For example, I have the right to own a car, but I am not obliged to – this is an option-right; I have the right to life, and am obliged to protect it – this is a duty-right. I will expand on this distinction later.)

Nevertheless, some general principles are available to deal with collision problems, in addition to the Principle of Totality just mentioned, and which do indeed offer a solution to some of the difficult cases such as those raised above. First, the moral law takes precedence over positive law. For instance, it would be permissible for Alan to park his car illegally if it was necessary to get his dangerously ill child to the hospital in time. What if Alan was only taking his child to the doctor for a routine examination? Then the position would be that the risk to the orderly movement of traffic would outweigh the importance of the visit to the doctor. Another way of putting this is to say that there is not even an *apparent* conflict in such a case, because that would only exist if two laws appeared to oblige simultaneously; but whilst there is an obligation to park legally on every occasion, there is no obligation to have one's child routinely examined *at any specific time*, whereas there would be an obligation *then and there* to get a dangerously ill child to the hospital. And if there were no risk to traffic? Again, the disrespect shown to the law by flouting it for a relatively minor reason such as a routine doctor's appointment would make the illegal parking morally wrong, though not seriously so. Note that the concept of universalisability ('What if everyone did the same?') is of little use in such problems. If everyone felt free to park illegally when they needed to get their dangerously ill children to hospital, there might well be traffic chaos; but man-made law would still have to give way to a higher objective, namely the preservation of life.

Some positive laws, such as those against murder and theft, directly mirror moral laws; others, such as traffic laws, only do so indirectly, by giving concrete effect to the general moral law requiring the state to provide for the orderly transactions of its members. Hence, to be more exact about the application of the above principle, it is the positive law that is not also a *specific* injunction of the moral law that must, *qua* positive law, give way to the latter. So, in the illegal parking case, it is the parking law *qua* man-made law which gives way to the moral law requiring the father to save his child's life. On the other hand, the positive law against assault mirrors the moral law, and if it gives way to the moral law obliging the father to preserve his child's life by getting him to the hospital in time, it is not *qua positive law* that it does so, but *qua inferior moral law*.

Which brings us to a second principle that is needed to resolve collisions, that where the apparent conflict is between two laws of the same category, the more important, urgent or necessary law prevails. Suppose Alan needs to get his dangerously ill child to the hospital in time, which he can only do by trespassing on Brian's land, but that Brian physically obstructs him. May he push Brian out of the way, thereby committing an assault? He can (and hence it is not reasonable to regard the case as insoluble as such, whatever difficulties might arise in particular situations), because the right (and obligation) to preserve life overrides the right (and obligation) to preserve bodily integrity. Here the laws are of the same category, namely moral (that one or both may be mirrored in the positive law is irrelevant). Indeed, both are laws pertaining to the general good of life. Nevertheless the sub-good, as it were, to Alan of the life of his child is closer to him, more directly connected to his well-being, more urgent to him in the proper living of his life, than the sub-good of being preserved from relatively harmless bodily intrusion is to Brian. (Doesn't the child have a say in this? it might be asked. Of course he does, and it is precisely the child's own right to be cared for by his parent that generates Alan's right, which is the right technically in collision with Brian's, to carry out an act of caring.) In general, the core good of life itself (existence) is more important to the individual than the good of bodily integrity (which is why the Principle of Totality mentioned above is correct), and bodily integrity is more important than the good of property – all of which goods, it should be repeated, belong to what I have called the good of life (in general). Does this mean that, *in extremis*, Alan could even burn down Brian's house in order to get his child to the hospital? The scenario sounds bizarre, but perhaps we can conceive of a situation in which destruction of the house was the only way to get across the land. Strictly, since the good of Brian's possessing his house intact is not as important as Alan's saving his child's life, this would in principle be permissible. (Consider the more realistic case of soldiers who destroy enemy equipment in wartime: they are indeed infringing the enemy's human right to own property, but since it is for the graver purpose of preserving their lives, it could hardly be called illegitimate.) Nevertheless, as moral theorists we are bound to consider serious situations such as these very carefully, in as much detail as possible, before making a decision (and Alan would have to consider the situation as carefully as circumstances allowed). Where two important goods are in collision, it may seem that either can give way to the other, or it may be tempting to make a hasty decision. It is easy – and an age-old tactic of the critics of systematic moral theory – to come up with improbable situations that make decision-making difficult, for that is in the nature of ethics. One must, as noted above, expect to be able to find an answer even where none seems to be forthcoming, but this may require a careful consideration of facts and circumstances. To say this is not, as devotees of rival moral systems such as consequentialism often do, to brush difficult cases aside as so remote from reality as to be safely ignorable for practical purposes. Remoteness has nothing to do with it. Rather, the point is that one must be judicious (the word is used advisedly – consider the admirable way in which common-law judges enter into minute consideration of the facts of each case) in assessing the circumstances and competing claims, and aim to show *why* a certain problem *does not really arise in this case*, or why the proposed solution is plausible, contrary to one's initial reaction.

The principle that goods in the same category are more or less important to the individual is simply another way of stating that there is a *hierarchy of values* within each good. Life is more important than health; health is more important than property. Family is more important than friends; friends are more important than strangers. Of course, in individual cases the ranking can change *within limits*, but only because a subgood lower in the hierarchy may in certain circumstances contribute to the good life *in the way in which the higher one normally does* though fails to do on a particular occasion. For instance, Alan might have an uncaring family, or have been abandoned, and find that certain friends are far more important to him than any relative, because in his case they fulfil the very role that family *normally* does. Indeed, it is exceptions like this that, as it were, prove the rule that there is a standard hierarchy of values within each good, against which the exceptional cases are to be measured in order to assess how a particular person's life goes.

But what about the general goods themselves? Is there an objective ranking for them? More will be said about this in chapter 4 when we consider the good of life, so I shall confine my remarks here to those relevant to the collision question. The basic point to make is that the general goods are equally fundamental. This means the following: although a person's particular circumstances might cause or require him to place more emphasis on one good rather than another in his own life, he cannot legitimately abrogate one good in favour of another; and by 'abrogate' in this context I mean 'wholly ignore, destroy, or directly attack at its core'. This constraint applies both to his own life and to others'. The various goods specify not only rights, but *obligations* that a person must fulfil if he is to be said to live a good life: living healthily, working, enjoying recreation, appreciating beauty (including the beauty of nature), learning, having friends, aspiring to a spiritual life, that is, one going beyond the merely worldly. For him to attack any of these goods, in his own life or that of others, even if for the purpose of promoting *another* of those goods, would be to commit an intrinsic wrong, to attack the very order of the moral law which is imposed on human beings for the fulfilment of their nature.

Returning then to the case of Alan, who needs to get his dangerously ill child to hospital and can only do so by crossing Brian's land, we can see the following restrictions. Suppose Brian were to obstruct Alan in such a way that only by killing Brian could Alan get his child to hospital; could he commit such an act? He could not, because this would be murder pure and simple, the trading-off of Brian's life against his child's. Suppose Alan needed a car to get to the hospital and Brian's was available; could he take it? We noted above that the higher law of the preservation of life supersedes the law protecting property, meaning that Alan could, if the situation were indeed desperate, use Brian's car without asking permission (though again, he would be bound to apologise later and perhaps to make some sort of reparation, in recognition of the inferior law). But could he then keep the car permanently? He could not, since that would be theft pure and simple, a direct attack upon the good of life: by permanently depriving Brian of his property he would be showing a complete disrespect for Brian's very humanity, abrogating a good central to any person's living well.

To take another example, suppose Alan and Brian were both sitting a test; for Alan, failing would mean the shattering of his entire career aspirations. Could he cheat by looking at Brian's test paper? He could not, since that would be a case of deception pure and simple, a direct attack upon the good of truth, which demands honest dealing between people. No matter what *other* goods Alan could promote by cheating, he could not abrogate the good of truth as a means to that promotion.

Examples could be multiplied, and since such cases are at the heart of applied ethics I will consider a number of them in the companion volume. For the moment, I conclude by noting how different a moral theory encompassing the ideas and principles expressed above is from a theory such as consequentialism. On the theory outlined here, rights are always and everywhere *inviolable*. They may be *infringed* in certain circumstances, but those circumstances are *limited and well defined* (whatever the difficulties of practical application, which must never be confused with theory): in cases of apparent conflict, the higher law prevails, and this only because the higher law protects a good that is closer to the core of a person's dignity as a human being. May not the consequentialist also argue as follows: 'On my theory as well rights are always and everywhere inviolable. Every infringement of a right that does not maximise is by definition a violation, hence morally wrong. One may only infringe where the infringement will maximise, and hence by definition the infringement will not be wrongful'?

For the consequentialist to argue in this way, however, would be seriously to misrepresent both his own theory and the stark and irreconcilable difference between it and the theory being defended here. The argument presumes what it should not, that in consequentialism there is such a thing as rights in the first place – and this, we have seen, is not the case. No type or token of a human act, for the consequentialist, has any moral force or claim upon any person save insofar as it maximises (directly or indirectly) ingredient X. Given this fundamental claim, the idea that there are separable modes of human behaviour that have an intrinsic moral compellingness, but that might in certain circumstances give way to competing modes of behaviour, can have no place. What are these 'claims', what life of their own do they have outside the consequentialist calculus, and by what right do they force themselves upon one's conscience? Thus it is that *every* type or token of human action, for the consequentialist, can be traded off against another, if the calculus requires it. And even if the consequentialist were able to isolate a class of modes of behaviour that had some intrinsic moral force (that, perhaps, were directed at the pursuit of 'goods', in some sense), they would *always and everywhere* be infringeable for the sake of maximisation. In what sense would there be inviolable claims, then, if moral theory never guaranteed their respect, but only gave them, as it were, respect *pro tanto* – a respect that lasted only as long as the contingency of circumstance?

On the theory being defended here, on the other hand, the infringement of rights is always a limited, temporary and well-defined affair. This is because it can never be allowed when fundamental rights are involved whose infringement would strike at the very heart of the good they are designed to protect and promote: there are some actions that are wrong whatever the consequences, and others that are right regardless of the consequences. Further, infringement is always restricted to cases of apparent conflict, where rights clash; and rights can only clash in unusual and transient circumstances (much of what passes for conflict of rights in contemporary theory is no such thing). Again, infringement carries with it the need either to seek permission to infringe, or to apologise or compensate afterwards. Once the infringement is over, the infringed right immediately takes its place again (which it never lost, though the place was temporarily superseded) as inviolable and protective of its bearer.

The central point is that, on the present theory, rights are never infringeable in consequentialist terms. There are things it would be wrong to do even if they maximised, and things it would be right to do even if they did not maximise. Alan's child might have the intelligence of Albert Einstein and the aesthetic sensibility of Mozart – but he could not cross Brian's land to get him to the hospital if he had to kill Brian in order to do it. Conversely, his child might be severely physically handicapped, brain-damaged, and with a life expectancy of months rather than years; and yet he would be permitted to cross Brian's land to get him to the hospital, if it did not mean killing Brian to do so, no matter how much distress and inconvenience Brian might thereby be caused. There are innumerable cases in which such a contrast can be brought into relief and which do not involve anything like fanciful speculation or the postulation of improbable circumstances, and which even reflect actual situations with which we are daily confronted: cases of racial exploitation, the abuse of children, pornography, the self-gratifying infliction of pain on others, and so on. And, as we shall see, cases of the sort to be discussed in *Applied Ethics*.

3

Basic Concepts In Moral Theory II

3.1 Intention and Foresight

3.1.1 Good, evil and the will

The good of a thing is, as we have seen, to be found in its operations and activities, and whether those operations and activities further its proper end, or fulfil its nature. Since man is not merely a living being who grows, is nourished, can be healthy or unhealthy, and so on, but is a *free* being, capable of choice, we must look for the good or evil of man, *qua man* (to use Aristotle's famous phrase) in his free choices, those of his operations and activities that are under the control of his *will*.

Moral goodness and badness, then, belong primarily to acts of the will. In this sense Kant was right to say that the only thing that is good without qualification is a good will.[1] But acts of the will extend over a far greater range than Kant typically recognised. The act may be one of desire, love or hope, to take but a few examples; an internal act of love (towards an absent friend, for instance) can be as much a free act as a physical embrace.

The moral quality of any act that is commanded by the will, then, derives from the quality of the act of will itself. More precisely, since every act of the will has an *object*, it is the act of the will understood as comprising a certain object that determines the quality of any other act that the will commands for the purpose of realising that object. If my will is, for instance, directed at the obtaining of another person's lawful property, then that act of the will, being directed at the prospect of theft, is morally bad, whether or not I do anything to realise what my will has in its focus, that is, whether or not I steal, or even try to steal, that property. And if I gaze covetously on someone else's property, wishing it were mine, that internal act of desire is also bad, being under the command of my will.

It is more common today to speak not of acts of the will but of *intentions*, though this is just another name for the same phenomenon. The idea expressed above of the primary goodness or badness of the act of will, then, can also be expressed by saying that it is the *intention* with which something is done that gives moral character to an action.

In applied ethics (involving analysis of concrete cases of the kind examined in the companion volume) we are primarily concerned with *external* acts, those doings and refrainings in the public arena that are the exteriorisation of acts of the will or intentions. Why should this be so, it might be asked, if it is really only intentions that matter morally? The question is misleading, however. To return to the famous Aristotelian example given earlier, although a diet can be called healthy only insofar as it promotes the health of the person who follows it, it would be absurd to conclude that we should not be interested in healthy diets as such because their healthiness is only derivative. Similarly, although the moral character of what people do derives from the moral character of what they intend, we should still be concerned with what they do, morally speaking, *in light* of what they intend.

And what a person does, externally, the *effects* he has on the world through his agency, are not matters of indifference because they will be characterised by that good or evil, in the primary, non-moral sense, which is the object of all human action. As we have already outlined, there is a range of ends that fulfil human nature. Considered as such, independently of any action towards or away from them on the part of individuals, they contain their own goodness; and their absence contains its own evil. Indeed, it is impossible even to comprehend what *makes* an intention morally good or bad if the reality of objective, non-moral good or evil is not apprehended in the first place. It is the inherent goodness of certain ends that makes them proper objects of human striving, so that the person who strives after them *does* good, or acts morally; and conversely for ends that are bad. In themselves they have no *moral* character – it is only when they come within the compass of human choice that they take on, as it were, the moral aspect of that choice. To take a simple example: an avalanche that causes the death of many people is *in itself* a bad thing; but it is not *morally* bad, since avalanches do not choose to be avalanches and to kill people. If a person, however, *decides* to cause an avalanche and thereby to kill people, say by yelling on a fragile mountain slope on which there are a number of climbers, he will have acted immorally, and all things being equal, committed murder.

It is wrong, therefore, for critics of the idea that morality attaches primarily to intentions rather than external actions, to object that it follows from this idea that a person who is resolved to commit an evil act might as well go through with it. To go through with it would indeed be to bring about objective evil, that which is bad for people: the moral primacy of intention does not deny the reality of the effect that the execution of our intentions has on others. But this is perfectly compatible with the idea that, morally, the external act adds nothing *qualitative* to the inner act of the will. Hence a person who is resolved to perform a good act is still praiseworthy even though the act is prevented by circumstance: for instance, someone who offers to give blood but is refused on medical grounds has still acted well. Similarly, a person who intends a bad act, say the burglary of another's house, has still acted badly even though he cannot find a way to break in. This basic truth is reflected in the legal system, which punishes the criminal attempt to do X as severely as it punishes the doing of X itself. It should be added, though, that the execution of an intention often adds something *quantitative* to the intention itself, since it usually requires greater and more prolonged effort to externalise an act of the will, and hence more concentrated dwelling on the good or evil one has in one's sights.

3.1.2   The Principle of Double Effect

There is a large sphere of human activity, however, to which moral responsibility attaches, but where intention is not the primary phenomenon at work. What has been described above is what might be called the *paradigm* of moral responsibility, namely the having of intentions to do (or the direction of the will towards) good or evil. But not everything we do, and for which we can be held accountable, we do intentionally. Alan is late for a lecture, and he drives his car so fast and carelessly to the university that he overshoots a traffic light and runs over a pedestrian. Barbara is anxious to make a good return for her company, and is so impressed by a report she reads that she overlooks some obviously misleading statements it contains and makes a bad investment decision, costing the company thousands of dollars. Charles wants to cure his patient's migraines, so he tries an experimental drug knowing it will probably have severe side effects, which it does. In all these cases, as in so many others we can think of, the agent does not *intend* a certain result, but nevertheless brings it about through careless or negligent behaviour. Is he to be held responsible for that result?

The first thing to note is that there is here an asymmetry between good and evil results. Unintended *good* results can never morally affect the intention with which one otherwise acts: if a person intentionally does X, knowing that Y will (or will probably) result, and Y is a good effect, Y does not add to the moral quality of the act. This is so whether X is good or bad. Suppose Daniel is a computer hacker and breaks into a company's network with the intention of stealing data. Now it may well turn out that, as a result, the company is alerted to security weaknesses in its computer system and is able to plug the leaks, thereby saving itself much future damage. It is no use for Daniel to plead (as hackers typically do) that he also did the company a good deed, though unintentionally. Good side effects do not turn a bad act into a good one. But neither do they make a good act a better one. Eric may visit his sick friend in hospital, thereby cheering him up immensely, with the result that the friend's wife may also be pleased at this act of kindness. If Eric did not intend to please his friend's wife, then even if he later welcomes the result, he cannot be credited with doing her a charitable deed as well. (Note that if he welcomes it *in advance*, we would have reason to suspect that he not merely foresaw it but also intended it.) If the agent merely foresaw the good result, but it formed no part of his *practical reasoning*, then he would have gone ahead with the act *whether or not* he believed the good result would follow. He cannot therefore be credited with its occurrence even if he does end up bringing it about. What about evil results that follow from our actions? Here, we want to say that a person cannot escape all responsibility for the evil that unintentionally follows from a good act he intentionally performs. We want to say, in the cases of Alan, Barbara and Charles above, that they *are* to blame for the foreseen side effects of their actions. Indeed, we have specific terminology to describe that responsibility: we say they were *negligent*, or careless in what they did. And this terminology reveals the asymmetry between good and bad side effects: for whilst we have the concept of negligence to characterise bad side effects, that is, foreseen but intended consequences of intentional actions, we do not have a corresponding term to describe good side effects; there is no concept at hand for expressing the thought that Eric, by unintentionally causing his hospital-bound friend's wife to be cheered up, has added to the good quality of his act of visiting the sick.

What is needed, then, is a way of distinguishing between those bad side effects that *can* be laid at the foot of the agent, for which we can legitimately say that he was negligent or careless in bringing them about, and those that cannot, in other words, those that it is *permissible* for him to bring about. And there is in moral theory just such a way of making the distinction: the so-called Principle of Double Effect (PDE), a principle that is almost universally derided in modern applied ethics, dominated as the discipline is by consequentialist ways of thinking. Nevertheless, PDE can be shown to be plausible, to make sense of moral decision-making in difficult situations, and to be resistant to the many, often shallow, criticisms that have been levelled against it (often with almost complete misunderstanding of what the principle actually *is*).

The general idea is that an act that is in itself innocent may become bad when the following conditions obtain: (1) some evil effect is foreseen, at least fairly clearly, as likely to result from it; (2) one has a free choice whether or not to perform the act; (3) there is an obligation to avoid the act precisely to avoid the evil effect. But many evil though unintended effects may follow from a person's actions. Given that the axiom of morality is 'Do good and avoid evil', must you refrain from acting whenever an evil though unintended (but foreseen) effect will follow? Surely if we had to avoid every act that had any sort of evil effect, we would be reduced to almost complete inaction: there is hardly a single permissible (or good) act that is never accompanied by evil effects, even if remotely. Hence the axiom, 'Do good and avoid evil', must be understood to mean, 'Do good *as far as you can* and avoid evil *as far as you can*.' The first half pertains mainly to the distinction between acts and omissions, which will be considered in the following section. It is the second half, however, that is explicated in terms of the Principle of Double Effect. First the principle will be stated; then I will elaborate it, giving some examples of its application; then it will be defended against the most common criticisms.

PDE consists of four conditions, each necessary and together sufficient for the performance of an act that has good and evil effects:

(1) The intended action must in itself be either good or at least permissible (for convenience, let us use the term 'morally indifferent' to cover acts that are either permissible or good).

(2) The good effect – that is, the effect of the initial action that is in itself indifferent – must follow from the act at least as immediately as the evil effect. The immediacy is not *temporal* but *causal*: the evil effect must either be caused by the good effect, or else be caused directly by the act

that also directly causes the good effect. What is *not* allowed is that the good effect be caused by the evil effect, because then the agent would have to *intend* the evil effect as a *means* of bringing about the good effect. But the end never justifies the means – you may not intend evil under any circumstances, irrespective of the good that can be achieved – and so the act would not be permissible.

(3) The evil effect must never itself be intended, or willed as an objective, but merely *permitted* to occur. Even if the evil effect did not *cause* the good effect (contrary to (2)) it might still itself be intended *along with* the good effect; but then the agent would again be intending evil and so the act would be immoral.

(4) There must be a proportionate and sufficiently serious reason for permitting the evil effect, in other words for performing the initial indifferent act that has a good effect. One would not have such a reason if one performed an act with a relatively insignificant good effect but a gravely evil effect.

Conditions (1) and (3) are the easiest to understand and apply. (1) says that the intended action must be morally indifferent. Suppose the commander of an Urbanian warship has sunk an enemy freight ship that also contains civilian passengers. While the passengers are in lifeboats he orders the boats to be shelled, and most of the civilians are killed or wounded. Since he has directly intended the killing of non-combatants, which is wrong, he has committed an act of murder and wanton cruelty. So even if his act has the good effect of shortening the war (the enemy may be intimidated into suing for peace), the commander cannot justify his action by appeal to the good effect, since the former was in itself evil. Any foreseen but unintended evil effects – such as public outrage and the bringing of shame on his country – do not even enter into the moral equation, given the wrongness of the initial action.

Suppose, to change the case slightly, the commander was an enemy spy and so *intended* to humiliate Urbania by his act of murder; here he would *also* have violated condition (3) (in addition to (1)), since the evil effect (the shaming of his country) was itself the object of his will. Or, to take a different example, suppose the manager of a political campaign arranges for money to be distributed to the poor so that they will vote for a corrupt candidate. Here the giving of money to the poor is itself a good act (hence indifferent). The good effect (relief of poverty) is not achieved by *means* of the bad effect (electing a corrupt candidate), but in fact the other way around (condition (2)). However, condition (3) is violated, because the evil effect is itself *intended* as an objective – to elect an unworthy candidate.

It is conditions (2) and (4) that contain the core of PDE, and whose grasp and application is a more subtle matter. Some of the subtleties will come out in later discussion, but for the moment let us illustrate the conditions with relatively straightforward examples. Suppose Alan lives with his rich uncle, who is an alcoholic. Alan stocks the house with alcohol, knowing that he will inherit a fortune when the uncle has drunk himself to death. Now the initial act of filling the house with alcohol is itself morally indifferent. It has a bad effect for the uncle by occasioning his death and a good effect for Alan by bringing him his inheritance sooner than he would otherwise have received it. However, the good effect (obtaining the money) is achieved *by means of* the bad effect (his uncle's death), and so condition (2) is violated and the act is wrong. (All violations of (2) will be violations of (3) as well, but not vice versa.) Alan may well protest, 'I did not intend to hasten my uncle's death; I merely foresaw that it would happen', but his words are belied by his actions and the circumstances. On the assumption that he had no *other* reason for placing the alcohol in the house, and that he was clear-sighted about the necessity of his uncle's death for him to obtain the money, then he must be attributed the intention to hasten his uncle's death. 'Whoever intends the end intends the means' is a fundamental principle of moral psychology; in the absence of an alternative explanation, the person who does what he knows is the means to a certain end must have intended to use those means *as means*. Note, then, that the mere fact that the good effect follows the evil effect *in time* is not what is morally important: it is the *causal* order that matters.

Or, suppose Alan visits his terminally ill friend Brian in hospital in order to cheer him up. Brian's wife mistakenly believes Alan simply wants to be written into Brian's will, and when she hears about the visit the next day she is distressed. Alan may have foreseen that Brian's wife would think this, but his act is still permissible. And if Brian's wife was in the hospital room at the time Alan walked in, so that her distress was caused at exactly the same time as Brian's mood was lifted, Alan's act would again not be wrong. Alan has not used the wife's distress as a *means* to cheering up Brian. This is very different from those many occasions on which a person deliberately upsets another in order to please someone else (or himself), which is wrong (even if the person upset may, in some way, deserve what is coming to her!).

Again suppose, to return to a familiar example, that Charles is rushing his dangerously ill child to hospital in his car, knowing that he is driving so fast he may knock over a pedestrian; but if he goes any slower, his child will die before he can get help. If a pedestrian is indeed knocked over and killed or seriously injured, there will be two effects of his morally indifferent action of driving his car fast: the saving of his child's life (assuming he gets to the hospital on time) and the death of the pedestrian. Since the latter was not a *means* to the former, he is not guilty of intentional homicide; the death was not necessary *in order* to save the child, nor did Charles think it was. Suppose, however, that his child desperately needs a kidney transplant and there are no available kidneys. Brian, seeing another child running across the road, thinks that if he kills the child he will have kidneys available for his own child – so he deliberately runs over and kills him. Here condition (2) is violated, since he has used the young pedestrian's death as a means to save his own child's life; Charles has committed an act of murder.

The fourth condition says that there must be a proportionate and sufficiently serious reason for permitting the evil effect. Though we are not always obliged to prevent evil, we are obliged to prevent a serious evil by a small sacrifice of some good. Hence some proportion between the good and evil effects is required, and if it is lacking the act is wrong by reason of its *circumstances*. How do we determine whether a proportion does exist? Here we must recall what was said in chapter 1, that we can only expect as much precision as the subject matter allows. Sometimes we may simply have to take the most *likely* position on a given action, in light of as many of the circumstances as we can ascertain. Moreover, as we said, the agent himself, the one who must decide what to do, often under great pressure, will have less freedom to ascertain the facts that an outside observer or a moral theoretician. What we can do for the purposes of present discussion, however, is to offer some general principles that help in determining the application of condition (4) and to consider some examples. Further, in considering some objections to PDE, we will be able to show how the condition is *not* to be interpreted: for by considering what it is *not*, we will be better able to see what it *is*.

First, the greater the evil effect, the greater must be the reason for permitting it. Like all the general principles for applying condition (4), and like PDE itself, this is really just common sense. If you are allowed to permit a serious evil, you must have a serious reason for doing so. Second, if the evil would probably happen whether or not the initial act was performed, a lesser reason for acting is permissible. Third, the agent needs a greater reason to permit the evil if omitting the initial act would definitely and effectively prevent the evil. Recall that we are obliged to prevent evil as far as we can; if our initial act is the only way the evil can occur, we need a very good reason for going ahead with that act. Fourth, if the evil is only a probable effect of the act, the reason for acting need not be as great as if it were certain; and if it is merely possible, far less reason for acting is needed than if it were likely. Fifth, a greater reason is needed to permit evil if the agent is under a *prior duty* to prevent it, than if he is under no such duty. A policeman, for instance, whose very job it is to prevent crime, also needs a very good reason for permitting it (saving a person from a burning house while the neighbouring house was being burgled would be an example). Sixth, if there is any other way open to the agent to obtain the good effect without causing the evil, he must take that way; otherwise there is no good reason for permitting the evil. (Again, this is obvious: there is no good reason for Charles to endanger pedestrians while driving his child to the hospital, if his child can get adequate treatment at another hospital a few minutes' walk away.)

Let us look at some examples of actions where condition (4) is satisfied as well as the other conditions, and so which PDE permits. An international football game is organised between traditional rivals Ruritania and Urbania. The organisers foresee a small amount of drunken and rowdy behaviour, but their intention is to entertain the crowd and to raise the prestige of the sport. Now the organisation of a football match is in itself morally indifferent and so permissible (condition (1)). The good effect, namely entertainment and increase in the prestige of the sport, is not caused *by* the bad behaviour, but by the playing of the game; the bad behaviour is merely another effect of the game (condition (2)). The organisers intend to entertain the crowd and to increase the prestige of the sport (good effect), but they do not intend to cause drunken and rowdy behaviour (evil effect); rather, they merely permit the bad behaviour to occur. Indeed, if any bad behaviour breaks out they will almost certainly try to stop it, which itself is evidence that they do not *intend* to cause it (condition (3)). The entertainment of the spectators and the increase in the prestige of the sport proportionately outweigh, in importance, the likelihood of sporadic misbehaviour (condition (4)). The good effect of the game might not be of great moment in itself, but balanced against the bad effect it is sufficiently important to outweigh it in the given context. If, on the other hand, the organisers knew that serious violence, leading perhaps to death, might well break out, (4) would be violated and they would be obliged to cancel the game.

Another case. A battleship is torpedoed by the enemy, causing water to rush in and threaten to sink the ship. The commander orders the bulkheads in that part of the ship to be secured, although he foresees that some of the men trapped there will be drowned. His intention is to keep the ship afloat, thereby saving the lives of as many of the crew as he can. This act is indifferent in itself, thus satisfying (1). The death of the men (evil effect) is not a means to saving the ship (good effect); rather, their death is a side effect of the act of securing the bulkheads, thus satisfying (2). The commander does not *intend* to kill the men; indeed, he regrets having to take such drastic action and would save the men first if he could also save the ship; so (3) is satisfied. Finally, the saving of the ship and of as many men as possible proportionately outweighs the likelihood that some men will die. The death of the men, in itself, is a serious evil, but may be permitted if a far greater good can be achieved, namely the saving of most of the men, and of the ship so that it may continue in battle. Thus (4) is satisfied. Note the application of some of the principles mentioned earlier for deciding whether condition (4) is fulfilled. The death of the men is very serious, and nothing short of a grave reason such as the saving of most of the crew would suffice to allow it to occur. (If no lives could be saved by securing the bulkheads, just the ship, that would not in itself satisfy (4).) Most of the men would die anyway if the bulkheads were not secured, which counts in favour of the legitimacy of the action. The ship's commander is under a prior duty to prevent the death of his men, so again he cannot and does not appeal to a lesser reason for acting. And there is, by hypothesis, no other way of saving most of the crew and the ship without causing the death of some men, which means he is not prohibited from acting on that head.

Now let us look at two cases where condition (4) is violated. Alan is employed as a lifeguard to protect the bathers at a beach. It is a warm afternoon and there are not many bathers, so he decides to take a nap while on duty. One of the bathers gets into difficulties and shouts for help, but by the time Alan is awakened the bather is drowning. Alan rushes into the water, but it is too late. He says in his defence that the bather swam beyond the buoys marking the safe bathing area. Alan's excuse is invalid, because he was under a *prior duty* to watch over the bathers (one of the principles mentioned above). Taking a nap is morally indifferent in itself, but in the circumstances he cannot avail himself of this fact. He would have needed a much more serious reason, then, for running the risk of someone's drowning (evil effect) than merely getting some rest (good effect). If, for instance, he had been feeling very ill and needed to rest, that would have been a valid excuse. Compare this to the situation in which Brian, who is *not* a lifeguard, naps while another bather acts carelessly and drowns. Because he is under no prior duty, Brian's own desire for rest is proportionate to the risk of harm run by a complete stranger for whom he has no special responsibility. This is because the balancing of good and evil effects *has* to be made according to the particular circumstances of the agent. Drowning as such is a far more serious evil than napping is a good, but the application of condition (4) is *not* an impersonal judgement made from the 'God's-eye' perspective. It requires an assessment of the circumstances in which the agent finds himself, including his special abilities, duties and responsibilities. (Compare this to the consequentialist assessment of the situation, about which more later.) It follows that Brian's nap can become less an excuse for not saving the drowning bather the more other relevant factors change, such as his having actual knowledge that a particular person might well come to grief while he slept, the ease with which he could help without exposing himself to serious risk, and so on. We will see in the next section how this sort of reasoning, relevant to judgements of *proximity*, ties in to the distinction between acts and omissions.

A second example. Brian, a businessman with his own private jet, orders his pilot to fly him in dangerous weather to a meeting at which he can finalise a business deal that will net him a small profit. The trip is completed safely, but both the pilot (and Brian) have been exposed to serious risk of death. Now flying a plane is morally indifferent (1). The completion of the deal and making of the profit (good effect) is not obtained by means of exposure to risk of death (bad effect) – it is a direct effect of the initial flying of the plane (2). Neither Brian nor the pilot intend to kill themselves (3). But (4) is violated, since there is not a sufficient proportion between the risk to life and the slight financial advantage to be gained. There will always be some cases where the risk in flying is justified by a financial advantage of sufficient magnitude, but not here.

3.1.3   Criticisms of PDE and replies

We have looked at a number of cases illustrating the application of PDE in general and its individual conditions in particular. Many more can be thought of, since PDE cases are the very stuff of our daily lives. (See if you can imagine others, and try tinkering with the facts to see how changes affect the way we should judge whether conditions (1) to (4) are satisfied.) When we come to discuss (in the companion volume) some of the life-and-death cases that arise in applied ethics, we will make use of PDE and the venerable tradition of moral thought that has gone into its elaboration. But what of criticisms? To be sure, the principle has come under heavy attack by contemporary writers, especially consequentialists, who see in it nothing but obscurantism and hair-splitting. Are their criticisms justified? I cannot look at all of them but the principal ones, which are repeated ad nauseam in the literature, must be discussed.

Are PDE judgements really consequentialist?

A common objection is that, in the words of Peter Singer, 'a consequentialist judgement lurks behind the doctrine of double effect'.[2] When applying condition (4), isn't the proponent of PDE merely doing what consequentialists do, balancing the good and bad effects of an action to see whether it is permitted? Certainly it would be quite misleading to assert that PDE prohibits the balancing of good and bad effects. But then it is no part of the system of morality defended here to say that such balancing judgements can never be made. Governments, and other organisations entrusted with the welfare of a large number of people to whom they bear a duty of strict impartiality, rightly make such balancing judgements all the time. A decision to build a road or a runway, to clear a slum, to erect a power station – decisions such as these, which have a public impact, carry with them benefits and harms, and it is up to the decision-making body to make a judgement that causes the greatest benefit and the least harm, all the while respecting the rights of those affected by the decision.

This observation does not, however, sustain Singer's objection. The first point is that consequentialism, at least in its more pure form, requires more than a simple balancing of good and bad effects. It is essentially a *calculative* theory, holding that benefits and harms can be *quantified* so as to produce a precise and unique result for every proposed action. The consequentialist ideal is to have a *unit of measurement* that can be used across all consequences so as to produce a result in respect of every given course of action. It is for this reason that economists who theorise about morality are nearly all consequentialists, seeing all benefit as economic benefit and all harm as economic harm. It is for this reason that they, and consequentialists in general, have alighted upon *betting behaviour* as a means of measuring what people value: how much money would they put at stake for a given chance of obtaining some result? It is also for this reason that consequentialist bioethicists, who form the majority in this field, commonly speak of 'quality of life years' ('qalys') and similar measures for reducing the value of all human existence to a common denominator.[3] They have not mistaken the ethos of consequentialism and its promise of a *decision procedure* for ethics by which an agent can, in a finite number of steps, calculate the right thing to do. Classical utilitarianism, the forerunner of modern consequentialism, did not by accident focus upon pain and pleasure as the ultimate constituents of morality; for pain and pleasure could, it was thought, be quantified, say by measuring behavioural responses according to a calibrated scale along the lines developed by behavioural psychologists. And it is no coincidence that utilitarians such as R. M. Hare and Singer himself should regard *preferences* as the criterion of moral evaluation; for preferences can, in theory, be *summed*, with each person's preference for a given outcome counting once and once only, and the result tallied along the lines of some form of ethical democracy.

Certainly many consequentialists, perhaps those more concerned with concrete cases than those occupied by high-level theory, still harbour the hope of finding that elusive unit of measurement by which all of morality might be reduced to a single fundamental equation. Theorists, however, are slowly but surely in the process of abandoning any claim to mathematical precision, and indeed any claim ever to have been in the business of finding it. Consequentialists typically distinguish themselves from utilitarians by saying that they embrace a more inclusive theory of what is good: not merely pleasure, not merely preferences, not merely economic welfare, but a whole range of goods along the lines defended by more traditional moral philosophers. Perhaps there is no common denominator, they argue, but this does not prevent the weighing of 'intrinsic goods' such as friendship and knowledge, in order to see which outcome is more important in a given situation.

So, to take a case where this sort of reasoning might be applied (I owe the example to Brad Hooker), suppose Alan has to decide where to live, and that all things are equal except the fact that in place A he will have more friends than in place B. Should he not choose A for that reason alone, namely that it would maximise friendship for him? Note that for the example to serve the consequentialist's purpose at all, everything else needs to be held stable; so, for instance, the *quality* of the different friendships is left out and only numbers are considered. If all of the friends in places A and B are equally good friends giving equally good friendship, surely it is better to have four friends in A rather than two in B? The non-consequentialist can take the point and immediately qualify it. Again, it is no part of the system of ethics defended here that an individual can never be faced with such a decision, and that mere numbers can never justify one course of action rather than another. Sometimes – *sometimes* – numbers are all that count. The death of four people is, all things being equal, worse than the death of two. To take the famous 'trolley case' of Philippa Foot, a person in charge of a runaway trolley (or tram) heading down a track on which four people lie, is morally bound to switch the trolley to a different track on which there are only two. (This is not to say he would be morally guilty of intentional homicide if he kept it on the track bearing four; at *most* it would be negligent or perhaps reckless killing.) The person who defrauds his employer of $10,000 is, all other things being equal, more blameworthy than if he had defrauded his employer of $100. To say this is hardly to legitimise either action; it is merely to say that there are degrees of blameworthiness that sometimes correspond only to quantity of harm done, just as there are states of affairs that are objectively worse than others merely because of the quantity of harm that occurs.

But the non-consequentialist gloss should be apparent. Such assessments are a *fractional* part of moral theory, not just in their obvious rarity, but conceptually. The permissibility of balancing good and bad effects *always* presupposes the fulfilment of the other three conditions of PDE. One can never use balancing to justify an otherwise evil act, which is a corollary of the first condition, namely that the initial act must be good or at least morally indifferent. The murder of an innocent person, for instance, in order to use his healthy organs to save the lives of five others, can never be justified by balancing numbers of lives: in such a case, where rights must be respected, numbers count for nothing. Nor can balancing be used to override the prohibition on using evil as a *means* to procure some good. And the agent can never balance good effects against *intended* evil effects.

Furthermore, on the assumption that alternative actions do satisfy the requirements of PDE, quantitative balancing is conceptually irrelevant to the vast majority of cases, in which matters are necessarily far too subtle to be handled by a strategy of maximisation. To return to the case of Alan's deciding where to live, suppose his choice is between place A, where he would learn more than in place B (since it has a better college) and place B, where he would have more friends than in place A. Consequentialists of a pluralist inclination, who embrace a variety of 'intrinsic goods', admit the implausibility of reducing the value of each course of action to a common denominator in order to calculate the optimal decision. But, they ask, does this matter? Can't a weighing of goods be carried out all the same? Again, if by 'weighing of goods' the pluralist consequentialist means what the traditional moral theorist means by 'judgement of relative importance', then the answer is yes, with the caveat that there will be a certain amount of inherent uncertainty in most cases. If Alan has placed a higher priority on education than on friendship he should choose place A, as long as he does not neglect friendship altogether (and vice versa). If he does not have any particular priority, then he must not make a choice that will damage his pursuit of either good, either by allowing himself a sub-standard education given his state in life and future needs, or by allowing himself to fall into a solitary and friendless existence.

Judgements of relative importance are a regular feature of our decision-making as to what sort of life to lead, and they require a careful assessment of the particular facts of each case. But this truism is far from the claim that some sort of *calculation* can be made according to anything remotely like a consequentialist decision procedure. Judgements of quality are conceptually *bound up* with the overall assessment of what to do. For Alan, even if *quantity* of friendship or of knowledge could be measured (how? by number of friends made? time spent in friendship-related activities? number of facts learnt? number of exams passed?), this would not be the whole, or even a central part, of what he had to assess. Clearly, the *quality* of an outcome is crucial (what *sort* of friends?; what *sort* of knowledge?) and quality is not quantity, so it is not remotely subject to the sort of measurement the consequentialist requires.

Perhaps the pluralist consequentialist never meant anything more controversial by 'measurement' or 'calculation' in the first place. Perhaps these terms were never meant to designate more than 'judgement of relative importance'. As unconvincing as such a response is, it also indicates the elusiveness of contemporary consequentialist thinking. Faced with serious objections, the consequentialist beats a retreat to plausibility by claiming that he is really a pluralist, that he does not believe in common denominators or 'moral mathematics', and that he believes in intrinsic goods. Let him say these things, but let the elusiveness be noted. And let it also be noted that the debate surrounding these issues is an ongoing one for consequentialists, on which traditional moral theorists should be no more than spectators, unwilling to pronounce, and reluctant to aim at a moving target.

The weighing of consequences, then, is *doubly* fractional in moral theory. First, it does not play a conceptual role in the vast majority of cases, where far more complex and subtle issues than mere quantity are at issue. Second, even in those cases where it does play a role, it does so only *after* all other moral requirements have been satisfied: weighing goods might occasionally tip the balance in favour of this or that action, but it can never turn a bad action into a good one, and it can never be used as the sole criterion of right and wrong.

A final point about the 'balancing of effects' question is worth noting, though there is no room to pursue it. As we saw in the case of Brian and the drowning bather, it would be legitimate for him to nap even though another bather might expose himself to the risk of drowning (on the assumption that there was no prior duty or other relationship of proximity). What this means, as I suggested, is that the balancing of good and evil effects is not *impersonal* or *agent-neutral*, as it is in consequentialist thinking. Brian's moral position depends on what *he* as agent is required to do *given* his own circumstances, relationships, knowledge, and so on. But for the consequentialist, why should Brian be allowed to nap at all, if he foresees that another bather – whoever he might be – may come to harm? Speaking *impersonally*, a few minutes' rest is trivial compared to saving someone from drowning, compared even to the *slight chance* that someone may get into trouble. This is another example of the problem that consequentialism is too demanding: the consequentialist is as hard-pressed to explain why *anyone* should take a nap on the beach as he is to say why we are not all *obliged* to drop our families, our friends, our careers, all our special obligations and relationships, and spend the rest of our lives helping starving people wherever they are in the world. This central objection to consequentialism cannot be explored here, though I will make some more remarks later; for the moment it should simply be noted that far from being an unattainable *ideal*, the demandingness of consequentialism is a recipe for *chaos*.

A contrived distinction that is psychologically implausible and a cause of hypocrisy?

The second objection to PDE is neatly stated by James Rachels, when he asks: 'If [an] act is wrong with one intention, how can it be right with another? It is hard to see how the transformation from wrong to right can be made simply by "purifying the intention".[4] (The phrase comes from the seventeenth-century philosopher Pascal, who satirised PDE.) The same idea is echoed by the legal philosopher Glanville Williams when he says that it is

> altogether too artificial to say that a doctor who gives an overdose of a narcotic having in the forefront of his mind the aim of ending the patient's existence is guilty of sin, while a doctor who gives the same overdose in the same circumstances in order to relieve pain is not guilty of sin, provided that he keeps his mind steadily off the consequence [that is, the patient's death].[5]

Hence, he concludes, if PDE 'means that the necessity of making a choice of values can be avoided merely by keeping your mind off one of the consequences, it can only encourage a hypocritical attitude towards moral problems'.

Peter Singer puts what is essentially the same objection by saying that the distinction between intended and foreseen side effects is 'contrived'. 'We cannot', he says, 'avoid responsibility simply by directing our intention to one effect rather than another.'[6] He gives the example of a company that releases chemical pollution: would the executives be excused on the ground that while their objective was to improve efficiency, hence promoting employment and keeping down the cost of living, the pollution itself was an unwanted side effect? But the obvious reply to this case is that the executives have violated condition (2): the pollution (bad effect) is used as a *means* to the improvement of efficiency, and so they cannot be heard to say that the former was 'merely an unwanted side effect' of furthering a worthy objective. What an agent *says*, as condition (2) makes clear, is often belied by what he *does*. Singer's point exemplifies what goes wrong so often in attempted refutations of PDE: you must pay attention to *all four conditions* when evaluating an action, with the result that PDE will *not* be seen to license or condemn actions to which a contrary attitude is required. (What if the pollution really were not intended as a means to improving efficiency, but simply permitted to occur as the effect of some other innocent act, such as restructuring the company's operations, that was intended to improve efficiency? The application of PDE would mean that if the improvement in efficiency were relatively minor and the pollution severe, the proportionality requirement in (4) would have been violated.)

This objection – that the intention/foresight distinction is psychologically artificial and contrived, and so irrelevant to moral judgement – is not so much an argument as an assertion of incredulity that intention can have any relevance to the moral quality of an act. The model Rachels and Williams have in mind is of an agent's possessing a stock of mental states, called intentions, which he can fiddle about with at will, dropping one, adding or creating another, and that PDE simply rubber-stamps one fiddle while cancelling another. To say that this is a simplistic way of viewing the relation between intention and action is an understatement. Intentions are indeed mental states, but they are not mere internal labels tacked on to pre-existing actions in order to avoid moral responsibility. The very *nature* of the action, at the outset, depends on the object that is willed during physical performance. Is the agent merely moving his finger? Or is he also pressing it against a piece of plastic? Is he also hitting a keyboard? Is he typing a number? Is he altering an account? Is he defrauding his employer of a million dollars? Human agency is not about brute physical movement: it is about intentional, willed action, and it is only by attending to and characterising the *objects* of the will, what the agent *intends*, that we can even begin to give an accurate taxonomy of human actions. That is, it is only by attending to intention that we can *separate* human actions from mere movements that are not part of the agent's purposive behaviour (the agent may have burped while he typed the number, but that is hardly relevant!), and so not within the ambit of moral evaluation. Nor can we classify different *kinds* of human action without considering their intended objects. It is not as though the consequentialist can ignore this point either. After all, not any old consequence is ripe for moral assessment, and not any old description of consequences will do. Did the agent merely open his mouth? Did he produce a sound? Did he cause an avalanche? Did he kill people as a result? The consequentialist will hardly accept the agent's plea that the proper description of his act is: 'bringing about a spectacle that I found highly amusing'. The only way of carving up responsibility, then, is by attention to what the agent *has in mind* by his actions – what the object of his will can properly be said to be.

It is curious, then, for consequentialists such as Rachels (and Williams, as revealed by the above quotation) to be heard to ridicule the role of intention in moral evaluation, when they need just such a concept to distinguish between those consequences for which the agent is responsible and those which his bodily movements merely cause; in other words, to make sense of their own theory. But since the operation of intention is nothing like the way it is portrayed in their criticism, neither they nor their opponents need be concerned on that score. Certainly an agent can change intention both before and during an act (though not after the act is substantially completed). But we should not lightly judge that such a change has been made. If Alan drives his child to the hospital and runs over a pedestrian in the process, we need to judge whether he killed the pedestrian intentionally or accidentally; and who would say that this did not make a moral difference? But what counts as evidence for his state of mind? Not just his mere say-so. He may *say* he only foresaw that someone might be run over, but if it turns out the pedestrian was Brian, his most hated enemy, and that only the day before Alan had been heard saying, 'If I ever see Brian, I'm going to fix him up good and proper', we would rightly baulk at Alan's protestation that the death was unintentional. Of course it may *still* have been an accident, but the point is that all relevant circumstances have to be taken into account; the evidence for a person's state of mind does not consist solely in his avowal, no matter how forcefully it is made. (Even *sincere* avowals might be wrong. Consider the alcoholic who says 'I won't touch another drop' or the inveterate gambler who swears 'I won't gamble another cent.' Whether it is because of a physical addiction, self-deception or simply a bad habit, sincere avowals of intention cannot always be taken as the last word.)

Similarly, if Alan were to say that he had indeed been harbouring murderous intent towards Brian, but that when he saw him he had a pang of conscience, at the same time reminding himself that his purpose in being at the wheel was to get his child to the hospital, not to exact revenge on an enemy, we would be hasty to rely on his statement that he had changed his intention, without investigating surrounding factors. (What was his state of mind soon after the death? Did his child recall his having said anything relevant at the time?) Again, there may *be* no extra evidence available for assessment: a change of mind is not often a public event, as it were, attended by radically changed circumstances. But the difficulty attached to assessing a person's intentions is not one of principle – it is one of *evidence*. It is sometimes difficult also to know what a person believes, wants, hopes or fears; but this should not make us sceptical about whether we *can* ever know a person's state of mind, including whether it has changed. For the opponent of PDE, then, to treat intentions as fleeting mental events easily changeable irrespective of circumstance, and hence as too elusive for moral theory, is to raise *wholly general* questions of scepticism about a person's mental life, questions that are relevant to every moral theory but persuasive against none.

Contrary to Williams, then, the 'purifying' of an agent's intentions does not amount to his fixing his mental gaze upon one object while 'keeping his mind steadily off' another. To take the medical case he cites – though we will deal with it more fully in chapter 2 of *Applied Ethics* – it is not as though a doctor who intends to kill his patient (whatever the motive) can evade responsibility by, as it were, thinking hard about the analgesic effect of the narcotic while putting the patient's death out of his mind. If responsibility were that easily evaded, hypocrisy would indeed be the norm of human action. But it is here that the maxim that you can know a person by their deeds is of utmost relevance. One of the primary ways of distinguishing what an agent intends from what he merely foresees is by asking: Did the agent do anything to *minimise* or even to *suppress* the occurrence of the side effect? Did the doctor, for instance, administer only enough of the drug to relieve pain, or did he give a dose far beyond what was necessary? Did he take other steps to try to keep the patient alive? If death was an inevitable consequence, did he make it clear to others (especially the patient's relatives) that he was only trying to relieve pain and that no other drug was available that would be equally effective but less of a threat to life? Similarly, in the case of Alan, did he drive with as much care as he could consistently with getting his child to the hospital in time? Or, when he saw Brian walking along, did he swerve so as to point the car in his direction? How can the need to answer such vital questions be compatible with the idea that the presence of an intention is no more than a matter of private mental gymnastics?

Is intention logically irrelevant to moral judgement?

In the criticisms of Rachels and Williams, however, there is a third objection to PDE lurking behind their protestation that the doctrine is psychologically implausible, namely that intentions just don't matter logically in moral evaluation. Consider Rachels's example of Jack and Jill who both visit their sick grandmother, Jack with the sole intention of cheering her up, Jill with the sole intention of being included in her will. 'Thus Jack and Jill do the very same thing', says Rachels. They both cheer up their sick grandmother, the consequences may be the same – in particular the influencing of her will – and Jack even knows he too might be made an heir; but it is not his intention to bring this about. Rachels continues:

Jack's intention was honourable and Jill's was not. Could we say on that account that what Jack did was right, but what Jill did was not right? No; for Jack and Jill did the very same thing, and if they did the same thing, in the same circumstances, we cannot say that one acted rightly and one acted wrongly. Consistency requires that we assess similar actions similarly.[7]

Although, adds Rachels, the difference in intention is relevant to assessing *character* – Jack's being honourable and Jill's being venal – this is 'another thing entirely' from assessing the morality of the *action*, which is the same irrespective of intention, as long as the same thing is done. Intention, he concludes, is thus irrelevant to the evaluation of action.

To see the weakness of Rachels's objection, we need only note that it simply begs the question against PDE. Rachels *presupposes* that intention is irrelevant and that only the 'action' – rather, the *outcome* – is relevant. The supporter of PDE will insist that, contrary to Rachels's assumption, they did *not* do the same thing, the actions of Jack and Jill are *not* similar; more precisely, though similar in some relevant respects, they are dissimilar in others, namely the highly relevant question of intention. If PDE could be refuted as easily as Rachels thinks there would, as Jorge Garcia trenchantly points out, be a similar ground for refuting *any* moral theory, including consequentialism! For consider Alan and Brian who visit their sick grandfather. The grandfather loathes Alan, so Alan's visit brings far more displeasure than if he had stayed away, making his action wrong (according to act utilitarianism; modify accordingly for other species of consequentialism). But the grandfather loves Brian, whose visit causes far more pleasure than anything else he could have done at the time, making his action right. But (goes the Rachels-style objection) Alan and Brian *did the same thing*, didn't they – namely, visit their sick grandfather? So how can consequences be relevant? Rachels's objection, then, being apparently sharp enough to cut through all moral theories, is in reality too blunt to harm any.

What Rachels's criticism does, however, is to highlight the need for a proper understanding of the role of intention in moral theory and the need not to confuse it with *motive*. For an act to be truly morally good, it must be good in all its elements, and these are three: object, circumstances and end or motive. These can be called the *determinants* of the morality of an action, the individually necessary and jointly sufficient conditions for its morality. To speak of the object of an act is really to speak of the act itself, stripped of its end and its circumstances. We can then say that ethics deals with such acts as murder, theft, adultery, lying, racial discrimination, and so on. But it would be wrong to identify the object with the *outcome* or *consequences* of an act, since any act can have all sorts of consequences: murder may produce great pleasure, perhaps net pleasure overall for everyone concerned, but this does not define its object. And helping a friend in need may cause overall displeasure or harm; these are matters of *circumstance*. The object, rather, is that which the will *primarily* has in view when an action is performed, which corresponds, in an agent who is not deluded, immature, or otherwise incapable of appreciating what he is doing, to what *kind* of action is performed. Even a consequentialist, who performs an act in order to produce overall pleasure, for instance, has a primary object in view: he appreciates that his act is the knowing communication of a falsehood, for instance, or the obeying of an order. Without this primary object of the will, human action becomes inexplicable: we could never distinguish one act from another, an agent could never tell you just *what* he was doing.

Human acts receive their essential moral nature from their object. This is because rational agents are always moved to action primarily by a consideration of the action in itself rather than its circumstances or end. For instance, Alan may believe that by taking money from his employer he can give assistance to starving people in Africa; he may also believe that since the amount to be taken is small in comparison to his employer's overall revenue, the circumstances do not make the act especially harmful; and he may justify his deed by appeal to act consequentialism. But before he can even *begin* to act, he must first realise that what he is proposing to himself is the taking of another person's property without his consent and (presumably) against his reasonable will (which is the definition of theft). Only *then* can he go on to consider other factors that he sees as relevant. But as for the agent, so for the person who evaluates the agent's act: he must first see it as an act of theft, whether or not he or the agent *uses* that term, and then go on to consider other factors. Similarly, if Brian lies to his wife concerning his whereabouts in order to be free to go to the pub, then it is an act of lying that he has committed, which gives us the *type* of thing he has done, and this must be appreciated before one can consider his end, which is to be free to go to the pub. Now on the theory being defended here there are acts, such as murder, theft and lying, which by their very nature are bad, not by reason of their end, outcome or other circumstances. They are direct attacks upon human goods such as truth, life and property, and cannot be justified by appeal to other factors. They may be *mitigated* or *aggravated* by these, the agent may be more or less blameworthy (less if Alan stole a few dollars, more if he stole millions), but the act will be intrinsically and absolutely right or wrong according as the *object* is right or wrong.

The circumstances of an act include a number of different kinds of fact surrounding its performance, such as: who performed the act; where; when; using what means; in what manner; and with what outcome. These contribute to the morality of an act in one of four ways. (1) An indifferent act, that is, indifferent in its object, may become morally good or bad through the attending circumstances. To go shopping is itself indifferent; to do so when you should be sitting an exam is bad. To stop eating fatty foods is indifferent; to do so when you have heart disease is good. (2) An 'objectively good' act, that is, one good in its object, may become bad. To take up vigorous exercise is good; to do so contrary to a conscientious doctor's strict instructions is bad. (3) An act that is objectively good may receive added goodness of a different kind because of some circumstance, and an act that is objectively wrong may receive added wrongness of a different kind. To avoid buying unnecessary luxuries is good, a virtuous act of temperance; to avoid it when you cannot afford it and would otherwise go into debt is an act of temperance *and* of prudence. To study hard for your exams is good, an act of diligence; to do so because your parents have told you to is also an act of obedience. (4) Circumstances may increase the degree of goodness of an objectively good act, and aggravate an objectively bad act. To give money to a poor person is good; to give all the money you have on you at the time is even better. To steal from someone is bad; to use violence in the process is worse.

It is common to confuse motive and object. This is understandable, because they often coincide. To take someone's money because you simply want to have it; to render assistance to someone in need because you want to help them; in such cases, there is no further end or purpose in view, and so motive and object coincide. But often the agent has some *further* purpose in mind when he does something, which is why action theorists use the term 'further intention' to denote this purpose. I study hard because I want to become a doctor; I go shopping because I want to buy some clothes; I go to the post office in order to post a letter. The motive is best understood as the good, freely chosen by the agent, that he wants to achieve by his act. Psychologically, the motive is, as the term implies, what *moves* a person to do what he does. The *object* is still the primary element that *defines* the act, that gives it its essential metaphysical and moral character, but the *motive* is what prompts the agent to do one thing rather than another.

The end or motive affects the morality of an act because it is an expression of the agent's *will*. If the motive is bad it will detract from, or even vitiate, the morality of an act. If it is good it can give a good character to the act. Of course, motives usually come in multiples, hence motivation is usually complex. There may be an end in sight, and a further end beyond that, and another beyond that. However many there are, they are all determinants of morality, and hence a necessary part of moral evaluation.

First, an indifferent act becomes good through a good motive and bad through a bad motive. To walk to the shops is indifferent. To do so in order to buy food for a needy friend is good; to do so in order to shoplift is bad. Second, an objectively good act is enhanced by a good motive. To study hard is good; to do so in order to please your parents is even better.

Third, an objectively good act, if done with an evil motive, is either totally or partially evil, depending on whether that motive is the total or only the partial reason why the agent acts. If it is the total reason, that is, the agent would not have acted if the motive were absent, the act is vitiated, in other words, made entirely bad. This is because the will is moved entirely by evil. If Brian walks Celia home at night, that is objectively good; if he does so with the sole intention of raping her, his evil motive makes the act wholly bad. If the evil intention is only the partial reason for acting, and the evil intended is not great, the act is essentially good but partially evil. For instance, if Alan gives money to a poor person partly to relieve his distress but also to impress his friends, the vanity of his motive makes his act partly good and partly bad. If the partial reason is seriously evil, this vitiates the otherwise objectively good act. So if Donald gives money to a poor person partly to relieve his distress but also as a bribe to gain his assistance in a burglary, the latter motive makes his act of generosity wholly bad.

Fourth, an objectively evil act can never be made good through a good motive. This is because the end does not justify the means, and evil is directly willed. The act may be *mitigated*, that is, not as bad as an evil act with an evil motive, but it remains evil all the same. For instance, it would always be wrong to commit perjury in order to help a friend avoid a charge, no matter whether the friend is innocent. And it would always be wrong to embezzle money in order to give it to the hungry.

A defect in *any* of the three elements of object, circumstances and end makes an act morally wrong. To say that only one of the determinants, say outcome, matters in morality is seriously to distort the nature of human action. We can see now why Rachels has wrongly assessed the case of Jack and Jill. To visit one's sick grandmother is in itself morally indifferent. But since Jack's motive is good, namely to cheer up his grandmother, his act becomes good. Since Jill's motive is bad, namely the deceptive and venal motive of being written into her grandmother's will, her whole act is vitiated. For Rachels to relegate motive to the question of *character* rather than action is to misrepresent the relationship between the two. Character is not an 'add-on' to morality. It is not something that we admire (whatever 'admire' may mean for Rachels if it does not mean 'morally approve') in addition to action. Character *reveals* action by showing us how the *will* of the agent is oriented: is the agent's will directed at good or at evil? Jill's will is set on evil, namely deception and the using of a person solely as a means to financial gain. Jack's will is set on good, on cheering up his sick relative. But, it might be objected, surely the act of visiting a sick grandmother is not morally indifferent; is it not objectively good, since in both cases she is in fact cheered up? This way of looking at the act makes no difference, however. For, as we saw, even an objectively good act can be made at least partly bad by a bad intention, and wholly bad if the intention is the sole actuating motive. Jill is motivated wholly by her venal and deceptive purpose, and so her act is vitiated. In Jack's case, his act is still good, but now motive and object coincide: his act of objectively cheering up his grandmother is also what he intends to achieve. So, whichever way one 'carves up' what is done, the moral assessment remains the same.

Metaphysical scepticism about the intention/foresight distinction

The fourth and final objection to PDE that must be considered is the problem of distinguishing intended from foreseen effects. How, it is objected, can the distinction be made? Critics of PDE appeal to cases in which it appears that the distinction can only be drawn artificially or arbitrarily. Consider, for instance, the case of a party of explorers trapped in a cave, whose entrance is blocked by a rather obese member of the group. Suppose that flood waters are rising and they are all in danger of drowning. One of the party sets off an explosion next to the fat man, who dies. Was his death intended or merely foreseen? How are we to decide?

Or consider the case of the runaway tram (or trolley), heading down a track on which five men are working. Suppose the driver can steer the tram on to a side track on which there is only one man: if he does so, and the one man dies, is he killed intentionally or is his death merely foreseen? How is this case to be distinguished from that of a doctor who has the choice of removing the healthy organs of one patient in order to transplant them into five others who may thereby be saved?

Again, there is the case of the man who places a bomb on an aeroplane, intending to benefit under the life insurance policy of one of the passengers, of which policy he is a beneficiary. If everyone on board dies, is he a mass murderer? And if so, how can such a case realistically be distinguished from that of someone who blows up a plane in order to benefit merely from a property insurance policy he has taken out on the cargo? If everyone dies, is he too not a murderer?

Hypothetical cases such as the above are usually raised in connection with the problems of abortion and euthanasia, and critics of PDE argue that it can only handle such cases at the cost of producing unacceptable results, or else that the results can be made acceptable only at the cost of dropping PDE.[8] I shall leave specific discussion of the alleged inconsistencies and related objections when we come to discuss (in the companion volume) abortion and euthanasia, as well as similar life-and-death issues such as self-defence and capital punishment. For the moment, though, a general discussion of the general way of handling double-effect cases such as those raised above is in order.

The first thing to note is that defenders of the intention – foresight distinction are indeed faced with some fiendishly difficult cases. The debate has engendered an enormous literature, and it would be rash to suggest that any solution of the problems raised by the distinction has commanded universal assent either among its supporters or among those who cannot see any way in which the distinction can be usefully drawn. Given the hardness of the cases that have plagued the debate for so long, a debate which shows no sign of vanishing, it is desirable to approach the general problem with substantial caution and reservation, and to try to deal with those cases only at a level of generality sufficient to maintain plausibility.

At a more concrete level, it should be said that critics of PDE are right to the extent that they highlight some of the inadequate ways in which its defenders have sometimes sought to draw the distinction between intention and foresight. The least adequate way is to appeal, as they occasionally do, to philosophical terms of art. One such term is 'closeness'. It might be said that the cave explorer who sets off a charge next to the fat man blocking the entrance has intentionally taken innocent life because the death is 'too close' to the act of causing the explosion to be merely foreseen. But what can be meant by 'close'? Is the death of a pedestrian too close to the act of driving one's dangerously ill child to hospital to be merely foreseen, so that the driver must have intentionally killed him? Either the term is far too vague to be given a precise and workable meaning, or it lets in cases that are clearly not ones of intentional killing. Others have proposed a term like 'invariable connection' as useful. But what does this mean? Is there an invariable connection between driving a tram at high speed towards someone on the track and the death of that person? If so, is the driver a murderer even though all he was trying to do was to save the lives of the five who were on the other track? Does an 'invariable connection' between act and effect mean that the effect must follow the act in 100 per cent of cases? Or 90 per cent? Or two-thirds? If 100 per cent, then can we say the cave explorer is not an intentional killer if there was one case in the past when, in an identical situation, a fat man survived the blast? Must the class of comparable cases be identical anyway, or will rough similarity do? Again, the vagueness of the terminology is apparent. Similarly with the idea that a killing is not intended if it is not absurd to suppose the death's not following the act, even if this is not physically possible in the circumstances. But there is nothing absurd in the thought that the life-insurance bomber might have failed to kill anyone, even though death was a physical certainty in the circumstances.

Supporters of PDE have looked for more rigorous terminology, but more rigorous terms bring their own difficulties. One might suggest 'logical entailment' as a criterion: if the effect is logically entailed by the act then it was intended. But no act ever logically entails a death – it is always at least conceivable that the person will survive what is done to him (unless the act is initially *described* as lethal, which would be question-begging). Another term that has been suggested is *control*: the agent intends all those effects over which he has control. But surely the person driving his child to hospital has control over whether pedestrians are harmed; the control criterion would rule as intentional all but accidentally caused effects, whereas most of the effects that we foresee but do not intentionally bring about are under our control to some extent.

One can play around with various concepts, seeing whether they capture our intuitive distinction between the intended and the foreseen, but the exercise appears fruitless. It would be more useful to begin with a broader brush in delineating the general way in which the distinction might be defended.

Part of that way involves casting doubt on the sceptical approach to the distinction. According to the sceptic, the intention – foresight distinction cannot be drawn in any principled way and so must collapse. More specifically, the tendency among sceptics is to claim that it is the concept of intention that is the problem, and that it is supposedly less difficult concepts such as belief, desire and knowledge that underpin all responsibility. But this is to ignore the fact that sceptical doubts can be cast on all of these concepts as well. Why should we think that it is easier to know what a person believes (or knows, since knowledge requires belief) than what he intends? It could not be because there are solid behavioural criteria for belief since, as we shall see, there are such criteria for intention as well. And it could not be because belief is any less a state of mind than intention – both of them are subjective states whose existence and content are usually known with more certainty by their possessors than by any outside observer. It turns out to be just as difficult, in many cases, to individuate a person's beliefs or desires as it is to individuate his intentions. Does the cave explorer who sets off the explosion next to the fat man believe that he will die? Or only that he will be blown into pieces? Or only that he will be dislodged? Does the driver of the runaway tram believe that the worker on the track will be killed, or only that he will be run over? Very similar sceptical moves that can be made against intention can also be made against belief, knowledge and desire, so any theorist who thinks that by doing away with the intention – foresight distinction he is on surer ground, is mistaken.

There is also a certain question-begging and even sceptical tendency among some theorists who want to maintain the distinction. Whereas they accept that there are clear cases of intentional action and clear cases where there is no intention (merely foresight or belief), they seek to treat hard cases by appeal to prior intuitions about responsibility. Surely, it might be said, the property-insurance bomber is as much a murderer as the life-insurance bomber: after all, he was reckless for their welfare, he endangered their lives, and so on. If that is not a case of intentional killing, what is? Surely that of the terrorist who sets off a bomb in a crowded street, with the intention of killing passers-by, no matter what other circumstances obtained? The tendency here is to treat cases as ones of intentional action because they are cases in which we want to hold the agent responsible for causing some serious harm. But such an approach reverses the proper order of explanation, because it seeks to explain intention in terms of actions for which we want to hold a person responsible, rather than saying that our judgements of responsibility should be assessed in terms of what a person intends. What, then, would be motivating our judgements of responsibility? Simply the brute intuition that someone is a murderer? Of course intuitions play an important role in moral theory, but they should not be used in a bootstrapping way: 'He must have killed intentionally, because he is a murderer.' Why should someone be called a murderer in the first place, if not because they have killed an innocent person intentionally? Simply to redescribe the case is not to explain it.

Further, the use of prior normative judgements in ascriptions of intention is really a sceptical move, rather than a move in defence of the reality of intention. It is to appeal to some other moral theory, perhaps consequentialism, to determine responsibility, rather than to support the sort of theory defended here in which intention plays a central role in responsibility. If a serious harm is caused, it is sometimes said, then, irrespective of the agent's state of mind, responsibility should be laid at his feet. But if this is how some cases should be treated, why not all? How does intention do any theoretical work whatsoever?

Defenders of PDE should, and usually do, insist on the *reality* of intention as a mental phenomenon, distinct from other states such as belief and desire. If this is true, then it is the reality of that phenomenon (among others) that should guide our judgements of responsibility. But the defence of its reality should not be undertaken by making everything depend upon the solution of the most difficult cases, especially those that turn out to be difficult on any theory. Hard cases, as it is often said, make bad law. Their resolution requires an investigation into complex issues in both the philosophy of mind and the theory of action, an investigation we cannot undertake here. Some plausible observations can, however, be made which are sufficient for the main purpose of guiding us through some of the life-and-death issues to be discussed later.

The first observation is that there appears to be a spectrum of cases, at one end of which are what we might call paradigm cases of the intended, and at the other paradigm cases of the foreseen. When I drink a cup of coffee, I do not intend merely to move my hand, nor merely to raise the cup, nor merely to place it to my lips, but also to swallow its contents. As I type this sentence, I intend not merely to move my fingers, nor merely to strike the keys of my computer, nor merely to produce symbols on the screen, but to construct a meaningful sentence. I do not merely *foresee* that any or all of these things will happen, nor do I merely *want* them to happen, but I *intend* them to happen, I *aim* at their happening, my mind is *focused* on their happening, even if I am not concentrating very hard on what I am doing. At the other end of the spectrum, I am late for a class because I have been detained in the bank. I *know* that I will be late, but I do not *intend* to be late; I did not *plan* to be late, and it was not part of my *plan* when I entered the bank, since I thought I would be early for my class and intended so to be. When I drive a car, I do not *intend* to have an accident, I do not *plan* it, I do not *aim* at it – but I foresee the possibility of an accident, perhaps even the probability or the certainty if I am driving fast in order to make it to the cinema before the film starts.

As we move away from paradigm cases of intention and foresight, how-ever, things get more difficult. Part of the difficulty stems from the failure to treat intention as a mental state as genuine as any other, or at any rate correctly to interpret what that genuineness consists in. Intention is not a function of language. A person can intend, say, to move a muscle without being able to formulate 'move a muscle' linguistically, without even know-ing what 'muscle' means – children do it all the time. A person can act intentionally without being linguistically competent at all. So intention cannot be a matter of a mere linguistic formulation that one proposes to oneself; nor can you fix your intention merely by *describing* what you are doing in a certain way – 'I don't intend to park illegally, only to place my car next to those yellow lines above which the sign says "No Parking".' Nor can one *retrospectively* determine one's intention by a redescription – 'I never intended to cheat, only to turn my head in the direction of the student's exam paper.' Of course one *might* not intend to park illegally, or to cheat, but the point is that the *identification* of an agent's intention does not hang on what description he gives of his action, either at the time or afterwards. The description is neither necessary nor sufficient. Rather, the description – how the agent characterises what he is doing – will be *one piece of defeasible evidence* for intention.

Concepts, on the other hand, go deeper than language. It is more plau-sible to claim that you cannot intend to do X without having the *concept* of X. Even the child who intentionally moves a muscle has the concept of muscle, which does not require any profound knowledge of physiology. I could not intentionally drive a car without having the concept of a car (again, this does not require that I have any substantial knowledge of car mechanics). The point here is that intention is a function of the agent's perspective on the world and on himself, and on the interaction between the two. But a person's perspective is crucially shaped by his concepts. Nevertheless, even if there were some deep connection between language mastery and the possession of concepts (there is no need to resolve the question here), the shaping of that perspective – and hence the formation of intention – would not be a matter of mere description, of merely proposing to oneself this or that proposition as describing the action at which one's mind is directed.

I suggested that the way an agent characterises his behaviour is one piece of defeasible evidence for his intention and indeed for his state of mind in general. There is other evidence as well, all of it defeasible, which points more or less strongly to the truth of what an agent intends. This is not to say that we must resign ourselves to hopeless scepticism about intention. The courts have to determine agents' intentions on a regular basis, and while no judge or jury would ever say that they knew a person's intention with such a degree of certainty as to exclude all possibility of doubt, given the impossibility of looking directly into a person's mind, nevertheless they frequently form assessments based on the strongest possible evidence. In this they follow – with a certain amount of legal refinement – our ordinary practice of judging each other's intentions in day-to-day cases. But there is no reason to believe that this practice is not applicable to the more difficult cases raised by moral theorists, which are no different in kind from those we ordinarily have to deal with.

There are various kinds of evidence we can have for intention. One, as I have said, is simply what the agent *says* he was doing, and in most cases this is strong evidence indeed. But a person can lie about what he intended, or perhaps even lack the self-knowledge to appreciate what he intended, where his intention is clouded by other states of mind. Hence we must pay great attention to *behavioural* evidence, and are bound to make the presumption that an agent usually intends what he *appears* to intend in the circumstances, given what we already know about his beliefs, desires, personal history, and so on. In judging intention we need to ask certain questions, an affirmative answer to any one of which is strong evidence that the agent intended the effect he brought about. For instance, we want to know whether the effect (such as a death) was part of the agent's *plan*, not merely as a probable or expected result, but as a *purpose, goal or objective* to be achieved. Was the effect something the agent was *aiming at*? The goal can be relatively immediate, and so figure in the agent's *means* of achieving something else, or it may be relatively ultimate, and so be an *end*. We also need to ask what the agent was *trying* to do: was he trying to kill the worker on the track, or merely to avoid killing the other five? If the effect had not come about – if, for instance, the worker had narrowly escaped being run over – would the agent have looked for some other way to realise that effect, to kill the worker? A slightly different question is whether, if the effect had not come about, the agent would have considered his act at least a partial *failure*, and whether, given that it did come about, he considered his act at least a partial *success*. We need to know whether the agent did anything, or saw himself as doing anything, *in order to* bring about the effect; or whether he saw the effect as a *way* of bringing about something else.

It might be objected that the defender of PDE is simply taking a scatter-gun approach to the intention – foresight distinction, in lieu of possessing a clear line of demarcation. The reply is that there *is* a clear line of demarcation, but the nature of things means that we can only ever have defeasible evidence – which may be weighty evidence nevertheless – of what side an agent's state of mind lies on. Hence we are forced to limit ourselves to the gathering of information that points in one direction rather than another, which means we need to ask a variety of questions and to be sensitive both to an agent's words and his deeds, as well as the circumstances in which he finds himself.

Given that we must be sensitive to these various and often complex matters, it is inevitable that the many hypothetical cases discussed in the literature, some of which were outlined above, suffer from the same flaw – they are underdescribed. And it is this underdescription that leads opponents of PDE – as well, occasionally, as defenders – to make hasty and unwarranted generalisations based on insufficient information. Take, for instance, the case of the judge who is ordered by a rioting mob to execute an innocent man, failing which they will kill many people. If the judge accedes to their request, it is natural to claim, without further investigation, that he is guilty of murder. But some opponents of PDE claim that the execution need not be described as intentional. After all, they say, the judge, if he had been able to frame the innocent man without killing him, say by creating the *appearance* of his having been executed, would have done so. So in what sense was the judge *aiming at* the man's death, any more than the driver of the runaway tram was aiming at the death of the sole worker when he saved the five others?

The reply is that the case is underdescribed. In what circumstances did the judge find himself? Was it known to him to be practically possible to frame the man without killing him? If so, did this knowledge enter into his practical reasoning? In order for the death to have been foreseen rather than intended, something like the following would have had to be the case: that he knew he could frame the man without killing him; that he handed him over to the executioner with explicit instructions that he only pretend to kill the man; and that these instructions were not carried out. Perhaps the executioner deliberately defied the judge. Or perhaps the pretence went badly wrong and the man was not saved from the gallows before death. And so on. In any case, we must remember that the judge, although he then would not have been guilty of murder, would still have been guilty of the seriously immoral act of condemning an innocent man. The main point, however, is that without a fuller account of the details we simply cannot *say* what the judge's state of mind was. He might later say that he never intended to kill, since he knew a pretence was possible. But if none of the additional factors such as those just mentioned intervened, we would we bound to ask: why did the death occur, if the judge knew he could have faked it? We would then have evidence that the judge's words belie his behaviour, that he was not telling the truth, since his knowledge of the possibility of pretence does not appear to have been part of his practical reasoning. The mere fact that he *could* have faked the execution should not influence our assessment of the case, if we have reason to believe he did not know of the possibility, or if he did that it did not enter into his practical reasoning. The mere possibility is just that – a possibility – and has no more relevance than the fact that the tram driver *could* have leapt out of the tram and killed the worker, if he did in fact escape the oncoming vehicle, is relevant to our assessment that the driver did not intend to kill him.

Suppose that the judge condemned the innocent man to death, that the procedure went ahead as for any execution, but that the man miraculously survived. Would the judge then have tried to kill him some other way? Would he have regarded his judicial act as a failure? The questions are different. We can conceive of circumstances in which the answer to one is affirmative, the other negative. He might have regarded the act as a failure, but not have tried to kill the man some other way – if, for instance, it was no longer practically possible. And he might have tried to kill him some other way without regarding his initial judicial act as a failure – if, for instance, he originally never intended to kill but new circumstances arose, such as the danger of greater civil disorder, that caused him to change his intention. Although each counterfactual question, then, gives us a useful test of intention, an affirmative answer to the first question would give even stronger reason to believe there was an initial lethal intent if it were the case that he would have tried to kill the man some other way *because* he would have regarded his initial act as a failure. We would then have very strong evidence that he intended to kill all along. If, however, the answer to the first question is no, the situation is slightly more complicated. We would naturally think that he never intended the death, just as the tram driver never intended the death since if the worker had miraculously survived, the driver would not then have jumped out of the tram and shot him. But the judge had to contend with a rioting mob, and what they believed may well have influenced his own state of mind. Suppose the mob stayed for the beginning of the execution, then, satisfied they had achieved what they demanded, went away and called off their riot before witnessing the miraculous escape. Then we would have reason to believe that the judge did indeed intend death at the beginning, not expecting the mob to call off the riot before they saw the innocent man dead and buried. Faced with this unexpected reaction, however, he may then not have had the man killed some other way, *relieved that his intention was frustrated.* He may never have *wanted* the man to die, but he did indeed plan it. His plan, however, was cut short.

But the moral of this version of the story is the fundamental philosophical truth that *intention is not the same as desire.* A person may not want to do something but nevertheless intend it, plan it, and try to execute it. If circumstances intervene, he may well *change* his plan. The judge, not wanting to kill the innocent man, and relieved that he was not longer under pressure to do so, may then have changed his plan and let the man go. But if he were to *reinterpret* his initial state of mind in the light of subsequent events not originally expected – if he were to protest, 'But I never intended to have him killed; see, later I let him go', we would have every right to be sceptical. Another lesson to be drawn, then, is that whether an agent's acts are intended or foreseen should be judged only in the light of facts known to the agent at the time he set his plan in motion. Had the judge known from the beginning that a faked or unsuccessful execution would have placated the mob, we would have evidence that he never intended death. Had it merely *turned out* that one of these results placated the mob, without prior knowledge by the judge, we have evidence he initially intended death, but changed his mind in the light of subsequent events. So, the mere fact that he would not have tried to kill him some other way had the victim survived does not of itself *prove* absence of intention, though it is still one useful question to be asked, among others. We need to know whether he would not have tried to secure death some other way *because* he would have regarded the victim's survival as a *successful* outcome of his judicial act.

It might be objected that in the above discussion the counterfactual test has not been applied precisely enough: the question must be whether it was the case, *at the time* the judge brought the original condemnation, and given what he believed then, that he would not have tried to kill the man some other way had he miraculously survived. But this will still not do, because the judge may only have been willing to go along with the mob's demands *once*, whatever the circumstances – in which he case he still intended death the first time around, but would not, had the victim survived, have tried to have him killed at a later stage no matter what else eventuated. Whenever an agent is only willing to try something once, whether out of fear, for a gamble, and the like, it will not be true that he would have tried again had he failed the first time. So the counterfactual test is just that, a test to be applied in the circumstances, not a sufficient condition of intention.

In the runaway tram case there is no correlate of the angry mob. Had the worker miraculously not been run over, the driver would not have tried to kill him some other way, but as we saw in the case of the judge, we need to inquire into the facts of the case. Our first and plausible reaction is to say he was not *aiming* at the worker's death, though he knew death was likely. But we can conceive of circumstances that might well point to a lethal intent. Suppose the worker was the driver's bitter enemy, on whom he had been planning revenge for some time; lo and behold, he finds him on the track and thinks, 'Aren't I lucky – I can both save the five workers *and* get rid of my enemy!' Here, killing his enemy would have been part of his plan, and circumstances would give strong evidence of that state of mind. Were the worker miraculously to survive, however, the driver still might not look for some other way to kill him, for the obvious reason that by killing him in the process of saving five he would have had a moral cover, whereas a blatant killing in the absence of a cover would more likely be detected. So he may then think, after the tram has gone past, 'I missed my chance, bad luck', and so change his intention. We could not then say that he never intended to kill all along, even though he didn't try to kill at a later stage. Hence the fact that, were an effect not to come about the agent would not have tried to realise it some other way, is again not sufficient for the absence of an intention to bring it about at an earlier stage. Nor is it necessary: the driver may not have intended to kill the worker when he first saw him, but suppose he discovered, *after* the worker escaped, that he was his bitter enemy – *then* he may have changed his intention and looked for another way to kill him, this time deliberately.

We can see again that the answer to the question, 'What would the agent have done if the effect had not come about?' does not tell us whether an act is intended in the absence of a consideration of (1) what the agent also would have *thought*, what the agent would have *known*, and what all the relevant circumstances would have been, including what other people in the situation would have thought and known; and (2) what the agent *actually* thought and knew, and what the circumstances *actually* were, including what others in the situation actually thought and knew.

The case of the fat man in the cave can be treated in a similar way, though it is notoriously more difficult. Did the explorer who set off the explosion (let us call him the exploder) intend to kill him? It is natural to think that he must have, and the more plausible view is that on most interpretations this would be so. There are, however, situations in which it would be reasonable to infer that he did not intend to kill, and we must again be sensitive to the facts. For instance, the exploder may have looked for other means to achieve the end of freeing the party. He may have tried to minimize the chance of death, say by placing a barrier between the fat man and the charge though it was still possible for the man to be blown out the of entrance. He may have used the smallest charge he could, consistently with its being efficacious in freeing the party. Of course, relevant information such as the above might not be available. We might have no more than the exploder's say-so that he did not intend to kill the man, only to free the party. Confessional evidence such as this is obviously weighty, if we can be satisfied that the exploder is not lying. Note that counterfactual questions, in this and other cases, must be asked with caution, whatever they are. The exploder might have intended to kill, even though, if he had had an alternative means of freeing the party he would have used it. We frequently do things intentionally which we *would* have avoided in another possible world; hence the often-used claim, 'I had no alternative', which in the vast majority of cases entails 'But I did intend it.' Had another means to freedom been available, presumably the exploder would have used it, unless, for example, the fat man was in any case a burden on the party, or threatening them in some way, and the exploder thought, 'Now's a good chance to get rid of him.'

If there are situations in which it is reasonable to infer that all the exploder intended was to free the party, are there cases in which it is reasonable to infer that all he intended was not to kill, but to blow the fat man to
pieces? Our earlier observations must be reiterated. Merely saying so does
not make it so: an agent cannot magically fix his intention, either before
or after the act, by describing (or redescribing) it in a particular way –
intention runs deeper than mere linguistic gymnastics. Further, an overly
fine discrimination of intention such as this would lead to the absurd
conclusion that hardly anything is ever done intentionally by anyone! For
instance, it might be said that no one ever intends to buy anything: all he
intends is to obtain what he wants, and this requires handing over money;
but if he could get what he wanted without the money permanently being
lost to him – if, for instance, the money miraculously went back into his
bank account – he would be more than happy. It might be said that no
one ever intentionally commits theft: all he intends is to acquire the use
and enjoyment of something, and that requires depriving the owner of it
for a certain length of time, which he foresees might be permanent – that
is, until the owner dies. But were the taker able to arrange for the property, on the day of his own death, to return to the owner (if the owner
outlived him), he would do it; and if he were able to arrange for the property to return to the owner the day before the owner's death (if the taker
outlived the owner), he would do that too. So how can anyone ever be
said to intend *permanently* to deprive another of his property?

Clearly something has gone wrong if the initial doubt about drawing
the distinction between intention and foresight leads to global scepticism
about whether we really intend to do what we paradigmatically intend.
So, remembering the central point that we need to make our judgements
of intention in a way that is sensitive to the facts, we need to ask in what
factual situations it *would* be reasonable to draw the inference that all the
exploder intended was to blow the fat man to pieces rather than to kill
him. Consider the case of a man who cuts off another's head. Can he
plead, 'But I didn't intend to kill him, only to decapitate him'? He can
offer this excuse, but that does not make it valid. Defenders of PDE sometimes hastily assume that he *must* have intended to kill and that any account that implies otherwise is flawed. But consider the following facts.
The decapitator is a surgeon working on an experimental procedure (albeit rather gruesome to us, but this must not interfere with our assessment of the fact of the matter) for replacing the body of a quadriplegic
with a healthy body from someone who has just died but had his bodily

functions maintained. (Again, let us leave aside the question of whether this is technically possible; but see the work of American neurologist Dr Robert J. White.) The person whose head he cuts off is just such a quadriplegic and the surgeon is trying to give him a healthy body. Now in such a case the intent to kill would be the furthest thing from the surgeon's mind – he would have intended the exact opposite. Of course, the bizarre nature of the case (although such experiments have indeed been carried out on monkeys and other animals) suggests that most cases where a person decapitates another just are intentional killings. But we must be careful not to assume they *must* be as a matter of metaphysical necessity.

An even more bizarre case would be needed to make it reasonable to infer the exploder really did intend merely to blow the fat man to pieces. He may have been a mad scientist who believed he had a technique for reviving the victim of an explosion, being able with a technical feat beyond our wildest dreams to reconnect the exploded parts of the fat man, with no harm done. In such a world blowing someone up would, for the exploder, amount to no more than temporary disassembly! He could, from his perspective, blow the fat man to pieces, free the party, and no one would be harmed.

Is the idea counterintuitive that the exploder might, in some situations, not be a murderer? Isn't the exploder clearly an intentional killer on all scenarios? But to insist on this looks like a case of simply *presupposing* that PDE makes artificial distinctions, that it has no moral relevance. At least it involves the concession that PDE *can* distinguish intention from foresight, contrary to the initial objection with which we began the discussion. The very bizarreness of the 'blowing to pieces' scenario shows that we would require strong evidence indeed that the plea, 'I did not intend to kill him – only to blow him to pieces', had any force. The scenario involving only an intention to free the party is, however, less bizarre, and the plea 'I only intended to free them' could accordingly have force in a greater and less remote range of circumstances.

On the other hand, to resist the evidential weight of circumstances that *do* suggest intention to kill – where the exploder thinks, as does the judge in the case of the rioting mob, 'I'm sorry, but you [the fat man] *have* to die, and I don't like it any more than you do' – may involve a confusion of intention and desire: any *regret* the exploder has after the death may simply mean he never *wanted* the death, not that he never *planned* it. (Compare the parent who smacks her child, saying 'I don't like this any more than you do': does this mean the parent only intends to deter the child from further misbehaviour, but not to cause pain? Or, rather, that the parent *does* intend to cause pain, but does not like it?) Equally important, however, is the point that moral judgement is not an all-or-nothing matter, by which is meant that if a person is not a murderer, it does not follow that he cannot be guilty of anything, in particular any heinous crime. The exploder will still have committed a grievous assault upon the fat man, namely exploding a charge right next to him, and this is self-evidently something that the exploder *must* have intended; in which case condition (1) of PDE will have been violated since the initial act was not morally indifferent, and the exploder will have imputed to him the foreseen consequences of his actions, including the fat man's death.

We can now briefly see how to treat the cases of the life-insurance bomber and the property-insurance bomber, mentioned above. I leave it to the reader to consider the cases in detail, and suggest only a few points to consider. The main one is that we cannot categorise these cases simply on the basis of bare information that in one case property insurance is at stake and in the other life insurance. Defenders of PDE are often tempted to draw a stark contrast, saying that the property bomber clearly does not intend to kill, since all he intends is to destroy property, whereas the life-insurance bomber does intend to kill since securing the death of the policy-holder is essential to his plan. Perhaps this is the case in some factual situations, but it will not be in all. It is quite plausible that in some cases the property bomber will think, 'The passengers must die; I want the property destroyed, and if I have to kill them to do it, then so be it.' On the other hand, he may well think, 'The death of the passengers will be an unfortunate by-product of my plan.' Merely *saying* some such thing to himself does not make it so, however, even if he has become philosophically sophisticated after reading some of the critiques of PDE. Rather, any inference as to what the bomber thought will depend upon various pieces of evidence, such as whether he looked for other, non-life-threatening ways to achieve his end, whether he tried to minimise risk to life and limb, or whether, from all of his words and deeds both before and after the event, he appears to have seen the passengers as an *obstacle* to achieving his goal, which obstacle had to be eliminated.

As for the life-insurance bomber, it looks as though death must be an integral part of the plan to obtain the insurance money. But one could imagine cases in which there was no lethal intent. Suppose the bomber used a bomb designed merely to stun the passengers into looking dead for sufficient time to allow him to collect the money. There would be no lethal intent and the bomber would not be a murderer. Again, we need good evidential reasons for such a conclusion: the mere fact that the bomber *would* have used such means if available but did not, does not license the conclusion that he did not intend to kill. Counterfactual tests, it must be repeated, are useful but must be employed with caution. If it is clear that the bomber would have tried a second time to kill the passengers if they had miraculously survived the first time, we would have evidence of lethal intent, defeasible, for instance, by evidence that the explosion was designed not to kill but to throw the plane off course for some reason. If it is clear that the bomber would not have tried to kill the second time around, we would have evidence of non-lethal intent defeasible by, say, evidence that he was simply too scared to make a second attempt to kill. That he would have used non-lethal *means* if they had been available does not, however, show that his plan was not to kill *given* the means he had available. The more plausible inference to draw from the possibility of access to non-lethal means is that the bomber would have *changed* his strategy and hence his initial intent (though the further end of collecting the money would have remained the same). In the absence of specific information pointing to an absence of lethal intent, however, it appears we should presume, from the nature of the case, that such an intent was present, just as, in the case of the property bomber, it appears we should presume the absence of lethal intent unless circumstances indicate otherwise.

We can now see how the runaway tram case differs from that of the surgeon who removes a patient's organs for transplantation into five others. Objectors to PDE sometimes say: 'All the surgeon intended was to get the organs. Had the patient miraculously survived, he would not have then given him a lethal injection, for instance.' Can the surgeon plead such an excuse? Suppose he believed he had a technique for restoring the patient to full health despite his lacking the removed organs. Technically remote though such a possibility might be, it would indeed suggest (defeasibly) that he did not intend death – though he would still be guilty of a serious assault upon the patient (thereby violating condition (1) of PDE). In the absence of an exculpatory fact such as this, however, what reason could we have for thinking the surgeon did *not* intend death? The fact that he would not have tried to kill the patient had he miraculously survived is only one factor to take into account. So is the fact that he would (let us assume) have used non-lethal means to remove the organs had the means been available. On the other hand, is it not reasonable to suppose that, given the circumstances in which the surgeon did find himself – lacking non-lethal means and knowing that survival was not even a remote technical possibility – he simply thought, 'The patient must die; I must kill him *in order to achieve my end* of saving the five others.' In the absence of strong evidence that he did not carry out practical reasoning such as this, we are justified in concluding that, for the surgeon, in his actual circumstances, the death was a *means* to his further end, the saving of five lives; hence it also violated condition (2) of PDE: even though the death would not have been a means to the further end in some possible situations, it was in the actual one. But in the case of the runaway tram, the death of the worker on the track was not a means to the saving of the five on the other track, even in the actual situation: it is far less plausible to suppose the tram driver thinking to himself, 'The worker must die *so that* I may save the five.' All he can reasonably be supposed to have thought – always remembering, though, that extra information may well change our view of the case – is, 'I fully expect that the worker will die, but all I am doing is diverting the tram on to another track, and *this much* is required to save the other five.' The surgeon may well regret the patient's death as much as the driver regrets the worker's, but regret does not imply absence of intent. Whereas the surgeon has the patient's death within the scope of his reasoning about what he must do in order to save the five, the driver does not. The driver would baulk at the very question, 'Why did you kill that innocent worker?'; he would likely respond, 'If you mean why did I murder him, I answer that I did not; I never intended his death.' The surgeon, when asked 'Why did you murder the patient?', would likely respond, 'If you mean why did I kill him, I admit that I did – I had to. But I reject the epithet of murderer, because what I did was justified by the greater good.'

A comprehensive solution to the problem of distinguishing intention from foresight would require an exploration of technical issues in the philosophy of mind and the philosophy of action, which there is no room to undertake here. All I have proposed are some general principles and guidelines sufficient to show that such a distinction *can* be made, and hence that PDE can be defended on that score. As was mentioned at the beginning, the immediate relevance of the sorts of cases discussed above is to questions such as abortion and euthanasia. When we come to look at these and other problems in *Applied Ethics*, the principles and method outlined above will be applied to a consideration of the objections that have been raised against the way the Principle of Double Effect handles such cases.

3.2   Acts and Omissions

3.2.1   Another derided distinction

The final principle to be defended as an integral part of the system of morality proposed here is the principle that there is a morally significant intrinsic difference between acts and omissions. Just as there are some acts that would be blameworthy if I did them – such as walking over to my neighbour's house and punching him on the nose without the slightest provocation – and others that would not – such as going to buy a carton of milk – so there are some omissions that are blameworthy and others that are not. As I type these words, I am not doing many (indeed an infinite number of) things: I am not walking through the park; I am not eating; I am not reading a book. But none of these inactions, as we may call them, are blameworthy (all things being equal, as we shall see). But suppose I had promised my friend to pay him back the $10 I borrowed and I simply failed to pay – that would be blameworthy. Or suppose I saw that the tree in my back garden was about to collapse on to my neighbour's house and I did nothing except stand by and watch it fall – if I *could* have done something, that too would be wrong. Or suppose your mother was desperately ill asked you to take her to the hospital, and you ignored her – again, that would be a serious wrong.

Just as it is sometimes difficult to say whether an act is right or wrong, so the same goes for omissions. I just gave some clear-cut examples of innocent and blameworthy omissions, but not every case is so obvious. Am I to be blamed for not giving money to a beggar I pass on the street? For not intervening in a brawl I can see going on outside my house, in which a person is being beaten up? Am I doing wrong by not giving money to any worthy causes this week? For not giving any, ever in my life? For not campaigning to free an innocent man whom I believe to have been wrongly convicted? For not joining a group of volunteers setting off to work on an irrigation project in a parched region of Morocco?

It is a commonplace among writers on applied ethics to deny that there is any *intrinsic* moral difference between acts and omissions, by which they mean that if there is any difference it cannot consist in the fact that something was an act or that it was an omission. Rather, any difference there may be consists in the *outcome* or *total consequences* of the act or omission. To use an example of Philippa Foot's (though she denies the critics' point, claiming instead that there *is* an intrinsic moral difference),[9] if letting starving people die in Africa because I give no money to aid agencies is not as bad as sending them poisoned food, this could only be because the latter would cause far more resentment and anger than the former, and hence more total harm, assuming (implausibly, in fact) that we would assess the number of deaths in both cases to be the same; but not because omitting to give the money was, *as such*, less bad that sending the poisoned food.

Thus the critics of the acts/omissions distinction (let us call it AOD) tend to base their criticism on consequentialist considerations. If an act and an omission have the same total consequences, they are either as bad or as good as each other. As for so-called 'side effects', such as anger provoked in others, they should not blur the issue. Further, 'side effects' differences can, for the consequentialist, usually be ironed out. If not giving money to help the starving were *seen* to be not intrinsically different from sending poisoned food – if people did in fact adopt the consequentialist outlook – then they would be as outraged by the former as by the latter. Indeed, most 'side effects' considerations against adopting consequentialist principles, say consequentialists, arise precisely because people have not been sufficiently 'educated' into accepting those principles.

Another matter where AOD is hotly debated is euthanasia, where critics hold that there is no intrinsic moral distinction between a doctor's withholding treatment from a dying patient and positively killing him. From this they conclude that if it is permissible to withhold treatment, it is also permissible to kill, and indeed obligatory when killing would involve less suffering that not giving treatment. Discussion of this specific issue will be deferred to chapter 2 of *Applied Ethics*. For the moment, I shall offer a general defence of AOD and reply to the most common criticisms.

3.2.2   Initial clarification of AOD

There are a number of points that need to be made concerning what AOD does and does not say, and theorists who have attacked the distinction have done a service to applied ethics at least insofar as they have both highlighted certain weak or irrelevant points made by its supporters and clarified the terms of the debate. One necessary clarification concerns the term 'omission'. AOD does not claim that there is something special about mere inaction. Nero would have been no less culpable if, instead of fiddling while Rome burned, he had merely sat on his imperial throne and done nothing. Some cases of inaction are every bit as bad as the worst actions, such as a mother's not feeding her child so that it starves to death, or a judge's omitting to call evidence from a defendant, in violation of natural justice. Nor does AOD deny that omissions can be causes of harm; both of the omissions just mentioned cause great harm. Of course not every omission causes harm: Alan's not showing up for work on a public holiday obviously does not do so. Indeed, it is hard to see how some omissions cause anything whatsoever: by not going to the shops this very moment, what effects am I actually causing? Are the shop owners losing revenue as a *result* of my not buying anything? Right now I am not learning to play the oboe – is that omission *causing* anything, such as the future collapse of an orchestra short on woodwind players?

Nor does AOD hold that omissions do not involve action. When Nero fiddled while Rome burned, he omitted to do anything to save Rome, but he also played the violin; and had he stayed still on his throne, he still would have been sitting. Suppose Alan and Brian are in a building when an earth tremor strikes and Alan ends up sprawled over Brian, pressing down on his windpipe. If Alan could move but does not, he has culpably omitted to save Brian's life; but he is also guilty of the positive action of sitting on Brian's windpipe. He did not cause the tremor to begin with, but he may well think, 'What a good opportunity to rid the world of such a nasty piece of work.' In this case the action and the omission are parts of the total cause of Brian's suffocating, and Alan is rightly blamed for both. But in the case of Nero, we do not properly blame him for *fiddling* – we blame him for failing to save Rome. When, in the parable of the good Samaritan, the priest and the Levite walked by without helping the dying victim of robbers, they were not guilty of *walking*, but of failing to help the victim. AOD does claim that omissions can at least conceptually be distinguished from actions, even if they always come together.

Critics of AOD are right to point out that neither the lack of identity of the person harmed, nor the fact that the omittor (to coin a term) does not have a specific person in mind as likely to be harmed, make a difference in moral evaluation. A man who runs amok with a gun in a crowded room might not have anyone in mind as victim. Similarly, a person who sees ten people drowning in a canal and fails to throw them a lifebelt lying next to him may not have a specific person in mind as a likely victim, but is nevertheless blameworthy. Further, it might be impossible to identify the victim – just *who* drowned as a result of not having the lifebelt? Nevertheless, *someone* could have been helped and no one was, which is a harm for which the bystander is responsible.

Another point to note is that while omissions involve a failure to intervene to change some pre-existing state of affairs, that state of affairs may or may not be of the omittor's own making. If Alan walks past Brian, who is lying in the street having been shot by a third person, and does nothing to help him, he is guilty of a serious omission. But the same is true even if it is Alan himself who shot Brian and now stands there watching him bleed to death. In the second case, Alan is not only guilty of the shooting, but of doing to nothing to help Brian afterwards. Indeed, the positive duty to act, about which more will be said shortly, is more stringent when it is the potential omittor himself who caused the damage in the first place. I may or may not be guilty of an omission if I do nothing to help you after I see your neighbour's tree fall on your house; but if I am your neighbour, and chopped down my tree so that it fell on your house (even accidentally), I am clearly guilty of an omission if I do nothing to rectify the damage.

Critics of AOD are also correct to point out that certain kinds of circumstance do not make a difference *in themselves* as to whether an omission is culpable or not. The mere facts that a potential beneficiary of your assistance is a long way away, or a stranger, or can only be helped with some difficulty on your part, do not of themselves absolve you of a duty to act. A parent has the duty to help her child in whatever way she can, whether the child phones her in distress from five miles away or five thousand miles. If Alan walks past Brian lying bleeding in the street, he is not under a duty to help only if Brian is his brother but not if he is a total stranger. And if the help requires going some distance to phone an ambulance, even if this means Alan will miss a night at the opera that he paid $100 to attend, he must still make the call.

3.2.3 The derided distinction defended

Should we say, then, that there is no intrinsic moral distinction between acts and omissions? This claim is central to consequentialist thinking, because for the consequentialist only outcomes matter, and if an omission is the cause of the same kind of outcome as an act, the act and the omission are to be given the same moral evaluation. In a system of morality such as the one defended here, however, outcomes are by no means all that matter, and this should lead us to suspect that there is indeed an intrinsic difference between acts and omissions, once all their relevant features are taken into account.

Consider the distinction between what are sometimes called 'negative' and 'positive' duties. One instance of the distinction is that between a person's duty not to do X to another and his duty to ensure that X is not done to that other. Another is that between a person's duty not to bring it about that someone lacks a particular thing P and his duty to provide someone with P. As an example of the former, Fred is under a negative duty not to burgle other people's houses; but he has no positive duty to ensure that other people's houses are not burgled. As an example of the latter, George is under a negative duty not to slander other people (hence depriving them of their good name), but he has no positive duty to go around speaking well of them (and so increasing their good name) at any and every opportunity. This suggests that there is an asymmetry between negative and positive duties; but we must be careful how we spell out the asymmetry.

It is not as though there are no positive duties that apply always, everywhere and to everyone. We have a duty to be kind to all people in all circumstances, to be patient, to be honest, and so on – in short, to be virtuous in our behaviour. We also have positive duties to act towards specific kinds of people in specific kinds of circumstances, simply because of the kinds of people and circumstances they are: a person must respect his parents, provide for his children, obey his lawful superiors, and so on. But positive duties do not enjoin specific kinds of action towards people in general, irrespective of circumstance. There are many ways of being kind, but this does mean that a person must help everyone at all times and places; indeed this is not something he *could* do. There are many ways of being patient, but we have no duty to go around being patient anywhere and always, or positively to seek out situations in which we can display patience. On the other hand, there are negative duties that apply anywhere, always and to everyone – not to steal, not to cheat, not to kill the innocent, not to rape, not to enslave, not to lie, and so on. These duties are not circumscribed by applying only to certain kinds of people or situations, but are wholly general.

This asymmetry between negative and positive duties – the fact that there are duties not to do certain kinds of thing to anyone in any circumstance, but no duties to do certain kinds of thing to anyone in any circumstance – stems from a basic fact about human agency. One of the axioms of morality is 'ought implies can' – there can be no duty without the capacity to carry it out. In general it is far easier to carry out negative duties than positive ones, since the former require simply require that a person do nothing, whereas the latter require a person to act, which means putting himself in certain situations, undertaking certain enterprises, extending himself in certain ways. Of course, carrying out negative duties is not always easy, and may require that you carry out certain positive acts – repressing your desire to help yourself to another's property, ignoring temptations, finding other things to occupy your attention, and so on – but in themselves negative duties merely require that you refrain from doing certain things, which, relatively speaking, is easier than performing tasks.

Being moral is not an all-or-nothing matter. All human beings have a general duty to do good, and indeed to strive for perfection, insofar as perfection is attainable by us mere mortals. The more a person strives for perfection, the greater the ways in which he will seek to carry out the duties entailed by the virtues – being kind to the point of enormous self-sacrifice, patient to the point of heroism, humble to the point of self-effacingness. And the more a person reaches these heights, the more we admire him, to the point even of calling some people saints. But while we should all strive for moral heroism, the fact that it is extremely rare does not mean that the vast majority of people are moral failures. It is possible to be virtuous without being a saint – in terms of its basic requirements, morality must not be too demanding. This is one of the insuperable difficulties often raised by critics of consequentialism, namely that it demands far too much of people even in terms of basic moral thresholds. Since the guiding principle of consequentialism is the duty to maximise value X (and remember that there are different views as to what X is), people simply fail in their fundamental duties if they do not maximise X in all of their actions. This often means that they are duty-bound to make enormous sacrifices in order to maximise X, whether it means reducing themselves to poverty in order to give all their money to charitable causes, neglecting their health, their friends, even their family, and undertaking strenuous and even dangerous activity in order to maximise X anywhere in the world. Recent writers, recognising that consequentialism seems far too demanding, have made all sorts of modifications to their theories in order to avoid this criticism, often appealing to rule consequentialism or other varieties that are less stark than act consequentialism, or to complicated theories of action. But the same, or similar, criticisms resurface and undermine the modified versions, and one can only speculate on the outcome of the ongoing consequentialist project of avoiding the demandingness objection.

Moreover, the demands of consequentialism appear even to outstrip the demands of perfect virtue that all human beings should strive to carry out: it turns out that consequentialism makes demands that are so extreme they fly in the face of morality itself, and so make the theory self-defeating. The duty to maximise X, as we have seen, requires even the violation of the rights of others, and other duties in general, in order that the goal be achieved. It may be heroic to leave one's family in order to live a life of self-sacrifice among the poor; but family members have rights, and a person has a duty to provide for his family, or at least to see to it that they are provided for. It would not be an act of heroism to leave them to starve in one's quest to feed the starving, but an act of callous injustice. Nevertheless, the consequentialist has to face the fact that, at least according to many popular versions of his theory, just such an act would be mandatory if the amount of benefit in the world caused by the feeding of the starving outweighed the negative utility resulting from the starving of a few members of one's family. The example is extreme and many consequentialists would reject it out of hand, but none as yet appear to have been able to ward off very similar sorts of counter-example to whatever version of the theory is proposed.

Morality, then, must not demand too much. It must not ask of us more than we are capable of doing, more than we are in a legitimate position to do given our other responsibilities, and it must not ask of us anything that involves violating the rights of others in pursuit of the 'greater good'. Nor, indeed, must it ask of us more than it is our legitimate *business* to do. I am under a duty to love my neighbour, and the term 'neighbour' covers more than simply the person living next door to me. But this does not mean that the entire world is my business, any more than it is the business of any single individual. Economists speak of a 'division of labour' – the creation of economic wealth requires that people specialise in doing certain things and not engage in work that is beyond their natural talent. We can also speak of a division of moral labour, as it were. It is primarily the duty of the authorities to maintain law and order, of the army to defend against attack, of doctors to heal the sick, of animal welfare agencies to look after stray animals, and so on. People free of family responsibilities are in a better position to live lives of self-sacrifice among the poor than those with such responsibilities, people who have devoted their lives to teaching are better able to educate than those without such training, and so on. The common good, which, along with the good of the individual, is the object of morality, is served by there being limitations on what any one person must do in contributing to it. And it may be positively harmed if one person takes on too much, by neglecting the other duties of his position in life. Hence a doctor inevitably neglects his duties to his patients if he goes to such extreme lengths to save one, say by trying every last technique no matter how slight the chance that it will do any good, that his other patients are deprived of urgent attention.

The sorts of life-and-death cases such as abortion and euthanasia that we will consider in *Applied Ethics* are typical cases in which the scope of our positive duties is narrower than that of our negative ones. I have a duty not to kill the innocent, whoever and wherever they are, but I am under no equivalent duty to save the innocent. To take Philippa Foot's example again, a person may not be under an obligation to save certain people, such as the starving in a remote country, but he is duty-bound not to send them poisoned food. When assessing whether or not an omission to do something is culpable, we need to see the notion of *failure* as central. A culpable omission is not merely a refraining from doing something, but a failure to act; and a failure to act implies that there is a *pre-existing duty* to act. James Rachels compares the cases of Smith and Jones, where Smith drowns his cousin in the bath to gain his inheritance, and Jones, for the same purpose, stands by and watches his cousin drown.[10] Surely, he says, they are equally morally blameworthy, so how can there be an intrinsic difference between acts and omissions? The reply is that an act and an omission can *sometimes* be equally wrong, but not *always*: and if their blameworthiness or praiseworthiness is not the same in *all* comparable circumstances, they must be intrinsically different. Even though circumstances, as we shall see, are a determinant of whether an omission is culpable (which is an instance of their being one of the determinants of morality in general, as we saw earlier), what this shows is that the *intrinsic* difference between acts and omissions is *brought out* in certain kinds of circumstance which, nevertheless, are the same for both the omission and the correlative act. This is contrary to the charge made by opponents of AOD that there is no intrinsic difference because in *all* circumstances the omission and the correlative act should have the same moral evaluation. Rachels acknowledges the force of the Foot-type counter-example, where the duty not to kill is far more stringent than the duty to save life, but answers it by changing the subject to Smith and Jones. He then goes on to say that life-and-death medical situations are nearly always more like the latter case than the former.

Changing the subject does not make the force of the Foot-type case go away. The point is that there are circumstances in which negative duties outstrip positive ones, and hence where an act would be more blameworthy than a comparable omission – indeed, where the omission may not be blameworthy at all – even if there are *also* situations in which this is not the case. What makes Jones's omission culpable is a pre-existing duty to save his cousin's life; and that duty stems from his *proximity* to his cousin and his ability to save him. 'Proximity' cannot be equated with family ties, nor with geographical location, nor with any other feature in particular. If it had been a stranger drowning in the bath, he still would have been obliged to save him, because in *this* case he was physically close enough to do so. If it had been his cousin drowning in a bathtub two miles away, and he knew about it, and was able to do something (call for help, go there himself), he still would have been obliged to act. If it had been a total stranger drowning two miles away, and (improbably) Jones knew about it, he would have a duty to call for help, but not to go personally to save him. And so his duties in matters of life and death recede as his proximity recedes, to the point where, if it were a total stranger drowning, and he knew nothing about it, he would obviously not have a duty to do anything. But neither Smith, nor Jones, nor anyone else, is ever permitted actively to drown another person, cousin or not. Proximity includes, but cannot be identified unconditionally, with physical closeness, ties of family, friendship or various kinds of responsibility, capacity to act, prior duties to others, prior responsibilities in general, and, of course, knowledge. A position of responsibility for another is an important situation involving proximity: an employer is culpable if he fails to provide for the health and safety of his workers, but not if he fails to provide for the health and safety of somebody else's employees; a teacher is culpable for failing adequately to educate his pupils, but not for failing to ensure that another teacher's pupils are adequately educated; and so on.

When it comes to medical situations, there is again a relationship of responsibility between doctor and patient, in which mere physical closeness does not play a large part. As Rachels correctly points out, a doctor's duty is precisely to help his patients, so failures to do so are often culpable. But not even a doctor has a duty to help his patients in *all* situations. Even doctors have other responsibilities, especially to their families and themselves. A doctor is not obliged to ruin his health in the service of his patients, nor to neglect his important family responsibilities. He is not obliged to undertake endless research to find a cure for every unusual malady that comes his way, nor to consult every specialist in the land, nor to exhaust his personal income on the latest equipment. Clearly his responsibilities are a matter of degree, and the facts of each case are of great importance; but the general principle is clear, that the proximity requisite for a duty to act will be limited by circumstance. In particular, we shall see in the discussion of euthanasia that it is limited by circumstances in which the doctor would have to take *extraordinary* measures to help his patient.

Opponents of the acts – omissions distinction often claim that there is no relevant difference between the two because, in the words of Peter Singer, 'doing nothing . . . is itself a deliberate choice'.[11] If, they argue, it is permissible deliberately to omit to save a life, it must be permissible intentionally to end it, where ending it involves less suffering. Although we will return to this in the discussion of euthanasia, the point is raised here because it indicates that they confuse the acts – omissions distinction with the intention – foresight distinction, and indeed Singer's objections to the former glide seamlessly into his objections to the latter. Objections to the two distinctions must, however, be kept separate: but the issue is clouded by the fact that those who confuse them are trading on two senses of 'intention'. In the first sense, an intentional omission is to be contrasted with an omission based on, say, ignorance or accident: Fred failed to turn up for the test because he did not know there was a test today; Gloria failed to stop the car because she was too busy changing gear; but Henry did not go jogging today because he wanted to go to the library. In this sense some omissions are, as Singer points out, deliberate choices to do one thing rather than another, and others are not. But in the second sense, an intentional omission is thought of as a deliberate choice to *bring about* some state of affairs as a result of the omission, and is to be contrasted with an omission in which there is no such choice: a parent may starve her child with the intention of killing him; a prison officer may deliberately fail to tell a prisoner that a parcel has arrived, with the intention to deceive or punish. But a person may omit to do something without the intention of bringing about the state of affairs resulting from it: Roger might not help to fix Stephen's television set, not because he intends the set to remain broken, but because he does not know how to fix it, or because he has to go shopping, or simply because he couldn't be bothered. Tania might not help Victoria study, not because she intends to contribute to

Victoria's failing the exam, but because she is too busy studying herself.

It is in this second sense that Foot-type cases are to be understood. If Bill does not give money to a charitable organisation for the starving, and even if (improbably) one could identify the precise harm done by that omission (an extra sack of grain is not bought, a particular village for which it was destined goes without), Bill may not have *intended* to bring about that harm. His omission may have been intentional in the first sense – he deliberately chose to spend the money on a new shirt – but not in the second. And whether or not the omission is culpable is a separate question; sometimes intentional omissions in the second sense are culpable, sometimes they are not. Culpability has to be assessed, as stated above, according to whether there was a pre-existing duty to act. So if a doctor refrains from saving a patient in particular circumstances, with the result that the patient dies, he may or may not have intended to bring about death. If he did not, then he may or may not be culpable, according to whether he had a duty to save *in those circumstances*. If he is not culpable, *it does not follow* that it would have been permissible for him to take active steps to kill the patient, any more than the lack of culpability (let us assume) involved in Bill's not giving money to charity for the starving implies that he would have been allowed – let alone *obliged*, as Singer, Rachels and others claim in euthanasia cases – to send the starving poisoned food.

The confusion we have just noted derives from the consequentialist assumptions of the opponents of AOD. Morality is not about the intentional causation of states of affairs with degrees of utility. If it were, there would indeed be little to distinguish an omission to save from an act of killing. It is about rights, about virtues, about character, motivation, human nature, our position in society, our responsibilities to others, our capacities, our knowledge, our priorities, and much more besides. Theories of the kind that have been dominant in applied ethics for thirty years are too thin and desiccated to capture the sorts of distinction and nuance with which ethical theory is replete. This chapter has provided only a bare outline of the central concepts and principles we will use in assessing concrete problems in applied ethics. What I hope the discussion so far has shown is that these concepts and principles are plausible, defensible against the common objections raised against them, and worth exploring to see how they can be applied.[12]

4

Close-Up on the Good of Life

4.1 Life as a Good

Consider a great work of art, such as Michelangelo's *Pietà*. What is special about it? What purpose does it serve, if any? We can think of several important functions that it has. First, it is a work of religious devotion, designed to inspire love of God. Second, it is a work of great beauty, naturally inspiring admiration of the sculpture's form, proportions and texture. More generally, it inspires a love of art as such. Third, it evokes a high regard for the author's creative talent, for the intellect, passion and skill which together were able to produce such a magnificent piece of work. All in all, the *Pietà* excites a sense of wonder, of awe, of reverence.

No doubt Michelangelo had all of this in mind when he created his sculpture, though in varying degrees. Thus it is true to say that the *Pietà* does serve several purposes; it performs various functions, as do all artistic works, even those of much lesser beauty than anything Michelangelo ever produced. But could we conceive of his famous sculpture's *not* serving any purpose? Imagine that the world one day became a place devoid of religion, where no person had any aesthetic sensibility, where artistic creation had ground to a halt, and hence where nobody admired the creative work of anybody else, both because there were no new artistic works to admire and because, even if there were any, no one would have the sensibility to admire them. Suppose the *Pietà* still existed in such a world, being regarded as no more than a quaint curiosity; people had become, let us suppose, so disconnected from their past that all they knew was that it was a figure of a man and woman, made a long time ago by an Italian man for no apparent reason. They might not grind it down for its marble – they might simply leave it standing in Rome among the many other curiosities of a bygone age. Would the *Pietà* serve any purpose in such a world? It is hard to see how it could. Would it, then, have lost any value it once had as a work of art? You might be tempted to say yes, but a little reflection should dispel the temptation. There is a difference between something's losing its value *for* someone and something's losing its value pure and simple. Certainly, in our imaginary world the *Pietà* would have lost its value for anyone. But would it have lost its value pure and simple? You might say: 'This question makes no sense. Sure, the *Pietà* has not lost its value for *me*, since I am not part of the imaginary world and I do admire art, and creative talent, and so on. But to ask whether it has or has not a value independently of its being valued *by* someone is a philosophical mistake.'

To settle the issue of whether such a question does embody a philosophical mistake would take us too far into aesthetics, but it can at least be said that there is good reason for thinking that the *Pietà* has intrinsic artistic value, that it has it from the moment of its creation and that it will continue to have it as long as it exists, even in the imaginary world just described. For one thing, there are few people who both think that the question of whether works of art have intrinsic value is a mistake, and who would not say that our imaginary world was an impoverished, artistically barren, soulless and altogether less-than-human place. But why would they describe that world in such a way unless they believed that its inhabitants *ought* to respond to the *Pietà* in the way that we do? And why would they believe this if they did not think the sculpture possessed intrinsic aesthetic qualities, qualities of harmony, proportion, pathos, reverence, spiritual transcendence, awesomeness – in short, beauty?

We can see, then, that the relationship between a work of art and its functions and purposes is a complex one. One the one hand, we want to say that the *Pietà* cannot be comprehended apart from the purposes it was created to serve, and without the capacity to respond to its typical functions – without an understanding of religion, or without an aesthetic sense – the *Pietà* would be nothing to us. On the other hand, we want to say that the *Pietà* is not merely the sum of its functions, or even the sum of its functions plus the responses it evokes in its observers; we want to say that it possesses intrinsic aesthetic qualities, that it has a value which those unable to respond to it simply miss. In other words, the *Pietà* has qualities by virtue of which it is intrinsically *apt* to produce certain responses, responses that are *appropriately* directed at any object that possesses such qualities. It is this that would make us say that if, in our imaginary world, someone came along and ground the *Pietà* down into fine powder, he would be an artistic vandal who did not know what he was destroying.

No analogy is perfect, but similar observations can be made about the good of life. What is life for? There are various ways in which the question can be answered, but one that is helpful for our purposes is simply this: life is for pursuing the goals that objectively fulfil us as human beings. Human beings are endowed with a marvellous array of faculties to be used for this purpose. We have an intellect that enables us to discern good and bad and to determine the means for obtaining the first and avoiding the second. We have a will whose proper exercise draws us towards the good and away from the bad. We have emotions that help our will to respond to our intellect, which they do by exciting in us a desire to obtain the good and to shun the bad. We are, it can be said, *built* for fulfilment, equipped with the capacities necessary for the achievement of those goals that are the objective of a distinctively human life.

Does this mean, then, that life has only an *instrumental* value? Is it valuable only because of what it enables us to achieve during its course? As in the artistic example, it would be wrong to draw such a conclusion. In the moral theory outlined in the previous two chapters, the concept of human good is central, and with it the associated concepts of human fulfilment, human nature, virtue, dignity, and others. Among the basic goods that were outlined, human life was seen as fundamental to the pursuit of all other goods, or a precondition of their pursuit. As such, life is the *starting point* for moral theory, or the place from which all moral evaluation begins. The actions we judge are the actions of living human beings, the goals we evaluate are the goals that, if pursued, tend to make a human life either fulfilled or unfulfilled.

None of this, however, implies that human life has only instrumental value, since it is important not to confuse two claims. The first is that human life is necessary for the pursuit of human goods, and the second is that it is sufficient. The confusion is often made by advocates of euthanasia, and we will consider it in that context in the companion volume. For the moment, the general point is that it is the second claim, not the first, that gives theoretical support to the idea that life has only instrumental value. For, from the claim that life is sufficient for the pursuit of goods, or, reversing the claim, that the pursuit of goods is necessary for life, one might be tempted to claim that if human life has value, then goods must be pursuable. But this is equivalent to saying that if goods are *not* pursuable, then life *has* no value – in other words, that life has value *only insofar* as it is lived in the pursuit of human goods; which is simply to say that it has only instrumental value. The second claim, however, that life is sufficient for the pursuit of goods, is false: merely being alive, as cases discussed in the context of euthanasia show, does not guarantee that the person who is alive will be capable of pursuing any other goods. Hence the claim about value that one might be tempted to base on it, that if life has any value it must be because the person who is alive is capable of pursuing goods, has no support.

On the other hand, the *first* claim, that life is *necessary* for the pursuit of human goods, is manifestly true – no one can pursue goods without being alive in the first place! But from this obvious truth, the only claim that follows about the value of human life is this: that if human goods are pursuable, then human life has value. Since human goods are indeed pursuable – not necessarily by every human being in every condition they are in, but by the human race in general – it follows that life does indeed have value, pure and simple; in other words, it is a fundamental good that is the precondition for the pursuit of all other goods.

This is not to say that life is not also instrumentally valuable; it is common to think, 'How good it is that I am alive today, because I can do such-and-such.' But the point is that the value of life is not *reducible* to its instrumental value – it has its own *intrinsic* value as a basic human good. We saw that all of the basic human goods are ultimately pursued for their own sakes, because together they make up human happiness: human happiness is not something over and above the goods, but is a complex condition made of those goods. Since the pursuit of any of those goods cannot be separated in thought from the idea of life itself – every pursuit of a good being a pursuit by a living human being – life is itself necessarily pursued for its own sake, as a constituent of happiness, along with every other good. Why do I pursue knowledge? For its own sake, since it is part of what fulfils a human being to know about the world around them. But what pursues knowledge is *me*, a living human being. So my life itself, which is conceptually inseparable from the pursuit of knowledge, must also be pursued as an ultimate constituent of human fulfilment, moreover as the basic precondition of fulfilment. In addition, there are many aspects of life, in particular the various elements of physical health and psychological well-being which, like knowledge, are pursued in themselves as ultimate constituents of happiness. In this way life reveals its dual role as a good: it is the basic precondition of the pursuit of all other goods, and it is a good in its own right, whose fostering helps us to flourish as human beings.

Some might object to the idea that life is, as it were, more basic than the other basic goods, on the ground that a person might reasonably rank it below the other goods in terms of the way of living that he has reasonably chosen for himself. But it is hard to see how life itself really could have a lower priority than the other goods. Take the case of knowledge and health. A person might place more emphasis on knowledge at some cost to health – studying long hours, not taking enough exercise, and so on – and this would indeed involve the ranking of knowledge above life in *one* respect, namely that of health, which is included in the good of life. But life *as such* could not be completely demoted in favour of another good. It would be a mistake, perhaps even senseless, to think that a person's *death* could ever enhance his pursuit of knowledge or of any other good. Examples that might seem to suggest the contrary are beside the point. Consider, for instance, the artist suffering from a terminal and debilitating illness, who forces himself to keep going for the sole purpose of completing his life's work. Such an attitude might be admirable; would it be an attitude that relegated life to a lower priority than the good of aesthetic creation? It is not as though the artist has come to see the only *point* of life as its allowing him to finish his work. Rather, his illness has been foisted upon him and seeks to *deprive* him of life, with the result that, through no fault of his own (such as deliberate neglect of his health to the point of becoming terminally ill), the instrumental value of life assumes priority. Compare this with the case of a depressed and suicidal parent, tired of life (for whatever reason), who says that the only thing that keeps her going is her children, whom she wants to see grow up; were it not for that, she says, she would commit suicide. Here other goods are actively being promoted above life itself, which is *given* a purely instrumental value. To that extent we should say that the parent has got her priorities wrong, since her attitude does not contribute to a flourishing life. Note that a mere transient attitude of despair is not enough to show that a person has wrongly demoted life below other goods; only if his attitude displays a settled disposition, a fixed turning-away from life, can we say his priorities are disordered.

The good of life, then, is fundamental in a way that other goods are not. Two individuals could live equally flourishing lives even though for one it is, say, art that is the most important thing, and for the other, knowledge. But life itself cannot be similarly demoted in favour of other goods. The good of life is part of the very moral framework within which the evaluation of action can take place, because every action is evaluated in terms of its contribution to a *good life*. No person can flourish without being alive in the first place, so if he deliberately undercuts his life in pursuit of other goods, he will soon have no goods to pursue whatsoever.

4.2 The Right to Life and the Sanctity of Life

The founding fathers of the Unites States said, in the Declaration of Independence: 'We hold these truths to be self-evident, that all men are created equal, that they are endowed by their Creator with certain unalienable Rights, that among these are Life, Liberty, and the pursuit of Happiness.' Echoing these beliefs, the United Nations' Universal Declaration of Human Rights (1948) states: 'Everyone has the right to life, liberty and the security of person' (Article 3); and given that the Preamble speaks of 'inalienable rights', it appears from the context that the Universal Declaration recognises the right to life as one of these. Now the fact that these important documents assert that there is an inalienable right to life does not, of course, make it so, but in this particular respect both documents recognise one of the central truths of morality. One way of putting this truth is to say that man does not have absolute dominion over his own life. He does not *own* his life as he owns his house or his money, and hence is not free to do with it as he pleases. Although this truth was recognised almost universally throughout human history, indeed up to the latter part of the twentieth century, it is a hard truth for many of us to accept, conditioned as we have been in recent decades by a combination of subjectivism, relativism, end-justifies-the-means morality such as that embodied in consequentialism, and the generally permissive approach to moral questions that has dominated the thinking of recent decades.

The idea that our lives are not our own, that we are not free to do with them as we wish, strikes many of us as bizarre. It is usually dismissed by contemporary moral theorists as part of that wrongheaded, or at least obsolete, doctrine of the 'sanctity of human life'. Various objections have been levelled against the doctrine, some important, some irrelevant or confused, and we will look at a few of the more significant ones. But the reaction to the doctrine as bizarre is itself curious. As we noted above, human beings are endowed with a marvellous array of faculties and capacities which, when they work correctly and harmoniously, make for a good life. One of the capacities that go to make up the good life is, tautologically, life itself. Hence we should expect similar fundamental truths to apply to life itself as apply to the other faculties and capacities that make human happiness possible. One is that these faculties must not be abused, attacked, disintegrated or disposed of. For example, man is endowed with reason, a capacity that enables him to know truth, to love it, and to pursue it. Because of it he can and does reach the sublime heights of scientific knowledge, philosophical and religious understanding, and artistic creation. That is what his reason is *for*: even thinkers who claim that human reason is a huge cosmic accident, the product of blind evolutionary forces, believe that it is a tool of inestimable price, by means of which mankind, through a combination of ingenuity, subtlety and creativity, has made up for its physical limitations and ensured its survival as a species in a hostile world.

Used correctly, reason contributes to man's happiness; abused, it leads to man's downfall. When a person uses his reason to lie, to cheat, to deceive others, to immerse himself in false systems of belief, when he allows himself to be taken in by falsehoods masquerading as news, fraudulent advertising, fads, fancies and trivia unworthy of serious thought, we think that he is abusing his faculty of reason. We think that it cannot be right for a person to pervert his reason in the service of error, that a person who does so is living, one way or another, a *diminished* or *undignified* life. Reason is not given to us to attack the truth for which it naturally strives, or to fritter away on the things of no consequence that obstruct us in the search for true happiness.

Why, then, should it be any different in the case of life itself? Since we have a right to pursue a given good, and since life is a good, we also have the right to life. But it does not follow that we also have the right to do with our lives as we please since, as with every other good, this would imply that we had the right not to live a good life, the right not to pursue the good; and this is as absurd as the claim that we have the right to believe error, to believe, say, that the moon is made of cheese or that pigs fly. (I am not here thinking of a case of invincible ignorance, but of a case where the person is confronted with persuasive evidence that what he believes is false and refuses to take it into account, or is 'put on inquiry' but refuses to make that inquiry, or is negligent in how he goes about finding out what is true, and so is vincibly ignorant.) Now most people would baulk at this suggestion: not only, would they say, is it *not* absurd to think a person has the right to believe that pigs fly, but to think the *opposite* is a sign of bizarre moral thinking. Here we need to pause. When we reflect a little on this question, we see that the almost universal notion that a person has the right to believe, for instance, that pigs fly is *not* the notion that a person has the right to perform what is in reality the mental act of embracing falsehood, and hence of perverting his faculty of reason. Rather, it is the notion that no one has the right to *interfere* with such an act, least of all to *coerce* a person into believing the truth. That is indeed a fundamental moral principle. But it is not the same as the idea that a person has the right to believe falsehood. Nor does it follow from the fact that no one has the right to force another to believe something, that the latter has the right to believe anything. To take an analogy, no one has the right to force another to be healthy (let us leave aside factors that modify this, such as a relationship of obedience like that of parent and child or of commanding officer and soldier); it does not follow that a person has the right to ruin his health. On the contrary, most of us would see the living of an unhealthy, self-destructive lifestyle as wrong, even though we would not claim that anyone had the right to compel a person living such a lifestyle to make a change.

Indeed, such is the strength of our beliefs about the morality of living healthily, that it comes as a surprise that so many of us should simultaneously hold that a person's very life is somehow not subject to the same strictures. Suppose Charles comes up to you in the street, holding a syringe and various paraphernalia, and says, 'Please inject me with heroin; I haven't tried it before and I'd like to get addicted, but I'm too nervous to inject myself.' Most of us would shrink immediately from helping Charles do himself such damage. We might say, 'Do it yourself', but that would not mean we *approved* of such an action, only that, while we disapproved, we could not compel Charles to desist. Or consider Diana, who is desperate to stay hooked for the rest of her life on, say, smoking or drinking. She knows that every so often she will have second thoughts and want to change her ways, but it is precisely at those times, she tells you, that you must make sure she has a plentiful supply of alcohol or tobacco at hand so as to make sure she stays hooked. Would you agree to her request? Suppose Diana says, when you ask her why she wants to stay addicted, that she has quite simply, for whatever reason, given up her right to be healthy. Would you think, 'Well, in that case, since she has renounced her right to health, I'm free to help her ruin it'?

If cases such as these are persuasive, then the natural question to ask is why life itself should be any different. If a person cannot legitimately give up on the pursuit of truth and understanding – and believing falsehood involves just such a renunciation – or on the pursuit of health, why should we think he can give up on life itself? Indeed, isn't the situation even more straightforward in the case of life? For with other rights, it is sometimes legitimate for us to allow their infringement to some degree. It is permissible for me to give up some of my liberty by joining the army, or by locking myself in my room and throwing away the key, say if I am trying to escape an attacker. It does not follow, however, that I have the right to sell myself into slavery. It is permissible for me to renounce some of my friendships, say because they are having a bad influence on me. It does not follow, however, that I have right to renounce all human warmth and affection – not even the most reclusive of saintly hermits has ever done that. In both cases, we naturally think there would be something less than human in the total renunciation of rights that attach to basic human goods such as liberty and friendship. The starkness of the case of life lies in the fact that there is no such thing as allowing a partial infringement or giving up some of the right: you are either alive or dead. In which case every giving up of the right must amount to renunciation or abandonment. And if renunciation or abandonment is illegitimate in the case of other basic goods, why should life be an exception?

What has just been said has clear implications for the issue of whether suicide is wrong, but it is not my purpose to explore that specific question; further considerations regarding the inalienability of the right to life will be raised when we come to look at voluntary euthanasia in chapter 2 of *Applied Ethics*. The main purpose of the above discussion has been to show in what general sense there is an absolute right to life. Like other basic human goods, the good of life cannot be destroyed, since this would involve a fundamental attack upon human integrity, so fundamental that such an attack would destroy not only the good of life itself, but the possibility of pursuing any other goods whatsoever. In this sense, the right to life is part of the very architecture of the moral theory being defended here. Every moral theory has its architecture, the basic conceptual framework within which it is elaborated. For the consequentialist it may be pleasure and pain, or desires, or preferences, or a system of rules that maximises these or some other ingredient. For the Kantian it is the autonomous human will, legislating the moral rules it will follow in accordance with the categorical imperative. In the present theory it is the framework of basic human goods which together constitute living well and in accordance with human nature, and in which the good of life underlies and preconditions the pursuit of all the rest. The good of life is, therefore, fundamental to the good life.

4.3   The Sanctity of Life and its Critics

Having briefly sketched the place of life in a general theory of the good, we need now to go into some more detail, elaborating just what the doctrine of the sanctity of life amounts to. Since it has come under such ferocious attack by contemporary moral theorists, the details can usefully be filled in by considering some of the most significant and common objections, after baldly stating the doctrine itself.

> *Doctrine of the Sanctity of Life (DSL):* It is always and everywhere a grave moral wrong intentionally to take the life of an innocent human being.

4.3.1   Innocence

A common objection to DSL is that it is ad hoc. Why is the word 'innocent' included? Surely, says the critic, this is because the supporter of the doctrine recognises certain exceptions to the principle that the killing of *any* human being is wrong: war, self-defence and capital punishment are the standard examples. So doesn't 'innocent human being' merely mean 'human being who does not fall under a predetermined exception'? And, says James Rachels:

> why should we accept the principle? If we had *already* decided, on *other* grounds, that euthanasia, abortion and the like are wrong, and that the only acceptable kinds of killing are in war, individual self-defence, and as punishment, *then* we might find the principle plausible. . . . But what if we have not already made that choice? Then we would have no reason to affirm that principle, and so the argument from it should not persuade us. It merely begs the question.[1]

And, he adds, it is 'silly'.

The reply is that DSL does not beg the question, any more than any other moral principle that, founded on rational considerations, does not cover certain kinds of case. Consider, for example, freedom of expression. Many, if not most, people (at least in Western societies) believe that everyone has the right freely to express their beliefs and opinions. Do they believe the right is absolute? What about the expression of beliefs – such as that all black men under twenty-five should be denied the right to vote – that are so offensive they carry a high risk of provoking civil disorder if aired publicly? What about the classic example of the man who falsely yells 'fire!' in a crowded cinema? (The usual reply is to say the person who yells 'fire!' does not really believe it and is simply trying to cause a riot. But suppose the person *does* believe it, and knows there is a standard procedure for orderly evacuation of the cinema, but wants to cause a stampede nevertheless?) What about someone who publishes detailed instructions on how to make your own nuclear bomb? Immediately supporters of freedom of expression would state that there are exceptions, or more precisely, that the principle must be carefully formulated so as not to cover certain categories of case, even though it is absolute for all other cases. Freedom of expression, they say, extends only to beliefs and opinions that do not, for example, incite anyone to violence, or directly harm another, or are likely to cause civil disorder, and so on. The right to privacy is another example. Does any supporter of the right consider that it is violated in the case of a suspected criminal whose house is lawfully searched by the police? Again, categories that are not covered by the right need to be specified, and not arbitrarily but for good reason.

The right to life is no different to the sorts of example just mentioned. Since life is a good for every human being, every human being has the right to life. But the right is only absolute in cases that do not fall into certain well-founded categories. In the case of war (about which more will be said in chapter 5 of *Applied Ethics*), a country that is the victim of unjust aggression (consider the German invasion of Poland in 1939) has the right to repel the aggression. Since the soldiers of the aggressing country are acting as representatives of and in the name of that country, then whatever their own personal opinions about the war, they participate in the guilt of their country, and the country that is aggressed against has the right to kill them in defence of its own integrity and the lives of its citizens.

In its essentials, the case of individual self-defence is arguably like that of war. I say 'arguably', because defenders of both DSL and the right to self-defence have two views as to how best to explain the latter. On the first view, the case of a person's defending himself from attack does not even come under the heading of 'intentional killing' and is for that reason outside the scope of DSL. What they claim is that it is never morally lawful intentionally to kill an attacker, only to use force that you know may be lethal. Thus self-defence comes under the Principle of Double Effect, and would be akin to the case of someone's driving her desperately sick child to the hospital at such a high speed that she increases the risk of a pedestrian's being killed (see chapter 3). Evidence used in support of this interpretation is that even if you knew for certain that someone was going to try to kill you tomorrow, you would not be allowed to carry out a 'pre-emptive strike' by going over and shooting them dead today. The right to self-protection exists equally in either case, so if you cannot kill intentionally in one you cannot in the other. Hence, if someone comes at you with a knife, and you have a gun, you may only shoot with the intention of repelling the attack or incapacitating the attacker, not with the objective of killing him.

On the second interpretation, a person may intentionally kill another in self-defence, and the explanation of the impermissibility of a pre-emptive strike is that a person who plans to murder another, but has not embarked on carrying out the plan, has not yet incurred the sort of guilt that brings the right to self-defence into play. A planned attack is not an attack, and so there can be no defence (though the intended victim can *plan* his defence); people can change their minds, they do not carry out all of the plans they make (perhaps they do not carry out a *fraction* of them!), and so an anticipatory strike would be murder.

These issues are exceedingly subtle and complicated and I will explore them further in chapter 5 of *Applied Ethics*. (So as not to keep the reader in suspense I should point out that I favour the first interpretation, though both interpretations' points about pre-emptive strikes are correct.) The central point for the moment is that, contrary to Rachels' criticism, there is nothing arbitrary or ad hoc about restricting the absolute right to life to the innocent. Some say that unjust aggressors *forfeit* their right to life. Other say that they *waive* their right to life by their actions. On the former interpretation, their case would be something like that of a person who forfeited the right to expect help from a close friend if he went about blackening his friend's name in public. On the latter, their case would be something like that of the American politician Gary Hart, who waived his right to privacy when he taunted the press by challenging them to catch him out in an act of adultery. (They succeeded.) Either way, we can see how a reasonable, principled case can be made for restricting the absolute right to life to those who are innocent, who do not offend against the very right they claim for themselves. (For a Kantian, it would be a kind of 'contradiction in the will' for an unjust aggressor to claim the right to life whilst attacking that very right in others.)

The term 'forfeiture' is arguably best reserved for cases of *punishment*. Capital punishment will be discussed in chapter 4 of *Applied Ethics*, but let us assume for the moment that the supporter of DSL also believes in capital punishment. Is this arbitrary or ad hoc? No more than in the cases of war or self-defence. Some have maintained that capital punishment just *is* a form of defence, namely of the State against a person who offends gravely against the common good. A strong argument against this is that in the case of a capital crime the deed is already done, so how could there be a defence when the attack is over? A better interpretation is that a capital offender forfeits his right to life for reasons that overlap, but are in important senses very different, from those justifying war or self-defence. These reasons, to be explored in detail in the companion volume, involve concepts of social order and the common good and are therefore based on fundamental moral notions. They are, then, not part of an ad hoc or specious justification for a kind of action whose acceptance is based, as Rachels claims, on the 'political expediency' of times long past. In short, if concepts such as forfeiture and waiver of rights, and others mentioned above and discussed in more detail in *Applied Ethics*, are meaningful, plausible, and properly located in a general moral theory, how can invoking them amount to an ad hoc manoeuvre designed to shore up a doctrine that one has already decided *must* be true no matter what?

So far I have concentrated on the negative justification of the use of the term 'innocent' in DSL: the doctrine covers those cases that do not fall under a well-defined exception. But there is also a positive side to the use of the term. For Rachels, its use is as arbitrary and unmotivated as would be the use of the term 'healthy' in a principle to the effect that it was always wrong to kill the healthy. This shows a lack of reflection upon what morality is all about. In the words of the Roman jurist Publilius Syrus, 'When innocence is frightened, the judge is condemned.'[2]

Justice is at the core of morality. Whenever an action betrays the innocent, such as when a judge condemns an innocent man, when a person has his good named blackened, when law-abiding citizens are subjected to brutality and interference by the state, we are outraged. But why? The reason is that morality is nothing if not a system of rules designed to protect people in their sole pursuit of the good. When they trample upon the rights of others, of course, they do not solely pursue the good – they damage its pursuit by others and show an obvious *disrespect* for the very system under which they otherwise seek protection. If, on the other hand, they simply live their lives in a peaceable, orderly and harmonious fashion, they are innocent and therefore entitled to the full protection of the system they respect and live by.

In particular, traditional morality is not restricted solely to those people who have the actual characteristics of the mature human being, the fully developed, and hence in a sense paradigmatic, member of the species. It is also concerned to protect the vulnerable, those who we often call 'innocent' in a more specialised sense: the young, the old, the sick, the handicapped, the less intelligent, the sleeping, the comatose, the drugged. If morality is not about protecting these classes of people, what *is* it about? Forty-five-year-old professors of philosophy with IQs of 130, still able to run a mile in under seven minutes? Justice, then, is fundamental to morality, and innocence is fundamental to justice. A system of rules cannot call itself truly moral if it is blind to the equal protection that is rightfully claimed by all human beings who go about their daily lives in ways which, although often radically diverse, have in common the feature that they are lives lived in the legitimate pursuit of the good. Only when a person subverts the good does he merit the condemnation of others; only when his subversion is serious does he merit interference either by the lawful authorities or by other persons acting in defence of their own well-being; and only when his subversion is the most serious that it can be does he merit the most serious interference. Otherwise, as an innocent person, he has the full force of the moral law on his side.

4.3.2   A life not worth living?

Leaving aside the sorts of case described above which fall beyond the scope of DSL, critics have attacked the doctrine on another ground, namely that it fails to allow for an important sort of case, one that strikes the doctrine at its roots. They claim that DSL is based on a serious misunderstanding of what it is that makes a human life valuable.

What matters morally, for these critics, is not whether an innocent human being's life is taken away, but whether what is taken away is a *life worth living*. This view is succinctly expressed by Peter Singer. There are, he says, some human beings who have 'lives not worth living'.[3] And if a human being has a life not worth living, it is sometimes right to kill him. This is especially the case when no one objects to the killing or is otherwise upset or disadvantaged by it; he says for instance: 'When the life of an infant will be so miserable as not to be worth living . . . if there are no "extrinsic" reasons for keeping the infant alive – like the feelings of the parents – it is better that the child should be helped to die without further suffering.'[4] The reason that other people's desires and preferences come into the calculation is that Singer is a preference utilitarian, so that the object of morality is primarily the maximisation of the satisfaction of people's preferences. It is therefore possible that a 'defective' (Singer's word) infant, with a life 'not worth living', should be spared death because to kill her would cause far greater mental trauma to her family than she would be spared the suffering involved in being disabled. But in a famous – or perhaps infamous – example, Singer discusses the case of a child with a condition as mild as haemophilia.[5] If, he says, no one objects to the child's being killed, and if killing her 'has no adverse effects on others' – especially her parents – it would be permissible to do so if the parents found their child a burden. Then suppose the same parents intended to go ahead and produce a disease-free 'replacement' baby. In such a case they would be in a position to *increase* the sum total of human happiness (the world containing the haemophiliac baby versus the world containing a 'normal' baby instead), and so killing their sick child and replacing her with a healthier one would be a *positive duty*. The parents, as good utilitarians, are bound to maximise the net benefit to the world, in particular the satisfaction of their own preference for a replacement. Singer in fact goes further: on his theory, someone whose life is 'worth living' and who *wants* to stay alive – say a mature handicapped adult who manages to cope happily with his disability – may still be killed if the total preference calculation shows that far more relief from being a 'burden' would be experienced by his family, his carers, and/or the state if he were killed than he would suffer by the overriding of his desire to go on living. For, as Singer says, 'if we are preference utilitarians we must allow that a desire to go on living can be outweighed by other desires'.[6]

We find similar thoughts in the work of Jonathan Glover, who asserts that 'if someone's life is worth living, then this is *one* reason why it is directly wrong to kill him.' Again:

> It is wrong to kill a baby who has a good chance of having a worthwhile life, but *in terms of this objection* [that it is wrong to destroy

a worth-while life] it would not be wrong to kill him if the alternative to his existence was the existence of someone else with an equally good chance of a life at least as worth-while. ... If the second baby has just as good a life as the first one would have done, then, in terms of the worth-while life objection, the death of the first baby has not mattered at all. And, if the first baby would have had a less good life, its death was in this respect a good thing. (original emphasis)

And when talking not about 'defective' babies (Glover's word) but about adults, the same considerations come into play: 'What is crucial is how much the person himself gets out of life', he says when discussing euthanasia; and 'What would his own future life be like, and would it be worth living?', he asks when discussing suicide. Furthermore:

If we accept that some people have lives so terrible as to be not worth living, it seems hard to deny the existence of a neighbouring grey area where a life may be worth living but is less worth living than normal. It would clearly be absurd to give priority in life-saving to someone whose life is not worth living. Yet it is hard, without making an artificially sharp cut-off point, to accept this while refusing to be influenced by the fact that someone is in a state only a little less bad.

So, like Singer, Glover thinks that even someone with a life worth living may not be spared, if the life is still 'very bad'. And the fact that Glover is at pains to stress that whether a life is 'worth living' is only one question to be asked is explained by his sharing Singer's belief that the other crucial question for the consequentialist is: what would the effect of killing someone be on other people? This in turn is answered by answering a number of more specific questions. Would their preferences not be satisfied? Would they be traumatised? or relieved? advantaged? disadvantaged? spared a burden? put in fear? reassured? And so on.

Quotations such as these can be multiplied, as they litter the works of the consequentialist critics of DSL. One would be justified in supposing, then, that they had a clear – at least a *tolerably* precise, if not necessarily black-and-white – test of what constitutes a 'life worth living'. Surprisingly (or perhaps *un*surprisingly) they do not. As Glover frankly admits, 'there is no adequate test for deciding the point at which someone's life is not worth living'.[7] For him, the two questions to be asked in the case of a person able to think about his own life are, first: Does the person want to go on living? And if there is reason to think he might be mistaken about how well his life is going: Would I prefer to be dead than have that sort of life? This is similar to Singer's approach, since for him, '[k]illing a person who prefers to continue living is therefore wrong' (though as we saw, not *always*). However, it may be that 'the person to be killed does not realise what agony she will suffer in future, and if she is not killed now she will have to live through to the very end'.[8] Glover speaks of 'a future so awful that the person cannot grasp what it will be like',[9] adding that he could not rule out that it might have been permissible to kill someone who was on the way to a Nazi concentration camp. It must be remembered, however, that the morality of killing the innocent amounts to more than a test of how things are *for* the innocent person himself. Singer is clear that it is wrong to kill a person who prefers to go on living 'other things being equal', by which he means not only that the person might be wrong about how well his life was going, but that his preferences might be outweighed by others who want him dead. And for Glover, the desire to go on living is an important but not final test of whether the person should be killed, since we have to consider the effects his death will have on other people.

All this talk of a 'life not worth living' has familiar overtones and associations, drawing (unintentionally, of course) on the Nazi concept of a 'life unworthy of life' (*lebensunwerten Lebens*), which was the guiding principle of their infamous euthanasia programme of the 1930s.[10] But whatever the importance or otherwise of its associations, we must evaluate the philosophical plausibility of such a concept; if it has no justification, the alternative account of the value of life given by the critics of DSL falls apart.

If we break down the critics' test of a 'life worth living', we see that it is in reality a hybrid, consisting of a subjective test and an objective test. The subjective test looks at how a person's life is going from their own standpoint, from their 'internal perspective', as Singer puts it. It is convenient further to break down the objective test into two parts. First, there is an objective evaluation of the life of the person whose death is being contemplated – let us call him the 'potential victim', for want of a less coloured but equally concise term, and let us call this test the 'victim test'. Then there is an objective evaluation of the effects of his death on others, in other words, a judgement about the interests, or more precisely preferences, of everyone concerned (or about some other ingredient, according to whatever version of consequentialism the critics supports) – we can call this the 'side effects test'. We need to bear in mind, then, that when consquentialists such as Glover and Singer separate the question of whether someone's live is 'worth living' from the question of what effects their life (or proposed death) has on others, they are keeping apart the test of how the potential victim's life is going *for them alone* (which has both a subjective and an objective element) from the test of how that life affects third parties. As consquentialists, however, these tests merge into one *overall* test of the worthiness of a person's life. Let us consider the criteria in turn, beginning with the subjective test.

The subjective test

This test looks, in Glover's words, at 'death considered from the standpoint of the person killed'.[11] For Glover, mere biological life only has value insofar as it is a vehicle for consciousness, and consciousness has value only insofar as it is a vehicle for a life 'worth living', which is a complex of other things he refuses to list on the ground that any such list is 'disputable' and 'ridiculous'; nevertheless, this is what matters morally. To carry out the subjective test is, for Glover, 'to make an attempt (obviously an extremely fallible one) to see [a person's] life from his own point of view and to see what he gets out of it'.[12] Still, the sorts of thing that he presumably has in mind as indicating what the potential victim 'gets out of life' are his plans, projects, desires, preferences, feelings, memories, sense of identity, and so on. If enough of these are present, and present in the right sorts of proportions and combinations, then for all Glover's coyness, one presumes he would say the potential victim had a life 'worth living'.

The problem is, exactly *what* should be present, and in *what* proportions and *what* combinations? To say that the test is 'extremely fallible', that its application is 'disputable' and 'could be endlessly argued over', that its 'difficulties . . . are obvious', and that 'any general formula seems either too indeterminate or too contentious, or both', is to make one suspect whether the subjective test has any meaningful content whatsoever. And given that it is human life at stake, one would have expected Glover to be less sanguine about a retreat to vagueness of such massive proportions.

It is one thing to talk about a person's plans, projects, desires, and so on, but what exactly should go into the subjective melting pot, and how? What relative weight is to be given to the various factors? Which, if any, of the scores of 'quality of life' tests proposed by various philosophers or medical ethics committees should a person use? Or does it all come down to a matter of brute feelings? Is the subjective test based on pure relativism? If so, it brings into play the objections against relativism raised in chapter 1, along with many more. If not, then there is supposed to be some sort of standard that should generate broad agreement among people as to whether nor not their lives were 'worth living'. While there may indeed be such agreement in uncontroversial cases, it is the controversial ones that are the most important, and where disagreement breaks out all over.

But it is not just that the subjective test is vague beyond what is tolerable in deciding matters of life and death. This is only part of the problem. Even more seriously, it is *unprincipled*. Consider Jonathan, a forty-five-year-old government employee recovering from a heart attack that has forced him to take early retirement, left him perpetually short of breath, unable to do any serious exercise, bedridden for several hours a day, uninterested in any of the things he used to care deeply about, such as going to the cinema, reading, and camping with his son, anti-social, bad-tempered with his wife, to whom he is always complaining and who is on the verge of leaving him, and frequently depressed. Is Jonathan's life 'worth living', on the subjective test?

We know that Jonathan's own judgement about how his life is going is the obvious starting point. But, as Glover notes, such judgements are 'especially vulnerable to temporary changes of mood', which means we have to consider his judgements 'over a fairly long stretch of time'. Now leaving aside the question of how long is 'fairly long', suppose we ask Jonathan whether his life is 'worth living' and he says it is. The main point is that we need to know exactly what it is that Jonathan is supposed to be judging. He might well say, 'I want to go on living', and this would have strong presumptive force in favour of the proposition that his life was 'worth living', but unless Jonathan is to be counted as irrational, doesn't he have to be able to give a *reason* for wanting to go on? Suppose we press him on this and he says, 'I just feel/believe/know that my life is worth living.' But that would involve a vicious circularity: Jonathan tells us his life is 'worth living' because he feels/believes/knows that his life is 'worth living'. But just what is it that he feels, believes or knows? We press him further and he says, 'I have plans for the future. I know I don't feel much like it at the moment, but one day I am going to buy a small shop. Anyway, I want to see my son grow up, I want to make up to my wife for my ingratitude, and

I want to make the most of however many years are left to me.' We ask: 'And if your wife insisted upon leaving you, how would you then judge your life? If your child grew up hating you, then what? Suppose you bought your shop but ill health meant you had to sell it after five years?' It is all very well for Jonathan to say, 'But none of that has happened'; we need to evaluate his beliefs over a 'fairly long stretch of time'. Now this may not mean waiting to see whether some or all of those and other scenarios eventuate. But it *does* mean waiting to see how Jonathan sees things after *factoring in* those other scenarios: their probabilities, how severe their effects would be on him, what other *good* things might happen to him, and so on. So Jonathan does need to take into account far more than the facts about how his life is right now. And it does not take much imagination to see how Jonathan could become very unsure, very quickly, about whether he thought his life was 'worth living'. It is not merely that he might be unsure *that* his life was worthwhile; he might be unsure *whether* it was, in other words he would very soon find that he did not even know how to go *about* applying the test. Exactly what principles or procedure is Jonathan supposed to apply? Unless the test is to collapse into an act of introspection of one's brute feelings, there must be some method, some reason that Jonathan can put forward. Otherwise all he can do is run through a list of things he considers important. And we can ask: 'But why does all of that amount of a life worth living?' If Jonathan can give no rationale for the list, and no explanation of how the list *generates the inference* that his life is worth living, the list remains just that – a list.

There is an even more devastating objection to the subjective test – that it *collapses into the objective test*. What we need to ask is (1) why a subjective test should be applied in matters of life and death when it is not applicable in the case of other goods; and (2) why a subjective test should be applied in controversial cases when it is not applicable in uncontroversial ones?

With regard to the first question, consider a good such as knowledge. Is knowledge worth having? Yes, because it is a good. I am not here talking about this or that piece of knowledge, which may not be worth having because, say, it is trivial or useless knowledge relative to some purpose. Rather, I am talking about knowledge as such. Knowledge is a human good and as such it is worth pursuing. But its being a good is not explicated in subjective terms. We do not make some subjective judgement based on our 'personal standpoint', or 'internal perspective', that knowledge is worth having. We do not evaluate whether knowledge is a good based on what we 'get out of' knowledge. Instead, we judge that it is good because reason tells us that it fulfils our nature as rational beings to know, to understand and to seek the truth. The same goes for all human goods: they are, as some philosophers put it, *intelligible* as goods through the act of reason. But if the basis for our judgement that other goods such as knowledge *are* goods is objective, why should it be subjective in the case of the most fundamental good of all, namely life? Why should life be an exception?

With regard to the second question, consider the case of Peter, for whom everything is going fine. He has a good job, a comfortable house, money in the bank, a happy marriage, loving children, and good health. Is his life 'worth living'? Presumably, for the critic of DSL, he is a *paradigmatic* case of someone whose life is 'worth living', and who therefore has nothing to fear from the critic's disbelief in DSL. But does the critic need to ask Peter to make a subjective judgement about what he 'gets out of life', in order to answer the question? Does he need to consider Peter's 'point of view' or 'internal perspective' at all? Surely the facts speak for themselves. But again, if in an uncontroversial case such as Peter's it is a wholly objective matter for the critic of DSL that this person has a 'life worth living', why does it suddenly become a subjective matter in what he considers more controversial cases such as those involving the handicapped, the elderly, the very young, and so on? It might be said: 'But it only *looks* like a wholly objective matter in Peter's case. One could easily imagine his suffering an existential crisis and becoming thoroughly sick of all the things he previously cherished, tired of life, bored, depressed and enervated. Isn't his personal standpoint the ultimate tribunal of whether he gets anything out of life?' To which the supporter of DSL replies that no critic, no matter how wedded to the concept of a 'life worth living', is going to fly in the face of objective evidence such as exists in Peter's case and take his own personal judgement on the matter as definitive. On the contrary, even if Peter persisted for many years in his boredom and depression, no one would disagree that the proper course of action would be to try to shake him out of his state by reminding him of how well things were in fact going for him.

What this line of thought brings out is the important fact that, no matter how confident a person is that things are or are not going well for him, *he can be wrong*. James Rachels, who denies the subjective test of a 'life worth living', puts it well in his critique of hedonism, the idea that what gives life value is pleasant experiences: 'In saying that achievement and friendship are good because they make us happy, hedonism gets things the wrong way round. They are not good because they make us happy [in the subjective sense of giving us pleasant experiences]. Rather, having them (and other things like them) makes us happy because we recognise them *as goods.*'[13]

Rachels' critique of hedonism can, however, be easily extended to any subjective test of whether a life is 'worth living'. Hedonism places ultimate value on purely subjective states of consciousness, and the counter-example to such a theory, as Rachels and many others have noted, is the case of a person who goes through life having had a monumental fraud perpetrated upon him: he thinks he is loved, honoured, respected, that his work is prized, his achievements great; whereas he is in fact a mediocre man with no real friends who has been the butt of an elaborate and vicious joke. Does he think his life has gone well? Yes. Has it? In reality, no. As for hedonism, so for any theory that make a person's own standpoint the ultimate tribunal, even if what the person evaluates are more than subjective phenomena, but encompass also objective feature of his life. The person may be quite wrong not just about how he feels, but about *what is true* of his life.

This is where it is crucial to distinguish between two senses of 'happy', the subjective and the objective. In the former, there is no distinction to be made between someone's *feeling* happy and *being* happy. If he *thinks* things are going well, then they *are* going well. But in the latter sense, the one outlined in chapter 2, there is a big distinction between feeling happy and being happy. Happiness is not a personal or subjective condition, whether consisting of pleasant states of mind or of a set of beliefs about how the world is. Happiness is a state of a person caused by that person's living an objectively good life, one in accordance with his nature as a human being. If the critic of DSL wants to devise a test of whether a life is 'worth living', then, it cannot be a subjective one; or if there is a subjective element, it cannot possibly be the dominant one. A person's feelings, beliefs, emotions, and the like, are only one, all too easily defeasible, piece of evidence as to how his life is really going.

The objective test

James Rachels makes the distinction, shared by all critics of DSL, between merely being alive and 'having a life'.[14] The first is a biological, the second a 'biographical' characteristic of a person. 'Having a life' consists in having plans, projects, aspirations, memories, desires, preferences, making choices, fulfilling ambitions, and so on. It is this complex of psychological and emotional features of a person which, says the critic, is what we value (or at least *should* value). Merely being alive in the biological sense, however, carries no moral weight. What is the value, for instance, of a life lived by a person in an irreversible coma? Or of an anencephalic or otherwise severely handicapped baby, doomed to live out its few remaining years deaf, dumb, blind and perhaps in severe pain? Or of an elderly person suffering from almost complete loss of normal mental function due to senility, with hardly any memory to speak of, unable to do anything for himself, crippled, frail, subject to endless bouts of pneumonia, and perhaps even bedridden? In what sense do such people 'have a life' that carries any moral value?

It is one thing to appeal to intuitions in such cases, to emotions, to thoughts about how you personally would feel about the possibility of being in that position – and another to provide an argument showing why such lives have less value than others, or even such low value that they are 'not worth living' and so could with legitimacy be taken away. An example of one of the many bad arguments used to buttress the opinion of critics of DSL concerning such cases is given by Rachels when he compares the deaths of a famous opera singer and of a brain-damaged woman in a coma. Suppose you learned that these two people had died: 'Would anyone', asks Rachels, 'really think that the two deaths were equally tragic?' Posing this rhetorical question, Rachels claims, shows that 'each of us already believes that different human lives have different values, whether we realize it or not. Nobody really thinks that all lives are equal . . . the division of "lives" into more valuable and less valuable is already an established part of our moral common sense.'[15]

Here Rachels has made a serious confusion between two distinct ideas: (1) that not all deaths are equally tragic; and (2) that not all lives are equally valuable. How does (2) follow from (1)? A death may be tragic because of the promise of a young life cut short, or of the forestalling of great achievements, or of the unforeseen or shocking circumstances of the death, or of some kind of 'poetic justice' in the death itself or its circumstances (consider the ancient Greek understanding of tragedy). We can accept all of this. But where is the principle licensing the inference from (1) to (2), the claim that not all lives have equal value? Rachels gives none, and it is hard to see what that principle could be, at least without a considerable amount of extra moral theory.

The extra moral theory that critics almost unanimously add to their judgements about a 'life worth living' is one or other version of consequentialism, the theory that what matters morally is, purely and simply, the maximisation of good effects, the greatest possible balance of good effects over bad. Since the test of maximisation is an objective one it is, the critics believe, a natural ally in the devising of an objective test of whether a life is not 'worth living'. It is appealed to by Rachels in his discussion of euthanasia and related issues, by Glover (whilst he supports, as we saw, a subjective test as far as the potential victim is concerned, this is embedded within a general consequentialist test of what the overall effects of death would be on all concerned), by Singer, Helga Kuhse, John Harris, and countless other critics of DSL.[16]

The problem facing the supporters of the objective test is to provide rational principles and a workable method for determining whether someone's life is 'worth living'. To this extent, their problem is the same as for those who support a subjective test. Whereas on the subjective test, however, what are evaluated are purely the various states of mind of the potential victim, on the objective test what is judged are whatever objective facts about the potential victim – possibly including, but not only, his subjective states – are deemed relevant to whether his life is 'worth living'. The question is, however: what facts? In this respect Rachels is as vague as Glover. Having and executing plans, setting and achieving ambitions, making the most of one's abilities, having a stream of memories that in some sense constitute an individual identity – all these and other factors are explicitly or implicitly claimed by Rachels and others to be elements in a biographical life. Since they contrast biographical lives with the absence of a life in the comatose, the severely handicapped, the senile, and so on, their definition of a 'life worth living' is partly negative: whatever it is that these unfortunate people 'obviously' do not have.

But general considerations such as these do not advance the debate very far. Exactly *what* factors, in *what* degrees (since most of them can be had in degrees, such as a stream of memories), and in *what* combinations? No answers to these crucial questions are forthcoming, and those medical ethicists of a more applied bent, who go so far as to propose 'quality of life tests' coated in a veneer of quasi-mathematical precision (see notes to chapter 3), tend either to resort to subjective assessments by potential victims themselves about what matter to them – on which there is virtually never anything like unanimous agreement – or to specious lists of factors that are eminently disputable and the subject of heated dispute among such writers.

It is here that consequentialism promises to come to the rescue, since it professes to offer a single, precise formula for reducing the various factors to a 'common currency' that can be weighed and calculated, as we saw in chapter 2. But there is, as we noted, no agreement as to what that common currency is. Is it the maximisation of preferences that matters, the satisfaction of interests, the fulfilling of desires, the having of certain kinds of feeling, the maximum balance of pleasure over pain as classical utilitarians assert, or something else? If Alan's life is not 'worth living', what *is* it about his death that is supposed to be objectively preferable to his staying alive? How is it identified? How is it calculated? The various candidates for ingredient X, the elusive object of maximisation, often come into conflict. Alan's death might spare him five years of severe pain, while at the same time depriving him of the chance to fulfil three important ambitions: to see his children grow up; to watch over the sale of his business; and to write the great American novel. Must both of these aspects of his life and proposed death be balanced against each other, and if so, how? Consequentialists retort that we frequently perform such balancing acts every day of our lives, or at least at important junctures, so it is churlish for their opponents to deny the legitimacy of such acts when consequentialists want to reduce them to an orderly procedure. The reply is that the opponent of consequentialism has no objection to the balancing of things that matter in life in an orderly way; what he objects to is any pretended attempt to reduce the things that matter to a *common currency*, a kind of 'moral dollar', against which everything that matters can be measured, and which gives the said balancing acts a spurious mathematical precision. We cannot in principle, for instance, calculate whether Alan's three ambitions are worth five years of severe pain, or whether five years of severe pain occasionally relieved by doses of morphine are worth the writing of a great American novel destined to make Alan a household name. To be sure, these examples are simple if not simplistic, but that is no help to the consequentialist; for as the example becomes more complex and subtle, the task of maximisation does not become *easier* – it becomes *harder*.

So far we have been considering the 'victim test', that part of the objective test which is applied to a person the 'worth' of whose life is under consideration. But there is still the other part to consider, the 'side effects test'. What effects will the life or death of the potential victim have on the world at large, in particular those most closely affected by what happens to him, such as his family, friends and those who care for him or give him medical attention? The consequentialist cannot in principle stop at considering the potential victim, because whatever ingredient X is which is to be maximised in respect of him is *also* going to be a factor in the lives of everyone else, the more so the greater the probability of their being affected by what happens to the potential victim. Furthermore, the fact that it is this or that person who experiences a loss or gain of X as the result of a given action, such as the killing of the potential victim, does not ultimately matter. All people have to be given equal consideration, so all that matters is the maximisation of an *impersonal* state of affairs – the greatest balance of X over not-X must be achieved *for the world as such*, not for any specific person. Let the X-chips fall wherever they may: what matters is that enough of them fall!

Much of what has been objected to in the victim test also applies to the side effects test, but further points should be noted. One concerns the ambiguity of the words 'harm' and benefit' as used by critics of DSL. Frequently they claim that what matters is whether the potential victim's death will be a benefit *to him*. Only then may he be killed. In other words, is the potential victim *better off dead*? Two related things need to be said about the idea of death as a benefit or harm to the person killed. The first is that it is incoherent. (How it is possible to talk about an idea that is incoherent is a puzzle that takes us beyond the scope of this discussion; suffice it to say that philosophers do it all the time!) When we say that a person benefits from something, we clearly imply that the person enjoys the benefit because he *exists* to enjoy it. You benefit from my returning the $10 I owed you; how could you do so if you did not exist? John benefits from having Jennifer help him study for the exam; how could he do so if he did not exist? If you die before I can return the $10 then you cannot benefit from my act; but your family might if I return it to them. But if a person must exist in order to receive all those things that can be benefits in the ordinary course of events, how can it be that death is an exception – that a person can *himself* benefit by being dead? If we could find exceptions to the rule, the case for death's being a benefit might be stronger, but it is hard to see what such an exception could be. One that is occasionally mentioned concerns a person's reputation: a convicted murderer may be given a posthumous pardon; a writer ignored during his lifetime might enjoy posthumous fame; so are these not benefits enjoyed by the dead? The reply is that there are natural, unforced readings of such cases that do not invoke the idea that the dead can enjoy benefits, which means that they do not support the opposing view. Certainly a person's *reputation* can exist long after his death, as can his legacy – so to say that a convicted murderer's name has been rehabilitated, or that a dead writer's fame has spread, does not imply that they themselves have benefited any more than if their estates are declared exempt from tax. There are parallel ways of dealing with other purported exceptions, which leaves us in the original position that the dead cannot themselves benefit from any-thing, including being dead.

The second point is that it is the incoherence of the idea that a person can himself be 'better off dead' that indicates how the side effects test comes into play. Any lingering thought that the possibility of someone's being 'better off dead' make sense trades on another meaning of the phrase – namely, that *other people* will be better off if the person is dead. This is largely what the side effects test is all about. Since what matters for the consequentialist is whether the world as such will be better if a person is dead, it is crucial to consider how other people fare if a person is dead. That is what is implied by writers such as Glover, who object that the potential victim's being dead does not prevent an assessment of whether that death was a benefit: all that needs to be compared are a world con-taining a stretch of consciousness in which there is, for instance, great pain and suffering, and a world without it. Hence the question for the consequentialist is: How does the world fare without this person? Now, radical consequentialists who deny any metaphysical or moral significance to the idea of personal identity (such as Derek Parfit) say that these states of consciousness can be broken down and evaluated as pure states of the world with no personal content to them.[17] On the whole, however, consequentialists writing in applied ethics have tried to preserve the im-portance of personal identity, so that for them a comparison of how the world is with and without the potential victim depends on summing up the various personal benefits and losses that derive from the presence or absence of that individual. Which comes down to the question of whether those who would be affected by the death of the potential victim would be better off without him.

Now, even to pose the question, Are we better off if X is dead? would seem to be so morally repugnant that one might think something had gone radically wrong with a debate that led to the raising of the question. To use the words of Elizabeth Anscombe that she applied to the moral theorist who thinks it an open question whether a judge is ever permitted to execute an innocent person (as consequentialists allow), someone who seriously thought it an open question whether the killing of an innocent person would be justified because others were better off without him, would show 'a corrupt mind' – they would not be someone worth arguing with.[18]

The reason the very thought that someone might be killed because others would be better off if he were dead is repugnant and offensive to

morality is that the protection of the innocent, if it means anything, requires that the desires, preferences and feelings of other people in respect
of that person must be reasonable. Consider the case of children, one of
the paradigm classes of the innocent. We all think, quite rightly, that children must be protected from harm, hence our outrage over such offences
as child abuse, child labour and parental neglect. How do children fare at
the hands of the consequentialist, in particular the preference utilitarian,
for whom all relevant preferences have to be taken into account in the
cost-benefit calculation before deciding upon the morality of an action?
The situation has recently been admirably outlined by Grant Gillett. He
points out the view of Peter Singer, who says:

> no one capable of understanding what is happening when a new-
> born baby is killed could feel threatened by a policy that gave less
> protection to the newborn than to adults. In this respect Bentham
> was right to describe infanticide as 'of a nature not to give the slight-
> est inquietude to the most timid imagination.' Once we are old enough
> to comprehend the policy, we are too old to be threatened by it.[19]

We see immediately what a view such as this means for children, explains
Gillett. If two children are competing for scarce health-care resources,
and one is handicapped and not as likely to achieve as high a 'net satisfaction' in life as the other, then on that score there would be a good reason
for discriminating against the handicapped child in favour of the healthy
one. Neither has any preference to go on living (in the sense of conscious
desire, which is what Singer and others deem relevant), so that is not part
of the calculation. More preferences would be satisfied in the case of the
healthy child as he grew up into maturity than in the case of the 'defective'
child, who may be able to look forward to a life filled with no more than
the satisfaction of bare necessities such as food and warmth. But what
about third-party preferences? The parents of the disabled child may want
her to go on living, so this counts for something. But so may the parents
of the healthy child, and this cancels out the others. Indeed, Singer claims
that we should not be led astray by the 'small, helpless, and – sometimes
– cute appearance of human infants'.[20] These feelings are, he says, irrational. What the parents of the disabled child ought to think is something
like (and here I am not quoting Singer but imagining a scenario):

> True, we are attached to our child – after all, she is cute and help-
> less. But this is irrational. Think of the drain on our time and re-

sources having to care for the child. Think of all the preferences she will never have, and hence never satisfy, compared to those of Mr and Mrs X's healthy child, who can go on to live a normal, productive life. And anyway, we can replace her with another child one day, whom we have no reason to think will also be handicapped.

Hence they should give way and forego the health care they wanted. And we can see how the health-care workers may themselves go through parallel reasoning, saying, for instance: 'On balance our preference is to help the healthy child, given the burden to us of looking after the disabled child, which may last for many years and not be very satisfying to us or to the child itself, in view of the meagre sort of existence which lies ahead for her.'

There are, of course, numerous ways in which third parties could think about the question of whether the handicapped child's life was 'not worth living'; all sorts of preferences need to be taken into account. But the point that all such reasonings have in common is that they are reasonings by third parties about the life of an innocent who does not herself have any preferences about her life, being an infant incapable of a conscious desire to go on living. (As Glover claims, 'a baby cannot want to escape from death any more than he can want to escape the fate of being a chartered accountant when he grows up. He has no idea of either.'[21]) As Gillett puts it, the 'worth' of children 'is largely going to be determined by the way that other significant moral agents value them', that is, agents who themselves have conscious preferences. A child will have some intrinsic 'worth', being able to feel pain and pleasure and to have certain basic wants met. But these are relatively insignificant in the total consequentialist calculation of preferences or other ingredients relevant to maximisation.

If this is how the side effects test of a 'life worth living' is to be implemented, however, why could it not, asks Gillett, be used to license, say, child abuse?[22] We know that for the consequentialist, 'no special regard attaches to the lives of small infants, although they might derive moral value from the preferences of their parents'.[23] Now, suppose a child is resented and unwanted by her parents, who do not even possess the 'irrational' feelings aroused by the sight of her 'helpless and cute appearance'. The child, then, has 'negative value' for the parents. Why, for the consequentialist, would they not be permitted to abuse and neglect her? After all, their conscious preferences would have to override the pain of the child, which, we are assured by Singer, would be no greater in many circumstances than that of a small, furry animal. Indeed, given that the child has negative value for the parents, what is to stop them killing her? Surely this could satisfy many preferences: to be free of a burden, to save money, time and energy, to be able to do other things like go on a holiday. The only conceivable restraining factor would be the preferences of other people, but then they need never know. Or the child might be valued by hardly anyone, as is the case in many run-down and deserted orphanages across the world. Or the child might be positively disvalued by almost everyone, especially if she were severely handicapped. If the preferences of third parties are what they are, then they must be taken into account as long as they are not illogical, inconsistent, based on irrelevant considerations like a cute appearance, and so on.

Now if all this seems repugnant to our basic sense of right and wrong, it is for good reason. On the traditional view of morality, when the life of an innocent person is at stake, the desires of third parties are of secondary importance and must conform to the primary principle that the right to life of the innocent is inviolable. Desires evoked by threats or duress, generated by lack of concern, other priorities, self-interest real or imaginary – all of these are per se unreasonable if they in any way form part of a process of reasoning that seeks to justify the killing of the innocent or other actions that constitute a direct attack upon an innocent's well-being, such as child abuse. On the traditional view, the life and well-being of the innocent child cries out for protection. On the consequentialist view espoused by critics of DSL, it has no intrinsic moral worth: whatever value it has is *extrinsic* and determined in large part by the desires, preferences and interests of others. Where the critic comes down in favour of the wrongness of killing the innocent, it may be because the killing would cause fear in others; or because it would undermine the legal system; or because it would ignore the relevant preferences of those most closely affected by the killing; or because it would generate communal outrage; but never because it would be, quite simply, the taking of innocent human life.

But surely, it might be objected, the critics of DSL do not take the desires and preferences of third parties at face value? The reply is that they do, although they sometimes equivocate. The official consequentialist view seems to be that there is no objective standpoint from which the moral theorist can pronounce that this or that preference is unreasonable. In the words of Bernard Williams, 'modern utilitarianism is supposed to be a system neutral between the preferences that people actually have'.[24] A preference might be inconsistent with other preferences held by the agent, it might not make sense, it might be vague – but in and of itself it is simply a preference, a reflection of the state of mind of the agent, and not to be judged by some standard of reasonableness other than whether it accords with the best moral theory. And this says, for the consequentialist (or more particularly, the preference utilitarian), that all preferences go into the melting pot, with no preference to count for more than any other (all other things being equal); more generally, there must be 'equal consideration of interests', as Singer argues.

On the other hand, consequentialists sometimes baulk at the idea that every preference must be given equal weight (other things being equal), no matter how unreasonable some preferences might be. Hence Singer: 'It may *occasionally* be right to prevent people from making choices that are *obviously* not rationally based and that we can be *sure* they will later regret'[25] (my emphasis). Note the many caveats: it must be obvious that the choice is unreasonable; we must be sure the agent will later regret their choice; and even then, we may override that choice only occasionally. Clearly there is a tension here, admirably explained by Williams when he says: 'To legislate them [some preferences] out is not to pursue people's happiness, but to remodel the world towards forms of "happiness" more amenable to utilitarian ways of thought. But if they are not to be legislated out, then utilitarianism has got to co-exist with them, and it is not clear how it does that.'[26]

This tension is exposed when critics of DSL such as Singer discuss the question of euthanasia, in particular the killing of 'defective' children (which I will discuss in chapter 2 of *Applied Ethics*). Sometimes Singer speaks as if the preferences of parents with respect to their disabled children should be taken at face value, and at others that their preferences must be reasonable. Unfortunately, however, on neither view does the life of the innocent child enjoy much protection. If parental preferences must be taken at face value, then just as in the case of child abuse mentioned above, if the parents disvalue their child, find caring for her a burden, are distressed by her suffering, and so on, then if they prefer to have it killed that preference should be respected, on the assumption (among others) that they are the people most closely affected by the decision and that there are no voices speaking up for the child substantial enough to outweigh what the parents want. On the other hand, if parental preferences must be reasonable, nowhere does Singer suggest that they must be reasonable vis-à-vis *the child*, only that they be reasonable by conforming to the overall consequentialist calculation of costs and benefits. Hence, he asserts, if parents have a haemophiliac child, who is not severely handicapped but does need special care and attention, the reasonableness constraint does not lead to the conclusion, consistent with DSL, that the parents are bound to look after that child no matter the extra effort involved. All it means is that the parents might reasonably choose to 'replace' the child with a *healthier* one! Either way, then, the haemophiliac child's own life does not have the sort of security that a moral system ought to provide. Any value the child has is determined not by her intrinsic status as an innocent human being, but by her place in the overall calculation of preferences. Needless to say, such a place makes the child's life highly susceptible to the 'slings and arrows of outrageous fortune'.

The side effects test of whether a life is 'worth living', then, is as untenable as any other test, including the subjective test and the victim test. All such tests have innumerable conceptual flaws and they all, in one way or another, issue in conclusions that deny the most basic protection to the most vulnerable members of society – the young, the sick, the disabled, the elderly, the comatose, and many others besides. If, as traditional morality holds, it is a mark of a civilised society that it protects the innocent – if, indeed, *being* an innocent has any claim whatever on our moral sense – then a society that based its attitude to human life of the concept of a 'life worth living' could never call itself civilised.

Some final points; and another objection

Before leaving the idea of a 'life worth living', some concluding points should be made. One concerns a serious objection to the very possibility of a test in this regard. Recall that the test, whether or not it combines both a subjective and an objective element, fundamentally involves as assessment of people's preferences: whether the potential victim prefers to go on living (reasonably or not as the case may be), or whether other people, such as parents, relatives, friends and carers, prefer that the potential victim should die (again, reasonably or not). Now, people's preferences, as with their moral views in general, are heavily influenced by the moral theory that is prevalent in a society. If we live in a society in which human life is regarded as being of ultimate value, then people will not merely feel more secure than in a society in which it was not, but their *actual moral opinions* will tend to conform to that standard and they will, on the whole, treat each other with the respect that the doctrine of the sanctity of life demands. And if they do not they will, on the whole, know their behaviour is wrong and feel appropriate remorse and guilt. However, in a society in which life is not of ultimate value but can be sacrificed for the sake of other interests, such as social cost, personal discomfort, burdensomeness, inability to cope in general, and the satisfaction of plans and projects that are incompatible with the existence of a certain person, not only will people feel less secure but the prevailing morality will *make* people less secure, because preferences will tend to accord with that morality. In other words, a person who conformed to the dominant view that human life had ultimate value would *act* in such a way that, for him, life had ultimate value. But if the dominant morality held that sometimes life might not be 'worth living', he would act in such a way that, for him, in some circumstances, life – whether his own or another's, say his child's or elderly parent's – was not 'worth living'.

This means the consequentialist critic of DSL has a problem. What he wants – and needs – is an impartial test of the value of a given life, uninfluenced by personal prejudice and bias, most importantly *his own*. If his own personal views actually *interfered* with the deliberations of others, how could he carry out an impartial test of what everyone wanted, all things considered? Consequentialism prides itself on being – so its supporters claim – *scientific*, not just in the broad sense defined in chapter 1, but in the narrow sense of being very much like a natural science in its methods and procedure. Now it would be highly *un*scientific for an experimenter in, say, chemistry, to let his own expectations of what he will find interfere with the results of his experiment – this would be called 'observer interference' and would effectively nullify the results he obtained. The question is: How is the consequentialist test any more free of a similar kind of observer interference? In the moral case, the observers or experimenters are any of us who conduct the 'ethical experiment' of testing whether someone's life is 'worth living'. Suppose we are consequentialists and conduct this test. It may be that we are directly involved in a real-life case. Or we may be discussing a real-life case amongst ourselves, or trying to work out the answer on our own. But the observer interference occurs, albeit in a more oblique way, even if we are doing no more than discussing or trying personally to solve a hypothetical case, whether as philosophers or as laymen. The same point applies: once the *very question*, Is X's life worth living?, is considered a legitimate question in a society, then not only will certain people feel less secure, but they will *be* less secure because they will tend to conform their moral viewpoint to the prevailing one and so begin to wonder whether, in fact, their lives are not 'worth living'; and only by a miracle would no one actually *come to think* that this was the case, say because they were a burden to others. Third parties will also tend to accord with the standard set by society (handed down by moral philosophers) and tend to *acquire* beliefs, in some cases, that some people's lives are not 'worth living', hence *preferences* that such people not go on living.

Note that the point is not that in a consequentialist society some innocent people will inevitably be *pressured* to decide that they are 'better off dead' or rather that others are better off without them. No doubt this is true, but my point is a conceptual, not a pragmatic one: in a truly consequentialist society, many people will *by definition* have the sorts of preferences that make their or other people's lives not 'worth living', just as the theory says some lives are to be characterised. Once potential victims and/or third parties begin to acquire the very preferences whose existence determines the answer to the initial question, it *becomes true* that the lives of certain people will, in some cases, not be 'worth living'. So how is the 'ethical experiment' impartial, unbiased and free from observer interference? On the contrary, consequentialism turns out to be a very powerful theory indeed, because merely by holding it, its supporters can generate the very results the theory says they should obtain. In other words, the consequentialist is in the remarkable position of being able to *confirm* his theory just by *holding* it. However, if this would be bad chemistry it would also be bad moral science, and the results of the experiment in both cases should be regarded as null and void.

The only response the consequentialist is apparently able to make to this conceptual objection is to appeal to the so-called 'levels thesis' made famous by R. M. Hare and adopted by Singer and others. They distinguish between two 'levels' of moral thinking, the 'critical' and the 'intuitive'. At the intuitive level, they argue, it is all right to have beliefs that encapsulate at least some of the principles of traditional morality, such as respect for rights. But when such principles yield conclusions at odds with the consequentialist calculus, then the thinking should move to the critical level, at which one adopts the standpoint of the impartial observer, looking at how the costs and benefits add up overall. The implication, then, would be that the alleged observer interference is prevented at the intuitive level since people are not supposed to put consequentialist questions at that level. Let them talk about rights, and respect for life, and so on, and no one will be made less secure.

A good example of the way this idea works relates to autonomy. Now, although the role of autonomy is misunderstood and exaggerated in modern society (we saw a hint of this earlier in the chapter, and I will pursue it in chapter 2 of *Applied Ethics*), the fact is that most people think they have a say in whether they live or die, perhaps a decisive one. They think respect for autonomy has its own special moral value (and understood correctly, it does). For the consequentialist, however, this is not the case: a person's own preferences and decisions are just one ingredient in the overall assessment of costs and benefits. But it everyone thought this way, people would live in great fear of their preferences' being overridden if the 'greater good' required it. So, says Singer, 'utilitarians may encourage people to adopt, in their daily lives, principles that will in almost all cases lead to better consequences when followed than any alternative action. The principle of respect for autonomy would be a prime example of such a principle.'[27] Let them *think* autonomy was an 'independent moral principle', he says – but if at the 'critical level' of moral evaluation it turns out that a person's preferences should be overridden, society should be so arranged that this can happen without an overall breakdown in mutual trust and confidence.

I have only suggested a way in which the 'levels' thesis might be used to combat the charge of observer interference, but it is not clear that all consequentialists would support such a way of thinking. The levels thesis, for that matter, is obscure in its own right, and to the extent that anyone other than consequentialists has been able to make any sense of it, it has repugnant implications as well as only limited application to the charge of observer interference. First, it has repugnant implications to the extent that it countenances a kind of moral schizophrenia in society, in which a consequentialist elite stands guard over the rest of us, allowing us to persist in our use of traditional ('intuitive') moral concepts, while carefully 'inculcating' (to use the consequentialists' own term) a disposition to abandon those concepts only when they lead to conflicts with the calculus of maximisation. Or perhaps the elite *redefines* our traditional concepts, so we think we are still using them even when we use them to make decisions completely at odds with their traditional application. Or perhaps they do not inculcate any dispositions, but so arrange social institutions that conflicts are inevitably resolved in a consequentialist way even while people still make personal use of the traditional concepts. In any case, such arrangements smack of Orwellian ideological tyranny, of 'doublethink' and 'Newspeak'. And even if the payoff of having such a society is that fewer people's lives are not 'worth living' than would be the case if everyone was an explicit consequentialist, the observer interference would still suffice to nullify the results of the 'value of life' test as applied in a whole range of situations. Some lucky people might not cease to value their lives; many others would not be so fortunate, if consequentialism at the 'critical' level were to have any application at all to real-life situations.[28]

A final objection to DSL that should briefly be mentioned is the contention that its defenders are confused over just what the status of the phrase 'life worth living' really is. Is the phrase meaningless? Or is it meaningful but simply inapplicable in a correct morality? If meaningless, what about its meaningful application to, say, animals, where we agree that in some cases an animal can be in such pain that it would be better off dead? And if inapplicable, what about our common use of the phrase and our agreement over its use? Since defenders of DSL often appeal to our basic moral sense that certain principles such as the sanctity of life are absolute and inviolable, shouldn't they pay some heed to our sense that sometimes, say in the case of someone suffering unbearably in body or mind, a person's life might not be 'worth living'?

The reply to this objection has several parts. First, whatever the disagreement among defenders of DSL, the proper attitude is that the concept of a life 'worth living' is incoherent if one pretends to analyse it in consequentialist terms, because of the very incoherence of the consequentialist calculus based on a single unit of moral currency. Second, if it is proposed to interpret it in a freer, less pseudo-scientific way, the concept may be meaningful but will still be inapplicable: life is a fundamental good and as such must not be directly attacked. As for the case of animals, this must be left to chapter 3 of *Applied Ethics*, but it can be said in anticipation that the existence of crucial differences between humans and animals means that even if an animal may sometimes be better off dead, it by no means follows that a human can ever be. Third, there are indeed respectable senses in which we all use the phrase 'life worth living', but these uses do not belong to some unacceptable moral theory. We might use the term to express profound regret ('I've upset her so much, my life isn't worth living'), a sense of urgent obligation ('If I don't make sure that letter is delivered on time, my life won't be worth living'), and even deep depression, where 'My life isn't worth living' is practically equivalent to 'Woe is me!', and often connotes little more than morbid self-pity. One can easily think of other cases; but the point is, if someone were to overhear such utterances in circumstances like those just suggested, and were then to kill the person who said – no doubt sincerely at the time – that his life was not worth living, the only appropriate response would be a charge of murder.

4.4   Persons and Human Beings

The final matter to be dealt with in this chapter concerns an important and frequently pronounced charge made by opponents of DSL against its defenders. The charge was made famous by Peter Singer and is levelled by virtually all the followers of Singerian bioethics. It is that defenders of DSL are, in his words, 'speciesist'. They accord an unwarranted special moral status to human beings simply because they are member of a certain biological species. This, charge Singerians, is as much a prejudice as claiming a special moral status for certain human beings because of their skin colour, sex, or religion. In Singer's words, '[t]o give preference to the life of a being simply because that being is a member of our species would put us in the same position as racists who give preference to members of their race'.[29] Much of the debate over speciesism occurs in the context of issues such as abortion, euthanasia, and our treatment of animals, where the question of the moral status of human beings in specific circumstances, or of other kinds of being, is the main concern. Hence a very abstract outline of what is wrong with the Singerian approach will be presented here, with only passing mention of particular cases; in *Applied Ethics* we will look at those cases in greater depth.

There is, claim Singerians, nothing morally special about belonging to a certain species. The reason is that species membership is a 'morally irrelevant characteristic' in assessing how a being should be treated. What *does* matter, on the other hand, are a being's *actual* (though not necessarily *actuated*) characteristics. Can it feel pain? Can it have desires? Is it conscious? Is it self-conscious? These are not, of course, the only characteristics the opponent of DSL might appeal to, but they are the ones that reflection suggests are morally relevant. The moral status of a being, it is asserted, must depend on its mental life. It is impossible, for instance, to wrong a potato by digging it up out of its natural habitat, tearing off its skin, cutting it to pieces and dropping it into a pot of boiling water. But why not, if the very same thing done to a five-year-old child would be a horrendous crime, and if done to a pig would at least raise questions as to whether the actions were performed cruelly, caused unnecessary suffering, and so on, with some people even saying it would be a crime against the pig in any circumstances? The point is not at this moment to assess whether eating animals is wrong, only to bring into relief the fact that we all believe, and rightly so, that if it is wrong to treat a being in a certain way this must be because there is *something* that is true of that being which makes the treatment in question immoral.

For the consequentialist, what must be true of a being for it to have moral status is whether it possesses properties ranging across a spectrum from basic sentience (the capacity to feel pleasure and pain), through various kinds of awareness and other mental activity (increasing in complexity), right up to the full self-consciousness displayed by adult human beings (such as middle-aged male philosophers). Since humans are not the only beings who are sentient or who have other kinds of awareness, it is argued that we must extend our sphere of moral concern beyond our own species to others; it would be mere prejudice not to do so. But there is another, equally important strand to the argument. The Singerian singles out certain properties as being of special moral value, those that make a being a 'person'. To be a person is to be self-conscious, aware of oneself as having an identity through time, having plans and projects, desires and interests to be satisfied. John Locke famously defined a person as 'a thinking intelligent being that has reason and reflection and can consider itself as itself, the same thinking thing, in different times and places'.[30] Singer accepts this definition and claims that persons have the greatest moral value of all beings.

Now, in ordinary usage we take 'person' to be equivalent to 'human being'. But Singer wants to put the term to specialised use; hence for the sake of clarity let us use the italicised term *person* to designate those beings who satisfy the Lockean definition, and *personism* for the claim that *persons* have the greatest moral value, with the corollary that a *person* need not be a human being, and a human being need not be a *person*. Singer and other *personists* hold that there might be, for instance, a race of extraterrestrial aliens who exhibited the characteristics of *persons*, and more importantly that some animals, such as apes, might be *persons*. Further, some human beings, for example the very young, the severely mentally disabled, the very old and the comatose, might not be *persons*.[31]

While many theorists have taken *personism* to be obviously correct, concluding that any moral position that gives special status to human beings simply because they are human is speciesist, others have criticised it, though for reasons that are often not persuasive. The appeal to ordinary usage, for instance, will not do. It may be that our use of the term 'person' to denote human beings is just an embodiment of our speciesist prejudices. To assert that it is fanciful to suppose we could ever come across alien creatures who had reason, reflection and self-consciousness is rash; even if it is at least *conceivable*, then the concept of a *person* must be distinct from that of a person in the sense of human being. Again, to say that *personism* is built on a false theory of personhood, namely Locke's, while true, is not quite to the point. Locke's theory contains truth as well as falsehood, and the anti-Lockean risks throwing out the baby with the bathwater. Locke's idea of personhood is, to put it crudely, the same as our idea of *personality*. For Locke, what makes Young Abe and President Lincoln the same person is that they are 'psychologically continuous' – they share a mental history or stream of consciousness that constitutes a recognisable personality. Now, this central aspect of Locke's theory (which is of course much more elaborate than anything I can sketch here) is indeed false, implying among other things that radical changes in personality (induced, say, by drugs, illness or changes in lifestyle) can *literally* turn one person into another. But whatever the errors of Locke's (and Lockean) theories of personhood, it is not clear that a Singerian ethic must rely on such a theory in all its detail in order to develop the moral position of *personism*. It is the basic definition of 'person' in terms of mental capacities that Singer and others draw from Locke and then put to moral use. Our main concern is whether, even if we assume that Locke's definition embodies an important truth – and irrespective of the details of his entire theory – that truth can be put to ethical work in the way that Singer and others want.

What *personism* does, then, is to place overriding emphasis, when assessing the moral status of a thing, on its psychological characteristics. And surely we should agree? If we believe that human beings have special moral status there must, as was argued, be something true of them that makes it so, and that something cannot merely be the presence of a certain kind of DNA. Nor can it be the presence alone of certain biological instincts, patterns of behaviour, and so on, that humans share with the rest of the animal kingdom. Anyone who values human life will inevitably focus on the presence of such things as reason, reflection and self-consciousness as somehow crucially relevant to moral status, and will say that if animals have moral status as well it will be to the extent that they partake of such characteristics. One could, of course, revere all life equally, in a quasi-Buddhist way, but such a position winds up in all sorts of incoherences and absurdities. Distinctions and gradations have to be made, and they are made on both sides of the *personist* debate. What all sides agree on is that the sorts of features of personhood that impressed Locke are just the ones that play a central role in assessing the moral worth of something, or at least in determining what sorts of thing have the *highest* status.

Granted this agreement, however, the idea that psychological characteristics are central to moral status has widely divergent interpretations. According to traditional morality, which Singer repeatedly derides, protection must be accorded to, for instance, the young, the sick, the sleeping, the drugged, and so on. And Singer, for the most part, agrees that such protection is necessary. But when we look at things from a *personist* perspective, we run into problems. After all, a sleeping man is not conscious, and so ipso facto not *self*-conscious; nor is someone whose mind is benumbed with drugs. A one-day old baby might be conscious of its environment, able to have sensations, and have a rudimentary concept of itself, but it is arguably not fully self-conscious, in the sense explained by Singer and also by Michael Tooley, whom he follows in these matters – that is, capable of seeing itself as a being with plans and projects, a future in which to satisfy its desires, and the like. Such human beings are, it seems, non-*persons*, even if, as human beings, we call them persons in the ordinary sense. Does this mean they do not have any special moral status? Does this mean they are no more than mere ingredients in the consequentialist equation, capable of being sacrificed for the sake of maximising overall benefit? One might think Singer did not believe so, and yet when it comes to babies, he has this to say: 'Killing a snail or a day-old infant does not thwart any desires of this kind [for the future], because snails and newborn infants are incapable of having such desires.'[32] So it looks like newborn babies are in the same moral category as snails as far as killing *per se* is concerned (leaving aside incidental moral factors such as the fact that the baby can feel pain and the snail not, which would make the painful killing of a day-old baby worse than the killing of a snail) – and this because of Singer's adherence to *personism*. In itself this ought to be evidence of what Anscombe calls a depraved mind, and so a *reductio ad absurdum* of the theory. But we need to dig deeper.

For a start, a central plank of the Singerian position is the moral irrelevance of *potentiality* as distinct from actuality. Traditionally, this distinction is very important. For instance, an actual member of civil society has certain rights and duties: the right to vote, the duty to obey the law, and so on. A five-year-old child is not an actual member of civil society. On the other hand, he is a *potential* member of civil society, and this entails his possession of other rights and duties, such as the right to be educated in a way that will help him become a responsible and law-abiding member of civil society, and the duty to heed his teachers and parents in matters related to such education (as in other matters). At a more basic level, the child has the right to be fed, kept healthy and physically protected so that he can grow up into an adult who will be, among other things, a member of civil society. Potentiality, then, brings its own rights and duties, those that are *proper* to the person (in the ordinary sense of 'person') at a given stage of development.

But potentiality as such is conceptually separate from rights and duties, and from morality altogether. A hydrogen atom is a potential part of a molecule of water. A brown table is potentially green, in the sense that a coat of paint will make it green. A lump of clay is a potential statue – sculpting will turn it into one. A sapling is a potential tree, and a tadpole a potential frog. Potentiality is a *metaphysical* concept and refers, in its broadest sense, to the ability of a thing, given the *kind* of thing it is, to have certain properties, enter into certain relations, and even turn into something else altogether – everyone of us is a potential corpse, and the plum tree in my neighbour's garden is potential firewood. On the other hand, no helium atom is ever a potential part of a water molecule, and a dog is not a potential frog. The *kind* of thing an entity is determines its potentialities.

Returning now to the ethical question, recall that for the *personist* all that matters, as far as the value of human life is concerned, are actual moral characteristics, not potential ones. Hence Singer's disregard for the *kind* to which a thing belongs, to the extent that this involves the idea that some members of the kind, for one reason or another, may not have the *actual* characteristics of typical, normally functioning members of that kind. For Singer, it is almost a kind of moral superstition to think that simply being in the kind confers moral status, if the being in question does not also *display* the typical characteristics of the kind's mature members. That is why *persons* matter, but persons do not: members of the kind *'person'* have, by definition, a set of actual moral characteristics that confer moral status, namely self-consciousness, rationality, and related properties. But there is a problem. Every adult human being needs sleep, including middle-aged male philosophers. Do these *persons* cease to have the rights of *persons* when they are asleep? It would be a bizarre consequence of Singer's theory if they did, and indeed he tries to resist the implication. In his essay 'On Being Silenced in Germany',[33] where he responds to this and other charges made by thousands of disabled people (and others) who have protested around the world at his public lectures, he says that his views 'cannot be a threat to anyone who is capable of wanting to go on living, or even of understanding that his or her life might be threatened'. Is a sleeping person capable, *while asleep*, of wanting to go on living? If he is not even conscious while asleep, how could he want anything, at least on a theory that says only actual characteristics matter? Does a sleeping person want food? If not, how could he want anything else? Singer seems to realize this problem, and later in the very same article makes an alteration: it is not being 'capable of wanting to go on living' that confers protection; rather, those who need not feel threatened by his proposals are 'anyone who is, or ever has been, even minimally aware of the fact that he or she has a possible future life that could be threatened'. As Jacqueline Laing puts it in her discussion of Singer, the sleeping person is protected, on this more verbose formulation, because prior to falling asleep he 'lays claim' to his life; his 'minimal awareness' is a kind of ethical insurance policy that protects him while asleep, enabling him to get through the night to the next day of full, waking *personhood*.

On closer inspection, however, it cannot be 'awareness of a future life' that gives protection for Singer, since otherwise an irreversibly comatose person would be protected too, since he was *once* aware of and concerned for his future life. But Singer believes the irreversibly comatose are not *persons* and can be killed if their death is 'for the best'. So what *does* protect the sleeping *person*, the drugged *person*, the temporarily insane *person*? It must, after all, be *potentiality* – the potential that the *person* has of regaining his *personhood* under the right circumstances. So whereas it seemed that potential was, for Singer, morally irrelevant, it now appears that the concept is doing very important moral work indeed, namely protecting the very beings he thinks have the highest moral status. (Not, as we saw earlier, that they too mightn't be permissibly killed, according to Singer, if their autonomy counted for less in the calculus than the preferences of others.) But then if potential is relevant after all, Singer has no ground whatsoever for rejecting the appeal to it by defenders of traditional morality who disagree with him that valuing the life of every human being equally reveals 'a morally indefensible preference for members of our own species'.[34]

Unless, that is, anti-*personists* (as Jenny Teichman aptly calls them, humanists) can be shown to use the concept of potentiality in an illegitimate way. We can be assisted in fleshing out the notion of potentiality as applied to human life by means of a thought experiment. Consider a human being, Peter, who is a *perpetual prisoner*. Peter was born in a room and has lived in that room ever since, being fed through a slit in the door. The room is wonderfully equipped to enable him, if he wants, to clean up, dispose of waste, and so on. If he needs anything, he can make a request by pushing some buttons. But he is never allowed out of the room. Although physically mature and strong, he cannot break out. Nor has he any prospect of escape, since it turns out that no one remembers the combination to the lock on the door, and the room is otherwise impregnable. Peter's physiological needs are met, but otherwise his life is tedious and frustrating, for obvious reasons. (Note that this case is but an extrapolation from terrible cases of child neglect that have in fact occurred.)

Is Peter, the perpetual prisoner, free? Certainly he can walk about in his room and do various other things, but clearly he is no more free than a bird in a cage. Does he, however, have the *right* to be free? Surely he does, even though, as a matter of fact, he is only potentially free. The potentiality exists even if we can predict with certainty that he never will leave that room. Peter, who is only potentially free, has the right to liberty. And yet one of Singer's principal arguments against the moral relevance of potentiality is that we cannot infer from the fact that something is a potential X that it has the rights of an X. There is, he says, no 'rule' allowing such an inference. After all, he adds, a prince is a potential king but does not have the rights of a king, and dropping a live chicken into boiling water is worse than doing so to an egg.[35]

What has gone wrong here? It seems that we can infer that Peter has the rights of a free man from the fact that he is potentially free, that only circumstance is keeping him imprisoned. Distinctions need to be made but Singer does not make them. A comatose person does not have the right to vote, nor does a one-year-old child. Someone who is insane does not have the right to fly an aeroplane. A seven-year-old does not have a right to join the army. Many rights belong to and are exercisable only by mature human beings in full possession of their faculties. People who are only potentially mature, or potentially rational, and so on, will not have those rights. To that extent Singer is obviously correct. But this is not the point he is trying to make. Americans are fond of pointing out the opportunities available in their country by boasting that every American is a potential president. But that does not mean they all *presently* have the right to sit in the Oval Office. On the other hand, there are many rights they *do* have as a direct consequence of being potential presidents: to run for public office; to publicise their campaigns, if they undertake any; to have a share in any public funds available for such campaigns; to hire people to help them; and so on. In a democracy, it is a good (though not obligatory) thing for people of ability to seek public office. Hence it is also a good thing for them to be able to exercise their *potential* for winning office by doing the things that conduce to satisfying that objective. That does not mean it would be good for someone to lie or cheat in order to win office: for one thing this would violate the Principle of Double Effect, and furthermore, lying and cheating are not genuine exercises of potential in the sense that is of concern here. We are all potential liars, but we do not have the right to lie. The genuine exercise of potential involves the fulfilling of a thing's nature by doing what is good for it, and attacking a good such as truth is a perversion of rational being's nature, not a fulfilment of it.

Peter, then, has the right to do what fulfils his nature, what is good for him, even though it may be guaranteed that he will never actually fulfil that nature. This is because of the *kind* of thing he is, a kind whose mature, normally functioning members have the capacity freely to pursue their lives. We cannot *begin* to understand what Peter's right to freedom consists in if we do not already have a grasp of the kind of thing he is. How do we *know* whether freedom would be good for him? Perhaps, for all we know, he is fulfilled living in the confines of his room, where his physical needs are catered for. How do we know whether he needs anything more than that? After all, it is not as though we have ever *seen* him strolling through the park smelling the flowers, driving a car, running, reading books, raising a family, playing games, and so on. In order to know what is good for him, and hence what his rights are, how he ought to be allowed to live, we have to know what *sort* of thing he is. And that knowledge will, by its very nature, take us beyond the individual before us to an examination of the characteristics he shares with beings who are similar to him. It is probably this sort of reasoning that once led explorers to realize that the members of primitive tribes they discovered were not after all sub-human animals, but normal human beings like them. They could not have done that without having a grasp of what makes a human being a human being, what the *kind* 'human being' signifies.

Just as Peter may be in the unfortunate situation of never being able to fulfil his potential, so many other human beings are in the same predicament. Some are in irreversible comas, or lacking in most of their brain matter, or basic motor skills. Some are very old and barely able to remember their names, some are insane and likely to stay insane, some are unlikely ever to get beyond simple arithmetic. Some spend most of their lives in a drunken or drug-induced stupor and are virtually guaranteed never to be rehabilitated. Some are extremely young and unable to communicate any of their wants and needs. Some barely live for a few hours. Some never see the light of day. In fact, very few people do indeed fulfil their human potential. Most lives are lacking in something that is good for us to have as human beings. Most lives are diminished in some sense. How does potentiality fit into all of this?

Not all potentialities are the same. The potential of a child to become an adult is different from the potential of a comatose person to recover consciousness. All a child needs is time and maintenance (food, physical protection, and so on), whereas a comatose person needs more than this – he needs repair. Time and maintenance are *good* for the child, and repair would be *good* for the comatose person. And these objective facts have nothing to do with the *prospects* of either. Even if a sick person survived the death of the last doctor on earth, it would still be good for him to be healthy. (I owe this example to Helen Watt.) And yet neither the child, if young enough, nor the comatose person, would be *persons* in Singer's and Tooley's sense. But the sorts of characteristics Singer and Tooley emphasise are, as was said earlier, crucial, though not in the sense they advocate. Rationality and self-consciousness – actually displayed – are properties of the mature, normally functioning member of the species *homo sapiens*. Were the child or the comatose person to be rational and self-conscious in the sense of actually exercising those capacities, they would be capable of recognising what was good for them by the very use of those capacities, even if they were otherwise unintelligent or incapable of following an ethical argument. They would have the *functioning equipment* to know what is good for them and, being free creatures able to choose to pursue what is good for them, they would have the right to make such choices.

But when Aristotle said 'man is a rational animal', he was not making a statement about only those mature, normally functioning members of humankind, when they are awake, and not drugged, and not insane, and thinking clearly, and forming plans, and making choices about what sort of life to live. He was defining the *essence* of humankind, in other words, he was telling us what human nature is, and hence what *every* human being is, simply by being a member of humankind. And it is a fundamental principle of classification, adhered to throughout the ages right down to our own, that kinds of living thing are defined by the properties of their paradigmatic, normal members, whether or not *every* member of the kind has those properties. (As Jenny Teichman puts it, all cattle are mammals – even the bulls. Of course the definition of *mammal* involves reference to methods of reproduction, so bulls are not abnormal, it is just that they do not share the relevant defining properties; but they are mammals nevertheless.) Why, then, should being immature or damaged (for instance) detract from the moral status of certain human beings if they are, by their very nature, every bit as human as their mature, normal fellows? There may indeed be a phenomenon that some theorists have called moral luck, but it would surely be a defect in any ethical system if it entailed that those human beings who by dint of circumstance are not yet fully developed, or injured, or old, should be subject to a kind of moral bad luck so grotesque as to deprive them of the protection routinely given to those of their conspecifics who are fortunate enough to be in full possession of rationality and self-consciousness. Here we can see the irony in Singer's claim that extending protection to all human beings *because* of the kind of thing they are involves a 'morally indefensible prejudice'; on the contrary, it is the *personist* who displays a prejudice in favour of the normal and the mature and against the disabled or immature. There is a further irony. It is a fundamental tenet of traditional morality that the most vulnerable members of society do not deserve *less* moral protection than everyone else; rather, they deserve *more*, precisely because of their vulnerability. It is difficult to see how a society that gave up this tenet could continue to call itself civilised.

As was said above, this has only been an abstract sketch of the case against *personism*. It has been argued that while characteristics such as rationality and self-consciousness define what it is to be a human being and undergird human rights, *all* humans participate in that moral protection by virtue of being what they are essentially, irrespective of the contingent circumstances in which they may find themselves. Some of us might only be potential *persons*, but we are all still actual persons, because we are human beings. As such we all have an interest in living and in doing whatever we are capable of to fulfil our natures, even if we cannot do everything. Whether there are other kinds of being who deserve similar protection will be examined in the companion volume, when we look at the animals issue. And the way in which traditional morality handles specific questions concerning human life also needs more detailed examination. It is to these that we turn in *Applied Ethics*.

Notes and Further Reading

Chapter 1

1 A useful little book criticising scepticism in ethics and arguing that we can know what is objectively right and wrong is Renford Bambrough, *Moral Scepticism and Moral Knowledge* (London: Routledge, 1981).

2 David Hume, *Treatise of Human Nature* III.I.I; ed. L. A. Selby-Bigge (Oxford: Oxford University Press, 1978; 2nd edn), p. 469.

3 For criticisms of the fact–value distinction, see P. Foot, 'Moral Beliefs', *Proceedings of the Aristotelian Society* 59 (1958–9), reprinted in her *Virtues and Vices* (Oxford: Blackwell, 1978), ch. 8; G. E. M. Anscombe, 'Brute Facts', in her *Ethics, Religion and Politics: Philosophical Papers,* vol. III (Oxford: Blackwell, 1981), pp. 22–5; B. Williams, *Morality* (Cambridge: Cambridge University Press, 1972), pp. 52–61 and *Ethics and the Limits of Philosophy* (London: Fontana, 1985), ch. 7; A. Macintyre, *After Virtue* (London: Duckworth, 1985; 2nd edn), ch. 5; J. Finnis, 'Scepticism, Self-Refutation, and the Good of Truth', in P. Hacker and J. Raz (eds), *Law, Morality, and Society* (Oxford: Clarendon Press, 1977), pp. 247–67, and *Fundamentals of Ethics* (Oxford: Clarendon Press, 1983), ch. 1.

4 Hume, *Treatise* III.I.I, p. 467.

5 W. V. Quine, 'On Empirically Equivalent Systems of the World', *Erkenntnis* 9 (1975), pp. 313–28, at pp. 327–8.

6 For the controversy surrounding the work of Margaret Mead, see her *Coming of Age in Samoa* (New York: Blue Ribbon Books, 1928; repr. Penguin, 1943); Derek Freeman, *Margaret Mead and Samoa: the Making and Unmaking of an Anthropological Myth* (Cambridge, MA, Harvard University Press, 1983), reprinted as *Margaret Mead and the Heretic* (London: Penguin, 1996) [the remark by Freeman is taken from p. 292 of both editions]; and Freeman, *The Fateful Hoaxing of Margaret Mead: A Historical Analysis of her Samoan Research* (Boulder: Westview Press, 1998). Freeman believes

that Mead was not only guilty of bad science, but of gullibility, because she was almost certainly given false stories by the Samoans: 'The Manu'ans [inhabitants of one of the groups of Samoan islands] emphasize, however, that the girls who, they claim, plied Mead with these counterfeit tales were only amusing themselves, and had no inkling that their tales would ever find their way into a book' (*Margaret Mead and Samoa*, p. 290). For a defence of Mead, see Martin Orans, *Not Even Wrong: Margaret Mead, Derek Freeman and the Samoans* (Novato, CA: Chandler and Sharp, 1996).

7   Hume, *Treatise* III.I.II, p. 470.

8   Peter Geach's refutation of emotivism and related 'expressivist' theories is in his papers 'Ascriptivism', *Philosophical Review* 69 (1960), pp. 221–5, reprinted in his *Logic Matters* (Oxford: Blackwell, 1972), pp. 250–4, and 'Assertion', *Philosophical Review* 74 (1965), pp. 449–65.

9   Jonathan Bennett's response (without naming the Frege/Geach point as such) is in his *The Act Itself* (Oxford: Clarendon Press, 1995), p. 17, from which the quotation is taken.

Chapter 2

1   Aristotle, *Nicomachean Ethics* 1094a, trans. W. D. Ross (Oxford: Clarendon Press, 1925), reprinted in R. McKeon (ed.), *The Basic Works of Aristotle* (New York: Random House, 1941), p. 935.

2   For a more detailed refutation of the charge that Aristotle is guilty of a fallacy, see D. S. Oderberg, 'On an Alleged Fallacy in Aristotle', *Philosophical Papers* 27 (1998), pp. 107–18.

3   Thomas Nagel's discussion of the Aristotelian notion of function (*ergon*) and his example of the corkscrew-bottle-opener is in his 'Aristotle on Eudaimonia', in A. Rorty (ed.), *Essays on Aristotle's Ethics* (Berkeley: UCLA Press, 1980), pp. 7–14.

4   G. W. F. Hegel, *Lectures on the Philosophy of World History: Introduction* (1830; trans. H. B. Nisbet, 1975), p. 94.

5   William James, *The Principles of Psychology* (New York: Holt, 1923), vol. I, p. 122.

6   The literature on the role of the virtues in ethics has grown steadily in recent years, though its value is uneven to say the least. The mere fact that someone calls himself (or is called by others) a 'virtue theorist' does not mean that he *is* a virtue theorist (the same is true in all areas of philosophy). The writer might have a defective notion of virtue, exaggerate its role in moral theory (the very term 'virtue theorist' suggests this), or apply the concept quite wrongly to concrete situations. On this matter see A. Macintyre, 'How to

Seem Virtuous Without Actually Being So' (Lancaster University: Centre for the Study of Cultural Values, 1991).

Caution is thus advised if the reader plans to delve into recent writing on the virtues, and such a plan would be ill-advised altogether if the reader has not already tried to understand Aristotle's account. For some of the better recent literature on the virtues the reader should consult papers by P. Foot (see especially her collection *Virtues and Vices*); Macintyre, *After Virtue* and later papers; J. Cottingham (see, for instance, 'Medicine, Virtues and Consequences', in D. S. Oderberg and J. A. Laing (eds), *Human Lives: Critical Essays on Consequentialist Bioethics*, London/New York: Macmillan/St. Martin's Press, 1997, pp. 128–43); also Finnis, *Fundamentals of Ethics*.

7   William Blake, *Jerusalem* (1804), p. 55 l.60.

8   Two good books on rights theory are J. J. Thomson, *The Realm of Rights* (Cambridge, MA: Harvard University Press, 1990) and J. Finnis, *Natural Law and Natural Rights* (Oxford: Clarendon Press, 1980).

9   Hans Kelsen, *General Theory of Law and State*, trans. A. Wedberg (New York: Russell & Russell, 1961), p. 6.

10 Peter Singer, *Practical Ethics* (Cambridge: Cambridge University Press, 1993; 2nd edn), p. 96 (all references to this book are to the second edition unless otherwise stated).

11 Peter Singer, *Animal Liberation* (London: Jonathan Cape, 1990; 2nd edn), p. 8.

12 J. J. C. Smart, in J. J. C. Smart and B. Williams, *Utilitarianism: For and Against* (Cambridge: Cambridge University Press, 1973), p. 71.

13 J. Harris, *The Value of Life* (London: Routledge, 1985), p. xvi.

14 Jonathan Glover, *Causing Death and Saving Lives* (London: Penguin, 1977), p. 83.

15 Amartya Sen's attempt to reconcile rights with consequentialism can be found in his paper 'Rights and Agency', *Philosophy and Public Affairs* 11 (1982), pp. 3–39; reprinted in Samuel Scheffler (ed.), *Consequentialism and its Critics* (Oxford: Oxford University Press, 1988), pp. 187–223. For a perceptive interpretation, on which I draw, see Cora Diamond, 'Consequentialism in Modern Moral Philosophy and in "Modern Moral Philosophy"', in Oderberg and Laing (eds), *Human Lives*, pp. 13–38, at pp.15–16. This paper also contains her interesting interpretation of Ross, showing that he is a consequentialist.

16 Philip Pettit's attempt to reconcile rights and consequentialism is in his 'The Consequentialist Can Recognise Rights', *Philosophical Quarterly* 38 (1988), pp. 42–55. The quotation is from p. 54.

17 On the distinction between infringement and violation, see Thomson, *Realm of Rights*, p. 122 and subsequent discussion. This is not to say that Thomson's general approach is endorsed here.

Chapter 3

1   Immanuel Kant's famous statement that the only thing good without qualification is a good will is to be found at the beginning of his *Groundwork of the Metaphysics of Morals* (1785; see any edition).

2   Criticisms of the Principle of Double Effect (PDE) by Peter Singer, including this claim, can be found in *Practical Ethics*, p. 210.

3   For a typical example of majority consequentialist thinking in bioethics, see A. Dyson and J. Harris (eds), *Ethics and Biotechnology* (London: Routledge, 1994), which I reviewed in *Philosophical Books* 37 (1996), pp. 56–9. A standard application of such thinking 'in the raw' can be seen in A. M. Hickey et al., 'A New Short Form Individual Quality of Life Measure (SEIQoL-DW): Application in a Cohort of Individuals with HIV/AIDS', *British Medical Journal* 313 (1996), pp. 29–33.

4   J. Rachels, *The End of Life* (Oxford: Oxford University Press, 1986), p. 92. His objections to PDE are at pp. 92–6.

5   G. Williams, *The Sanctity of Life and the Criminal Law* (London: Faber & Faber, 1958), p. 286. For an interesting discussion of Williams, Rachels and PDE in general, see J. L. A. Garcia, 'Intentions in Medical Ethics', in Oderberg and Laing (eds), *Human Lives*, pp. 161–81. His criticism of Rachels's Jack and Jill case is at pp. 169–70.

6   Singer, *Practical Ethics*, p. 210.

7   Rachels, *End of Life*, p. 93.

8   The hypothetical cases considered in respect of double effect, such as the runaway tram and the fat man in the cave, are discussed in numerous books and articles. A useful collection on references can be found in Helga Kuhse, *The Sanctity-of-Life Doctrine in Medicine* (Oxford: Clarendon Press, 1987), ch. 3, especially 3.2. See also P. Foot (who devised many of the most-discussed cases), 'The Problem of Abortion and the Doctrine of Double Effect', in her *Virtues and Vices*; also in B. Steinbock (ed.), *Killing and Letting Die* (Englewood Cliffs: Prentice Hall, 1980).

9   Foot's example of letting starving people die versus sending them poisoned food comes from her 'Problem of Abortion and the Doctrine of Double Effect'.

10 Rachels on acts and omissions: *End of Life*, chs 7–8. The cases of Smith and Jones are at p. 112 ff.

11 Singer on acts and omissions (from which his remark about omission as deliberate choice is taken): *Practical Ethics*, pp. 208–9.

12 Further useful points in defence of AOD can be found in Nicholas Denyer, 'Is Anything Absolutely Wrong?', in Oderberg and Laing (eds), *Human Lives*, pp.39–57, at pp. 42–6.

Chapter 4

1   James Rachels's objections to the addition of 'innocent': *End of Life*, pp. 67–77; the quotation is on pp. 69–70.

2   Quoted in J. A. Laing, 'Innocence and Consequentialism: Inconsistency, Equivocation and Contradiction in the Philosophy of Peter Singer', in Oderberg and Laing (eds), *Human Lives*, pp. 196–224, at p. 196. My remarks on innocence draw upon the thoughts expressed in that paper.

3   See *Practical Ethics*, ch. 7, e.g. p. 184; Singer and Helga Kuhse, *Should the Baby Live?* (Oxford: Oxford University Press, 1985), chs 2 ('Is All Human Life of Equal Worth?' – answer: no) and 3 ('Deciding when Life is Worthwhile').

4   Singer, *Practical Ethics*, p. 184.

5   Ibid., pp. 185–6. He uses the term 'defective infant' in the first edition of *Practical Ethics* (Cambridge: Cambridge University Press, 1979), ch. 7, and replaces it throughout with the term 'disabled infant' in the second edition, possibly out of fear of causing offence.

6   On the 'desire to go on living [being] outweighed by other desires', see *Practical Ethics*, p. 99.

7   Glover on 'lives not worth living': see *Causing Death and Saving Lives*, pp. 51–3, 158–62, 173–5, 192–4, 223–4 at pp. 53, 159, 173, 223–4 and 192.

8   Singer, *Practical Ethics*, p. 94; p. 201.

9   Glover, *Causing Death and Saving Lives*, p. 191.

10 On the Nazi euthanasia programme, which built on what had begun before they came to power, see the excellent study by Michael Burleigh, *Death and Deliverance: 'Euthanasia' in Germany 1900–45* (Cambridge: Cambridge University Press, 1994). The term 'life unworthy of life' was coined in the 1920s. The question of the extent to which Singer's views on euthanasia parallel those of the Nazis' has been discussed extensively in the popular press and magazines. For an overview, see D. S. Oderberg, 'Academia's "Doctor Death"?', in *The Human Life Review* (Fall, 1998), pp. 31–40, and other contributions in that issue.

11 Glover, *Causing Death and Saving Lives*, p. 46.

12 Ibid., pp. 52–3.

13 Rachels, *End of Life*, p. 48.

14 Ibid., pp. 5–6, 49–59.

15 Ibid., p. 64.

16 John Harris's critique of DSL is in his *Value of Life*; Helga Kuhse's is in her *Sanctity-of-Life Doctrine in Medicine*.

17 The radical consequentialist view that personal identity has no moral significance is represented in Derek Parfit, *Reasons and Persons* (Oxford: Oxford

University Press, 1984). For critical discussion of Parfit (of which there is a large literature), see J. Dancy (ed.), *Reading Parfit* (Oxford: Blackwell, 1997). A good recent critique of Parfit on personal identity and morality can be found in work by T. Chappell: 'Personal Identity, "R-relatedness" and the Empty Question Argument', *Philosophical Quarterly* 45 (1995), pp. 88–92; 'Reductionism about Persons; and what Matters', *Proceedings of the Aristotelian Society* 98 (1998), pp. 41–57; and *Understanding Human Goods* (Edinburgh: Edinburgh University Press, 1998), ch. 4.

18   Elizabeth Anscombe, 'Modern Moral Philosophy', originally in *Philosophy* 33 (1958), pp. 1–19; reprinted in *Ethics, Religion and Politics*, pp. 26–42, at p. 40, and in R. Crisp and M. Slote (eds), *Virtue Ethics* (Oxford: Oxford University Press, 1997), pp. 26–44, at p. 42.

19   Singer, *Practical Ethics*, p. 171.

20   Ibid., p. 170.

21   Glover, *Causing Death and Saving Lives*, p. 158.

22   Gillett, 'Young Human Beings: Metaphysics and Ethics', in Oderberg and Laing (eds), *Human Lives*, pp. 109–27, at pp. 112–16.

23   Ibid., p. 115.

24   Bernard Williams, in J. J. C. Smart and B. Williams, *Utilitarianism: For and Against* (Cambridge: Cambridge University Press, 1973), p. 131.

25   Singer, *Practical Ethics*, p. 200.

26   Williams, in Smart and Williams, *Utilitarianism*, p. 131.

27   Singer, *Practical Ethics*, p. 100.

28   On the idea of government by a consequentialist elite, see Williams, in Smart and Williams, *Utilitarianism*, pp. 138–9.

29   Singer, *Practical Ethics*, p. 88.

30   John Locke, *Essay Concerning Human Understanding* (1690; see any edition), I.9.29.

31   In using the special term *person* to cover those beings who satisfy Locke's definition and who are thus of special concern to Singer, I follow J. A. Laing in 'Innocence and Consequentialism', and in speaking of *personism* I follow Jenny Teichman, who coined the term: see her 'Humanisn and Personism: The False Philosophy of Peter Singer', *Quadrant* (Australia), December 1992, pp. 26–9; and also 'Freedom of Speech and the Public Platform', *Journal of Applied Philosophy* 11 (1994), pp. 99–105, reprinted in her *Polemical Papers* (Aldershot: Ashgate, 1997).

32   Singer, *Practical Ethics*, p. 90.

33   This essay first appeared in the *New York Review of Books*, 15 August 1991, pp. 36–42, and is reprinted as an appendix to Singer's *Practical Ethics*, pp. 337–59. See also Singer, 'A German Attack on Applied Ethics', *Journal of Applied Philosophy* 9 (1992), pp. 85–91; H. Pauer-Studer, 'Peter Singer on Euthanasia', *The Monist* 76 (1993), pp. 135–57; Singer and H. Kuhse, 'More

on Euthanasia: A Response to Pauer-Studer', *The Monist* 76 (1993), pp. 158–74; D. S. Oderberg, 'The Singer Controversy', *Quadrant* (Australia), September 1993, pp. 4–6; and the citations in nn. 10 and 31.

34 Singer, *Practical Ethics*, p. 60.
35 Singer on whether a potential X has the rights of an X: *Practical Ethics*, p. 153.

Index

Made in the USA
Lexington, KY
03 September 2013